Cambridge Imperial and Postcolonial Studies Series

General Editors: Megan Vaughan, King's College, Cambridge and Richard Drayton, King's College London

This informative series covers the broad span of modern imperial history while also exploring the recent developments in former colonial states where residues of empire can still be found. The books provide in-depth examinations of empires as competing and complementary power structures encouraging the reader to reconsider their understanding of international and world history during recent centuries.

Titles include:

B. D. Hopkins
THE MAKING OF MODERN AFGHANISTAN

Ronald Hyam
BRITIAN'S IMPERIAL CENTURY, 1815–1914: A STUDY OF EMPIRE AND EXPANSION
Third Edition

Iftekhar Iqbal
THE BENGAL DELTA
Ecology, State and Social Change, 1840–1943

Brian Ireland
THE US MILITARY IN HAWAI'I
Colonialism, Memory and Resistance

Sloan Mahone and Megan Vaughan (*editors*)
PSYCHIATRY AND EMPIRE

Javed Majeed
AUTOBIOGRAPHY, TRAVEL AND POST-NATIONAL IDENTITY

Gabriel Paquette
ENLIGHTENMENT, GOVERNANCE AND REFORM IN SPAIN AND ITS EMPIRE, 1739–1808

Jennifer Regan-Lefebvre
IRISH AND INDIAN
The Cosmopolitan Politics of Alfred Webb

Ricardo Roque
HEADHUNTING AND COLONIALISM
Anthropology and the Circulation of Human Skulls in the Portuguese Empire, 1870–1930

Michael Silvestri
IRELAND AND INDIA
Nationalism, Empire and Memory

John Singleton and Paul Robertson
ECONOMIC RELATIONS BETWEEN BRITAIN AND AUSTRALASIA, 1945–70

Aparna Vaidik
IMPERIAL ANDAMANS
Colonial Encounter and Island History

Kim A. Wagner (*editor*)
THUGGEE
Banditry and the British in Early Nineteenth-Century India

Jon E. Wilson
THE DOMINATION OF STRANGERS
Modern Governance in Eastern India, 1780–1835

Finance, Politics, and Imperialism

Australia, Canada, and the City of London, c.1896–1914

Andrew Dilley
Lecturer in History, University of Aberdeen

palgrave
macmillan

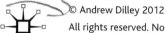
First published 2012 by
PALGRAVE MACMILLAN

Palgrave Macmillan in the UK is an imprint of Macmillan Publishers Limited,
registered in England, company number 785998, of Houndmills, Basingstoke,
Hampshire RG21 6XS.

Palgrave Macmillan in the US is a division of St Martin's Press LLC,
175 Fifth Avenue, New York, NY 10010.

Palgrave Macmillan is the global academic imprint of the above companies
and has companies and representatives throughout the world.

Palgrave® and Macmillan® are registered trademarks in the United States,
the United Kingdom, Europe and other countries.

ISBN 978-0-230-22203-8

This book is printed on paper suitable for recycling and made from fully
managed and sustained forest sources. Logging, pulping and manufacturing
processes are expected to conform to the environmental regulations of the
country of origin.

A catalogue record for this book is available from the British Library.

A catalogue record for this book is available from the Library of Congress.

10   9   8   7   6   5   4   3   2   1
21 20 19 18 17 16 15 14 13 12

Printed and bound in the United States of America

For Sarah and Beth

Contents

List of Tables

List of Graphs

Acknowledgements

The study of the interaction of politics and global finance which lies at the heart of this book may have acquired a new and unfortunate topicality in the wake of the 2008 banking crisis, but it has been much longer in the making. When the underpinning research was begun in 2002 the study of finance and the settlement empire were marginal in the historiography and lacked their current resonance. In the intervening period, I have amassed quite a few debts while ploughing what for a long time seemed a lonely furrow. Fortunately few of those have been financial, thanks in no small part to the AHRB (as it then was), and to my family during the period of doctoral research on which this book is based. I am also grateful to the Menzies Centre for Australian Studies for the Rydon Fellowship which helped bring the Australian sections of the book to completion. Reconstructing the politics of finance would have been impossible without the patience and assistance of numerous archivists, and in particular I must acknowledge the ANZ Bank's permission to cite material from their archives and for their excellent checking service. My intellectual debts have been more numerous. John Darwin and Ian Phimister have patiently provided wise, astute, and canny guidance throughout. I am particularly grateful for the stimulation and constructive criticism of Bernard Attard, Frank Bongiorno, Rachel Bright, Phillip Buckner, Peter Cain, Tony Hopkins, Joseph Martin, Thomas Pickles, Andrew Porter, Andrew Smith, and Sarah Stockwell, and the anonymous reviewer of this book. Many other fellow graduates and colleagues in Oxford, London, and Aberdeen have provided advice and encouragement. Successive cohorts of undergraduate students have acted as valuable sounding boards, with varying degrees of willingness. Finally, I must thank my wife Sarah for helping to reconstruct the *Dramatis Personae* but more importantly for her herculean patience and tireless support throughout, and for our baby daughter Beth. Life would be dark without them. This is their book as much as mine...

List of Abbreviations

AGM	Annual General Meeting
AIBR	*Australian Insurance and Banking Record*
AMLF Papers	Noel Butlin Archives Centre (Australian Mercantile Land and Finance Company Papers)
ANA	Australian National Archives
BCER Papers	University of British Columbia, MSS Col Rare Books and Special Collections, British Columbia Electric Railway Papers
Beaverbrook Papers	House of Lords Record Office, BBK (Beaverbrook Papers)
Borden Papers	National Archives of Canada, MG-26-H-1-(a) (R. L. Borden Papers)
CAR	*Canadian Annual Review of Public Affairs*
Carruthers Papers	Mitchell Library, MSS 1638 (Joseph Carruthers Papers)
CCJ	*Chamber of Commerce Journal*
CMA Papers	National Archives of Canada, MG 28 I 230 (Canadian Manufacturers Association Papers)
C.MRC.CS.	State Record Office of Western Australia, 1150/297/6 (Agent-Generals Papers): Midland Railway Company, *Correspondence between the Midland Railway Company of Western Australia and the Colonial Secretary...* (Jan. 1904)
Coghlan Papers	National Library of Australia, MS 6335 (Timothy A. Coghlan Papers)
Daglish Papers	State Library of Western Australia, MN 553/2397A (Henry Daglish Papers)
Deakin Papers	National Library of Australia, MS 1540 (Alfred Deakin Papers)
DDEAP	National Archives of Canada, RG 25 B (Department of External Affairs)
DHC	*Official Report of the Debates of the House of Commons of Canada* (Ottawa, 1900–1914)
Doxat Letterbooks	Noel Butlin Archives, N8 (Dalgety Papers, E. T. Doxat semi-official and private Letterbooks)

ESAB Papers	ANZ Group Archive, E/143/ (English, Scottish and Australian Bank Limited. General Manager's Letters to London)
Fielding Papers	Public Archives of Nova Scotia, MG 2 (W. S. Fielding Papers)
Frank Crowley Papers	State Library of Western Australia, MN 1379 (Frank Crowley Papers)
GL	Guildhall Library
GTRC Letterbooks	National Archives of Canada, RG 30/10712 (Canadian National Railways, Grand Trunk Papers, Chairman's Letterbooks)
Hays Letterbooks	National Archives of Canada, MG 30/a18 (C. M. Hays' Letterbooks)
HYGM	Half Yearly General Meeting
James Papers	Mitchell Library, MSS 412 (Walter James Papers)
Laurier Papers	National Library of Canada, MG 26-G (Wilfred Laurier Papers)
LCC	London Chamber of Commerce
MRC Papers	State Library of Western Australia, 1557A (Midland Railway Company of Western Australia Papers)
NAC	National Archives of Canada
O.R.CCCE, 1900	Guildhall Library, MS 18287 (Federation of Commonwealth Chambers of Commerce Papers): *Official Report of the Fourth Congress of Chambers of Commerce of the Empire* (1900)
O.R.CCCE, 1903	Guildhall Library, MS 18287 (Federation of Commonwealth Chambers of Commerce Papers): *Official Report of the Fifth Congress of Chambers of Commerce of the Empire* (1903)
O.R.CCCE, 1906	Guildhall Library, MS 18287 (Federation of Commonwealth Chambers of Commerce Papers): *Official Report of the Sixth Congress of Chambers of Commerce of the Empire* (1906)
O.R.CCCE, 1909	Guildhall Library, MS 18287 (Federation of Commonwealth Chambers of Commerce Papers): *Official Report of the Seventh Congress of Chambers of Commerce of the Empire* (1909)
O.R.CCCE, 1912	Guildhall Library, MS 18287 (Federation of Commonwealth Chambers of Commerce

	Papers): *Official Report of the Eighth Congress of Chambers of Commerce of the Empire* (1912)
PLV	Public Library of Victoria
Reid Papers	National Library of Australia, MS 1540 (George Reid Papers)
SDT	*Sydney Daily Telegraph*
SEYB	*Stock Exchange Yearbook*
S.L.W.A.	State Library of Western Australia
SMH	*Sydney Morning Herald*
S.R.O.NSW	State Record Office of New South Wales
Strathcona Papers	National Archives of Canada, MG 25 (Lord Strathcona Papers)
Syd.Ch.Com. Papers	Mitchell Library, MSS 5706/6/11 (Sydney Chamber of Commerce Papers)
TSDC	Deakin Papers MS 1540/15/3/3/15: T. A. Coghlan, 'The Transference of the State Debts to the Commonwealth' (28 March 1906)
UBA Papers	ANZ Group Archive, U (Union Bank of Australia Limited Papers)
Vict.P.R.O	Victorian Public Record Office
W.A.A.G. Papers	State Record Office of Western Australia, 1150 (Papers of the Western Australian Agent-General)
Waddell Papers	Mitchell Library, MSS 3144 (Thomas Waddell Papers)
Walker Papers	University of Toronto, Thomas Fisher Rare Books Library, MS Col. 1 (B. E. Walker Papers)
White Papers	National Archives of Canada, MG 27-II-D-18 (W. T. White Papers)
Whitney Papers	Public Archives of Ontario, F 5 (J. P. Whitney Papers)

Dramatis Personae

Max Aitken – Canadian-born financier, later Lord Beaverbrook

R. B. Angus – Director of the Bank of Montreal, 1891–1922

Frank Anstey – Australian monetary radical

Lord Avebury (John Lubbock) – Banker and former Liberal politician; President of London Chamber of Commerce, 1888–1893

A. J. Barber – Secretary to the Midland Railway Company of Western Australia

Thomas F. Blackwell – Chairman of the Council of the London Chamber of Commerce, 1898–1901; President of the London Chamber of Commerce, 1904–7

Edmund Barton – Protectionist Prime Minister of Australia, 1901–1903

Thomas Bent – 'Reform' Premier of Victoria, 1904–1909

Robert Laird Borden – Prime Minister of Canada, 1911–1920

Horatio Bottomley – London financier dealing in Western Australian mining shares

Samuel Bagster Boulton – Member of the Council of the London Chamber of Commerce

Lord Brassey – Liberal politician, Governor of Victoria, 1893–1895; President of the London Chamber of Commerce, 1901–1904

W. Capel Slaughter – Director of the Midland Railway Company of Western Australia

Joseph Carruthers – New South Wales Free Trade/Liberal Politician, Premier, 1904–1907

E. S. Clouston – General Manager of the Bank of Montreal, 1890–1911; Vice-President, 1905–1911

Timothy A. Coghlan – New South Wales Official Statistician, 1886–1904; Agent-General, 1905–1915, 1916–1917, 1920–1925

Henry Coupland – New South Wales' Agent-General, 1900–1903

George Cox – Director of the Canadian Bank of Commerce, 1886–1914; President, 1890–1907

Henry Daglish – Labor Premier of Western Australia, 1904–1905

Alfred Deakin – Victorian politician, Australian Protectionist/Progressive Prime Minister, 1903–1904, 1905–1909, 1909–1910

Edmund T. Doxat – Chairman of the pastoral finance company Dalgety and Co.

George Drummond – Director of the Bank of Montreal, 1882–1910; Vice-President, 1887–1905; President, 1905–1910

Lord Dufferin – Diplomat, Governor-General of Canada, 1872–1878; Viceroy of India, 1882–1888; director and chairman of mining companies associated with Whittaker Wright

Charles Duguid – London financial journalist

Ferdinand Faithfull Begg – Stockbroker; Treasurer of the London Chamber of Commerce, 1910–1912; Chairman of the Council of the London Chamber of Commerce, 1912–1914

F. W. Field – Canadian financial journalist with Montreal's *Monetary Times*

W. S. Fielding – Nova Scotian Canadian Liberal politician; Minister for Finance, 1896–1911

Andrew Fisher – Australian Labor Leader 1907–1915; Prime Minister, 1909, 1910–1913

John Forrest – Western Australian Premier, 1890–1900; Australian Protectionist/Liberal Treasurer, 1905–1906, 1909, 1913

George Foster – Canadian Conservative, Finance Minister, 1885–1896; Minister for Trade and Commerce, 1911–1920

Frank Gardner – London-based American mining financier concentrating on Western Australia

Francis A. Govett – London stockbroker, heavily involved in Western Australian mining

Arthur Grenfell – London-based financier; partner in Chaplain Milne Grenfell and Co; chairman of the Canadian Agency

Earl Grey – Governor-General of Canada, 1904–1911; father-in-law of Arthur Grenfell

W. L. Griffith – Deputy High Commissioner of Canada

Charles Melville Hays – American-born manager of the British-owned Grand Trunk and Grand Trunk Pacific Railways, 1896–1911

Herbert Hoover – London-based American engineer (later US President), leading light of Berwick Moreing and Co, who were heavily involved in Western Australian Mines

R. M. Horne-Payne – London financier, former partner of merchant bank, Speyers; Chairman of British Columbia Electric Railway (from 1897) and British Empire Trust Company (from 1902); played a leading role in the financing of the Canadian Northern Railway

William Morris (Billy) Hughes – Australian Labor Politician, Attorney-General, 1909, 1910–1913; later Prime Minister

William 'Iceberg' H. Irvine – 'Reform' Premier of Victoria, 1902–1904; Federal politician ('Corner' then Liberal), 1906–1914

Walter James – Premier of Western Australia, 1902–1903; Agent-General, 1904–1905

Earl of Jersey – Governor of New South Wales, 1890–1892; acting Agent-General of New South Wales, 1903–1905

H. V. F. Jones – London Manager of the Canadian Bank of Commerce, 1902–onwards

Wilfred Laurier – Canadian Liberal politician; Prime Minister, 1896–1911

W. R. Lawson – London financial journalist

H. B. Lefroy – Agent-General of Western Australia, 1901–1903

H. Lowenfeld – London financial journalist with *Financial Review of Reviews*

William Lyne – Australian Progressive (later Labor) politician; Federal Treasurer, 1907–1908

Stanley Machin – Deputy Chairman of the Council of the London Chamber of Commerce, 1906–1909; Chairman of the Council of the London Chamber of Commerce, 1909–1912

William MacKenzie – Canadian railway contractor and chairman of the Canadian Northern Railway

Donald Mann – Partner to Mackenzie, railway contractor, and director of the CNR

J. S. T. McGowan – Labor Premier of New South Wales, 1910–1912

Charles A. Moreing – Chairman of the engineering firm, Berwick Moreing and Co.

R. L. Nash – Leading Australian financial journalist

Robert Nivison – Underwriter, dominant force in the issuing of colonial bonds

E. B. Osler – Canadian Conservative and Director of the Canadian Pacific Railway

George Paish – Editor of the *Statist*, leading statistician

Cornthwaite Hector Rason – Western Australian Premier, 1905, Agent-General, 1906–1909

George Reid – New South Wales Premier, 1894–1899; federal Free Trade/Anti-Socialist party leader, 1901–1909; Australian Prime Minister, Aug. 1904–July 1905; High Commissioner, 1910–1915

Charles Rivers Wilson – Former diplomat, civil servant, and finance minister in Egypt; chair of Grand Trunk and Grand Trunk Pacific Railways, 1895–1909 and 1903–1909 respectively

Lionel Robinson – Australian-born stockbroker, based in London from 1900. Specialises in mining shares

T. J. Russell – Area Manager of the London and Westminster (London, County and Westminster from 1909) Bank; with Nivison a key figure organising Australian borrowing

John Scaddan – Labor Premier of Western Australia, 1911–1916

Thomas Shaughnessy – American-born manager of the Canadian Pacific Railway, CPR President, 1899–1918; Director of the Bank of Montreal, 1907–1923

Alfred W. Smithers – Stockbroker; Vice-Chairman of the Grand Trunk and Grand Trunk Pacific Railways, 1904–1909; Chairman 1909–1922; Chairman of the English Association of American Bondholders

Albert Spicer – Deputy Chairman of the Council of the London Chamber of Commerce, 1903–1904; Chairman of the Council of the London Chamber of Commerce, 1904–1905; President of the London Chamber of Commerce, 1907–1910

Lord Strathcona – Former Canadian businessman and politician; High Commissioner, 1896–1914; President of the Bank of Montreal, 1887–1905

J. W. Taverner – Victorian Agent-General, 1904–1912

George Turner – Protectionist Victorian Premier, 1894–1899, 1900–1901; Commonwealth Treasurer, 1901–1904

Thomas Waddell – New South Wales Protectionist/Progressive later Liberal politician; Treasurer, 1901–4; Premier, 1904; Treasurer 1907–1910

C. G. Wade – New South Wales Free Trade/Liberal politician, Premier, 1907–1910

Bryon Edmond Walker – General Manager of the Canadian Bank of Commerce, 1886–1907, Director from 1906, President 1907–1924

J. C. Watson – Australian Labor politician, Prime Minister, April-August 1904

Lord Welby – Civil Servant; Liberal politician; Director of the Grand Trunk Railway

William T. White – Canadian businessman; Conservative politician; Managing Director of the National Trust Company in Toronto, which had close links to the Canadian Bank of Commerce; Conservative Minister of Finance, 1911–1919

James Pliny Whitney – Conservative politician; Premier of Ontario, 1905–1914

Andrew Williamson – London financier; Chairman of Australian Estates Company; Director of Midland Railway Company of Western Australia

Frederick Williams-Taylor – London Manager of the Bank of Montreal, 1904–1913; General Manager, 1913–1929

A. J. Wilson – London financial journalist; editor of the *Investor's Review*, scourge of Australia

Bernhard Ringrose Wise – New South Wales Progressive/Protectionist politician and supporter of Deakin; resident in London, 1904–1908

Hartley Withers – London financial journalist

Edward Rogers Wood – Canadian financier; Director of the Canadian Bank of Commerce, 1909–1914; President of Dominion Securities 1902 onwards; expert on Canadian borrowing

Whitaker Wright – London mining financier concentrating in Western Australian and British Columbian mines in the late 1890s; an ungentlemanly capitalist

Introduction

In 1905 a satirical dialogue entitled *The Australian Case Against John Bull* was published in Sydney. Its radical author, Edward de Norbury Rogers, described a fictional meeting in a London office between a canny representative of Australia – Dr Commonwealth – and an equally buffoonish John Bull. Dr Commonwealth's 'case' revolved around the havoc wreaked on Australia by its £344 million debt to Bull's business partner, one Mr Wrathchild. Australians were forced to pay an annual 'tribute' of £15.5 million to Wrathchild and Bull, yet (according to figures drawn from Australia's leading statistician, Timothy Coghlan) only £16 million of capital had reached or remained in the continent. Thus, borrowing had only led to stagnation, poverty, and unemployment. Responsibility for the mess lay with Australia's 'commercial interests, the squatters, and upper classes', who were 'more or less identified with the money ring'. Interest payments meant that 'our governments are rapidly being converted into mere taxing machines for the benefit of absentee money-lenders'. As a result, Dr Commonwealth warned: 'It is justice, not the money tie, which keeps states and Empires together... your partner with his eternal and increasing demand for interest... is setting us against you'. Wrathchild's avarice was compelling the Australian Labor Party to 'take the lead in a universal revolt against the power of money', and, if nothing changed, 'your wonderful credit machine will be smashed to pieces and your Empire will pass from you'.[1] At the end of the dialogue, and after long discussions focusing on the iniquities of the gold standard, we are told by Rogers in an epilogue that Dr Commonwealth can do little, having come down with appendicitis (a lack of stomach?), that Wrathchild objects to any reduction of the debt, and that John Bull's hands are tied by 'the conventional red tape'. Surely, Rogers concluded, 'it is... time for those who wish to see Australia made worthy of the name "commonwealth" – a higher title than

Empire or Dominion – to seriously consider a change in the constitution'.[2] Rogers exemplified a distinctive strand of thinking on the Australian radical left. For him, borrowing only served the interests of Australia's upper classes, resulting in the subordination and exploitation of the masses while eroding loyalty to an unsympathetic or impotent John Bull. Australian workers had nothing to lose but their chains. Of course the revolution never came, the red tape (or crimson thread?) was never cut, and Australia remained within the capitalist fold and the British 'embrace'.[3]

The unlikely departure of Australia from the empire threatened by Dr Commonwealth would have been a major blow for Britain. By the early-twentieth century, the colonies of settlement had become crucial components of Britain's 'world system' (its agglomeration of global power and influence).[4] Their collective importance and distinctive position within the formal empire was recognised in the official adoption of the term 'dominion' at the 1907 Imperial Conference (for convenience, the term is used more loosely in this book as a synonym for self-governing or settler colony).[5] The change was intended to remove connotations of subordination, and reflected evolving constitutional practices. From the late-1840s, the concession of 'responsible government' had given settlement colonies a significant and increasing measure of internal autonomy.[6] The change also reflected a long standing bifurcation in British conceptions of empire. Victorian writers such as Charles Dilke and J. R. Seeley distinguished the settlement empire, or 'Greater Britain', from tropical colonies of rule (and particularly from India).[7] Greater Britain featured prominently in popular images of empire, indeed, the Raj's most imperious of Viceroys, Lord Curzon, complained that the, 'average Englishman... if he looks abroad... sees more and hears more about the 11,000,000 who inhabit the Colonies than he does about the 300,000,000 who inhabit India'.[8] Establishing the best means to cement connections within Greater Britain became a leading concern in the late-Victorian and Edwardian politics of empire, inspiring successive movements advocating differing forms of imperial federation.[9] This issue became more pressing when colonial contributions in the South African War (1899–1902) suggested that settlers' loyalty might become a tangible strategic asset.[10]

By then the soon-to-be dominions had become important economic partners, generating material benefits for British migrants, investors, and merchants. Their trade became ever more important. Collectively, by 1909–1913, the dominions accounted for about half of all British imports from and exports to the empire – 14 and 18 per cent of the overseas totals.[11] In an era of intensifying competition they remained one of Britain's few expanding markets.[12] They were an important destination for British migrants. Between 1853 and 1910, of 7.9 million people leaving Britain 44 per cent travelled to the dominions and after 1911 collectively they overtook the United States as the leading destination.[13] Meanwhile British investors invested heavily in the dominions: of an estimated £3.1 billion of capital exported from Britain between 1865 and 1914, 27.6 per cent was placed in colonies enjoying responsible government (constituting 71 per cent of all British investment in the empire).[14]

Thus, the dominions assumed a central place in Britain's world system in the early-twentieth century. Understanding their relations with Britain is fundamental to any understanding of the empire as a whole. As De Norbery Rogers suggested, the bonds forged by investment were a central but unstable pillar of this relationship. His tract was a small fragment of a transnational politics generated by capital export which bound Britain, or more accurately the City of London, with the settler colonies. The patterns, processes, and impacts of this politics, as experienced by Australians and Canadians in the 'long Edwardian period', and its relationships to the British empire and British imperialism, are the central themes of this book.

Historiography: Finance, imperialism, and the British World

Study of the relationship between Britain and the dominions, and the role of finance and empire in these regions in particular, declined through the twentieth century. Amongst Seeley's interwar successors, the dominions continued to be central. They assumed pride of place in the *Cambridge History of the British Empire*.[15] These works placed little emphasis on finance, and tended to narrate the organic evolution of a virtually assumed relationship. Keith Hancock devoted several pages of his *Survey of Commonwealth Affairs* to the 'interdependence and a linking of economic destiny of the creditor and the debtor country', but had little to say on that forces governing that 'linking' beyond that 'mastery' might be exerted over politically unreliable borrowers (such as China, Persia, and Turkey), a 'mastery' which by implication did not extend, say, to Australia.[16] Conversely British radical critics of empire focused largely on the dependent empire. J. A. Hobson's *Imperialism: A Study*, the lodestone of twentieth-century debates about finance and empire, denied that the dominions were subject to any form of financial imperialism; rather he feared that they would be co-opted as junior partners in imperial expansion.[17] It was left to Australian radicals and socialists to delineate and condemn financial imperialism in Australia.[18]

In part both Hancock and Hobson shared, and were bounded by, a conception of imperialism, or 'mastery', as actions undertaken by states.[19] After the Second World War, Ronald Robinson and Jack Gallagher's re-conceptualisation of empire provided an alternative means to examine anglo-dominion relations, in particular through their emphasis on 'informal empire'. They explained continuing close relations between Britain and the dominions following the concession of responsible government through a combination of 'economic dependence and mutual good-feeling [which kept] the colonies bound to Britain'.[20] Robinson later described white settlers as 'ideal prefabricated collaborators' committed to participation in the global economy, facilitating an imperialism which functioned through the 'meshing of autonomous private enterprises with the internal politics of quasi-autonomous governments'.[21] These, however, were brief forays laying greater emphasis on trade than investment. The focus of Robinson's and Gallagher's writings, along with those of several generations of historians of empire, was on the dependent empire.[22] Meanwhile, as the British connection waned, the gaze of historians in the former dominions often turned inwards.[23]

From the 1990s, the dominions returned to the heart of debates about empire. Two separate literatures have been responsible: firstly, a wave of publications on the 'British World' (along with parallel writings 'imperial networks'); and secondly – and predating the British World – ongoing debates surrounding Cain and Hopkins' account of British imperialism. In recent years the British World has assumed greatest prominence. The concept emerged in a series of conferences seeking to reconnect the historiographies of the dominions and the empire.[24] It draws heavily on J. G. A. Pocock's vision of a new British history, which originally stretched beyond Britain's shores.[25] The British World's spatial dimensions remain unclear, with some authors including pockets of Britishness globally beyond the settler colonies, or (at times) the United States, and others focusing heavily on the dominions.[26] In so doing, successive writers on the British World have rejected the tools of analysis bequeathed by Robinson and Gallagher. Contrary to their emphasis (shared by Cain and Hopkins) on the material forces binding Britain and the dominions, the British World, as Carl Bridge and Kent Fedorowich argue, was constructed 'from below' through dense connections forged by migration, professional and other associations, and a shared British culture which together formed a 'cultural glue' holding this world together.[27] Frequently writers on the British World have also reflected broader concerns to 'decentre' empire, focusing on intercolonial connections as well as those with Britain.[28]

This preoccupation with culture and identity may explain why economics has only recently found a place in this literature.[29] James Belich's study of 'Anglo-world', (which includes the United States) has usefully re-iterated the social, economic, and technological circumstances which made the British World possible.[30] In rather different fashion, Andrew Thompson and Gary Magee explore the economic dynamics of the British World (focusing largely on the dominions without entirely excluding the US), arguing that a shared culture (bounded by race) facilitated the formation of networks and information flows which in turn lubricated economic exchanges. The resultant 'cultural economy' had discernable economic effects, encouraging migration, trade, and investment.[31] Both works open new avenues of enquiry into the dynamics of the nineteenth-century global economy, and the degree to which this economy shaped, and was shaped by, cultural forces. Neither, however, seriously analyses the political repercussions of these processes.[32]

This reflects a broader tendency for the British World to evade politics and the issue of power. Several of its leading lights, Bridge and Fedorowich, and Phillip Buckner, are quick to reject the notion that anglo-dominion relations involved any form of subordination, explicitly rejecting the Robinson and Gallagher tradition and expressing a deep unease with Robinson's extension of the term 'collaboration' to settlers who considered themselves British.[33] Thompson and Magee briefly discuss power, commenting that:

> the logic of a 'networked' or 'decentred' approach to the study of empires is that metropole and colony acted and reacted upon each other in complex ways, and that sovereignty in the colonies, far from being static or stable, was subject to negotiation and renegotiation by a variety of settler and non-settler groups.[34]

However, pointing out the complex ebbs and flows of power does not obviate the need to analyse the dynamics underpinning those ebbs and flows, and emphasising negotiation tells us little about the nature of that negotiation: is the negotiation equal or does one party have an inherent advantage? By avoiding these questions, the literature on the British World has generally portrayed networking as a rather cosy activity.[35]

There is no reason to suppose networks necessarily behave in a benign way. A parallel literature on mid-Victorian imperial networks, while cutting across conventional divisions of metropole and colony, emphasises that networks and alliances facilitated struggles between like-minded interest groups (settlers, missionaries, humanitarians, and officials).[36] Similarly, Simon Potter has shown how the political struggle surrounding the Canadian government's agreement for freer trade with the United States in 1911 (reciprocity – of which more in Chapter 5) was fought out in a co-ordinated manner on both sides of Atlantic.[37] Networking, in other words, was frequently a political phenomenon, generated by, and facilitating struggles for power and influence. Further-more, a networked conception of empire, or the British World, may help reconstruct these struggles, but reveal little about the underlying forces shaping the networks.[38] These points are particularly pertinent when analysing the relations between debtor and creditor.

For this reason, analysing the politics of finance hinted at earlier necess-itates a return to older debates which underpinned the second revival of interest in the dominions. In particular it is impossible to overlook the work of Cain and Hopkins who placed financiers and the City of London at the heart of their re-interpretation of the history of British imperialism, and also (following the pattern of overseas investment) placed a heavy emphasis on the role of finance in anglo-Dominion relations. Revisiting their account of British imperialism in the dominions does not require an engagement with their central, and controversial, argument that the main contours of British imperialism were shaped by the interests of what they called gentlemanly capitalism (the intertwining of Britain's political and official masters with the financial and commercial elites of the City of London).[39] After the concession of responsive government, these regions saw little by way of British government intervention. As a result Cain and Hopkins offer a conceptually distinct analysis, suggesting that reliance on British capital allowed London finance to wield an informal imperial con-trol over Australia, Canada, and New Zealand, as well as over many Latin American countries. Following Robinson, they argue that 'rapid change in small, newly settled countries could only be achieved at the cost of dependence on British capital'. This dependence required borrowers to conform to the 'rules of the economic game set in London', especially when they experienced balance of payments problems, or difficulties borrowing or repaying debt. This conformity was maintained by 'col-laborative groups whose leverage was sufficient to keep these countries within the international system dominated by Britain' and who acted to 're-establish their credit-worthiness and restore their credibility locally'.[40] As well as Cain and Hopkins' own examples, Andrew Smith and Bernard Attard have more recently shown that Canadian confederation (1867) and the abolition of New Zealand's provincial governments in 1877 were both conditioned by connections with London.[41]

A number of criticisms though were made of Cain and Hopkins' original model. In particular, R. V. Kubicek and Jim McAloon suggested that the dominions were extremely effective in 'regulating their dependence'.[42] In response, Cain and Hopkins (drawing on the work of the political scientist Susan Strange) have sought to clarify their position, distinguishing two levels on which power operates in international relations. The first level, 'structural power', 'refers to the way in which a dominant state shapes the framework of international relations and specifies the "rules of the game" needed to uphold it'. The second, 'relational power', concerns 'the negotiations, pressures and conflicts that determine the outcome of particular contests within this framework'.[43] Thus, an emphasis on the dominions' dependence on capital and credit in London is perfectly compatible with tough negotiations and occasional acts of defiance. For Hopkins, 'what matters is whether the exercise of relational power is consistent with maintaining the framework... or whether it caused the rules themselves to change'.[44] Hard bargaining, and the fleecing of the occasional investor, does not preclude the possibility of a deeper form of subordination.

The use of Strange's model, formulated to describe relations between states, to analyse relations between a capital market and an overseas borrower however creates conceptual difficulties. Notwithstanding the inconsistencies and conflicts surrounding policy-making, states generally possess mechanisms to ensure they offer one policy response at any one time. No similar mechanism ensured consistency in the City. Thus the nature and dimensions of the 'rules of the game' have been called into question. As Bernard Attard points out, the 'rules' may prove to be little more than the 'minimum standards of creditworthiness' in the London capital market, something far removed from Hopkins' presentation of them as a holistic 'package'.[45] If those standards proved particularly narrow, then the result may be an imperialism of less than monolithic proportions.[46]

Robinson and Gallagher, Cain and Hopkins, and the British World literature have been cannily combined in John Darwin's recent account of Britain's world system.[47] The 'Britannic Allegiance' of the dominions is fully acknowledged as a foundation of British power, as are the economic resources of the 'Commercial Republic' of the City of London (which remains firmly divorced from officialdom).[48] Darwin follows Robinson and Gallagher in suggesting that 'self-interest and self-identification' bound the dominions to Britain.[49] He emphasises shared identity, but adds that 'the pull of London reinforced... attachment to the British world system' since 'nation building in the white colonies meant greater dependence not less on the British market and the financial machinery of the City of London'.[50] It is, however, worth asking whether a sense of

Britishness and reliance of London finance necessarily proved mutually reinforcing. Few borrowers fail, at times, to curse their bank managers. Could dependence on the 'commercial republic' not also test 'Britannic loyalty'? De Norbery Rogers certainly thought so. Darwin acknowledges the tensions in Australia caused by the economic crisis of the 1890s, but concludes that it did not result in a challenge to Australia's participation in Britain's world system.[51] This may be true. Nonetheless the way in which these tensions were played out dominion politics, and the way this process shaped the limits, politics, and practices of the British World requires closer examination. Stuart Ward's argument that Britain's application to the European Economic Community (EEC) undermined Australian belief in a 'community of interest' with Britain, and precipitated cultural and political change suggests the need to analyse the historical role of earlier tensions (without resurrecting a futile search for 'genuine' nationalism).[52] Even if 'self-interest and self-identification' generally proved mutually reinforcing, we need to understand the political context that made this so.

The politics of finance[53]

It is at this juncture that this book enters the debate. It offers a comparative study of Australian and Canadian financial relations with the City between about 1896 and 1914. The Dominion of Canada and the Commonwealth of Australia (federated in 1901) were the two largest single components of the settlement empire and were major recipients of British capital and migrants. They then were the most important elements of the 'Britannic Alliance'; the outer core of Greater Britain and the British World.[54] The 'long Edwardian' period covered in this book saw a new phase in the dominions' rise to prominence.[55] It also saw the last and largest boom in the export of British capital before the First World War irrevocably altered Britain's financial position in the world.[56] Thus, no understanding of the impact of finance in anglo-dominion relations can omit Edwardian Canada and Australia. Simultaneously, profound changes took place in Australian and Canadian political and economic life. Canada boomed and in the process attracted ever greater volumes of British capital. Conversely the (eastern) Australian economy stagnated following the depression of the 1890s, a situation worsened by drought. Its recovery from the early 1900s drew on internal resources until 1910. Canadian and Australian politics contrasted too. Canadian politics had long been constructed around a stable divide between Liberals and Conservatives within the framework of a federal state. This contrasted with Australia whose constitutional arrangements following federation in 1901 and party politics were both in flux. These contrasts, and differing relations with London, enable a number of features of the political impacts of the financial connection to be teased out against the backdrop of a crucial period for the Empire, the City, and political and economic life in Australia and Canada.

A single phrase lies at the heart of this book: the politics of finance. It is used to emphasise that finance generated a deep connection between the City and political life in the two dominions. These political patterns depended not only on the economics underpinning financial relationships, but also on the conceptions of political economy held amongst creditors and debtors. Moreover, the impacts of finance at particular junctures also depended on political struggles and economic circumstances, processes only fitfully in the control of financiers themselves. Using these principles, this book reconstructs the politics of financial dependence in Edwardian Australia and Canada. Part I outlines the economic and business bases on which the politics of finance rested. Chapter 1 charts the role played by British capital in colonial economic development in the late-nineteenth century, and in the period under analysis. Chapter 2 traces the financial networks linking particular sectors of the dominions' economies with the City. Part II switches attention to the City's conceptions of political economy and their associated contests which were central to the operation of the politics of finance. Chapter 3 examines the conceptions held in the City of Australian and Canadian political economy at particular junctures (the 'rules of the game'), while Chapter 4 explores the ways these conceptions interacted with various aspects of the imperial connection, and ideas about Britishness, as well as the way colonial representatives in London manipulated these ideas. In Part III Chapters 5, 6, and 7 analyse the politics of finance in Canada and Australia, identifying points of contact between the City and each dominion, the understandings of the roles played by British capital in economic development held by different groups, and the ways these connections and conceptions played out in political life.

The analysis presented here draws on the model developed by Cain and Hopkins. It concurs that the need to import fresh capital from Britain, and the legacies of past borrowing, did indeed shape many aspects of political life in both dominions. However, in order to analyse these political repercussions of debt, three modifications are necessary. Firstly, we need to play close attention to the conceptions of political economy held in the City. This expands the notion of the 'rules of the game' and separates them from the structural fact of financial dependence. The rules, as Chapter 3 shows, were cultural constructs which existed as shifting and partly formulated assumptions rather than a neat predetermined 'package'.[57] These assumptions delineated the contours of the City's influence. Secondly, in order to understand the impact of these conceptions of political economy – and hence financial dependence – a close analysis of the economics and politics of the borrowing nation is necessary. The structure of its economy affected the set of borrowers seeking capital in the City and hence the range of local actors in contact with London finance. The form and extent of the impact of financial connections on colonial politics also varied with economic cycles. Financial crises might catch a borrowing society in a vice (as Cain and Hopkins suggest), but booms led connections to be formed in London, and provided the perfect backdrop against which to argue that credit essential for economic, and indeed national, development. This leads on to the third point: that the ways in which the politics of financial dependence played out in a dominion's politics also depended on the ideas about debt and political economy prevalent in that dominion and their relative strength amongst political actors. Policy-making depended not so much on whether British capital was necessary, but whether it was perceived to be necessary and how far politicians were prepared to risk credit as a result. Thus as well as a shifting economic backdrop, political circumstances shaped the role played by credit and connections with the City.

The analysis also draws on, but qualifies, the literature on imperial networks of which the British World forms a benign subsection. In reconstructing the informational flows and financial networks linking the City with Australia and Canada, it contributes to the historiographical project at the heart of this literature. Equally the struggles charted here cannot be understood simply in terms of the antagonism of metropole and colony.[58] Colonial politics spilled into London, alliances and interests cut across oceans, while at the same time London's influence depended on the outcomes of struggles *within* colonial politics.[59] Nonetheless, the connections with and attention to London finance ultimately rested on the attractions of borrowing there and the necessity of managing existing debts. Thus, networks were *structured* by these relationships, and their patterns and practices reflected this structuring force.[60] Often they facilitated conflicts and arguments about credit and political economy. The networks and information flows charted here expose the practices rather than the underlying principles of the politics of anglo-dominion finance. At their core lay the central role of British capital in Canadian and Australian economic development. This is analysed in more depth in the next chapter.

Part I

The Economics and Business of Capital Export

1
Capital Imports and Economic Development in Two Settler Societies

The politics of finance did not take place in an economic vacuum. In order to understand the ways in which borrowing and relations with the City affected Australian and Canadian political life, it is necessary to rehearse the economic role played by British capital. This chapter charts the course economic development took in Australia and Canada from the mid-nineteenth century to the outbreak of the Great War, focusing particularly on the cyclical and sectoral patterns of economic expansion and the differing institutional contexts within which development took place. It also highlights the distribution (temporal and by sector) of British investment. While many broad similarities existed between Australia and Canada, differences in these patterns and contexts shaped connections with the City, and hence the ways in which it interacted with their politics. Before outlining the experiences of the two dominions, it is necessary to look more broadly at the development of 'settler societies' in the nineteenth century.

Settler capitalism revisited: Capital formation, overseas borrowing, and cycles of development

One of the most striking changes in the global economy in the nineteenth century was the unprecedented occupation of temperate lands in the Americas, Southern Africa, Australasia, and Siberia by European migrants. The growing weight of primary produce exports from these societies to the industrialised core of western Europe and the eastern seaboard of the United States became a central element in the emerging multilateral trading system that characterised the late-nineteenth century world economy.[1] Contemporaries were well aware of the development of these 'young countries' and were often beguiled by their capacity for dramatic growth.[2] In his 1920 classic, the *Economic Consequences of the Peace*, J. M. Keynes placed the development of the 'virgin potentialities' of the 'new world' at the heart of his account of pre-war 'internationalisation'.[3] Later twentieth-century commentators variously described them as 'regions of recent settlement', 'neo-Europes', 'newlands', and, for the dominions, 'neo-Britains'. Behind this nomenclature, with its varying elegance, lies the conviction that migrant-dominated societies indeed possessed a distinctive economic trajectory. All have limitations, particularly that their emphasis on newness risks omitting any acknowledgement of the (usually violent) dispossession of earlier inhabitants. In part with this in mind, Donald Denoon coined the phrase 'settler capitalism' to denote a distinct mode of production based on an export-orientated economy largely worked by populations of European descent exploiting land and other resources, often wrenched by force from indigenous peoples. This process relied on imports of capital (especially from Britain) as well as labour, rested on socio-political institutions orientated towards export production, and came of age between 1890 and 1914.[4]

The forces driving economic expansion in these settler societies have proved controversial. Frequently exports have been seen as central to their growth. An older generation of Canadian economic historians, following Harold Innis, considered that their country's development (social as well as economic) had been driven by the exploitation of a series of staples: cod, fur, timber, and wheat.[5] This staples thesis also incorporated a particular variation of the 'multiplier effect'.[6] The connections or 'linkages' staple production enjoyed with other sections of the economy generated further growth by stimulating industries servicing staple producers and their workers, or processing and exporting the staple.[7]

Critics of staples thesis revealed problems with the idea that growth in settler societies was of itself explained by the development of staple exports. Firstly questions were asked about where, exactly, the region of recent settlement was, and it was pointed out that it was rarely contiguous with the political units being analysed.[8] Hence, staples thesis seemingly had less to say about economic developments in late-nineteenth century central and eastern Canada, which had long been settled.[9] Secondly, the choice of staple was not necessarily simply a function of the interaction of geography and the demands of the world economy at a particular juncture. The temperate grasslands of Canada, Australia, Argentina, and New Zealand all came to be put to different uses in the late-nineteenth century. Specialisation in wheat, beef, lamb, dairy or wool production, as well as transitions between these uses, were argued to be the product of institutional differences, particularly contrasting state interventions, social structures, and forms of land holding.[10]

Thirdly, from the 1950s econometricians working on estimates of Gross Domestic Product (GDP), questioned the contribution of exports to growth in a variety of ways. Some analyses suggested that investment or changes in the size and composition of the population contributed more than exports to expanding output.[11] Analyses of GDP per capita (real average incomes) led to downward revisions of the level of development during booms in settler societies.[12] Transfers of capital and labour, it was argued, could not of themselves have augmented output per person, leading again to analyses focusing on the institutional factors increasing productivity.[13] Similarly, it has been argued that staples booms often failed to shift *underlying* per capita growth rates in an appreciable way.[14] Early and later defenders of staples thesis have replied that these analyses fail to estimate the role played by backwards and forward linkages. If other sectors grew faster, they might still have done so under the stimulation of the export sector.[15]

Several points ought to be made regarding such number crunching. First, the tendency to place GDP per capita at the heart of analysis of settler societies obscures one of their key features: their expanding output and occupation of space with the arrival of new migrants.[16] Second, while population expansion and capital formation may often have made greater contributions to growth, at times these processes were accelerated by *expectations* of returns from export development. Finally, there is a danger that the cyclical nature of the development of settler societies can become obscured by statistical manipulations. James Belich has usefully re-iterated the need to 'think in the rounds', arguing that rapidly developing 'newlands' (which are not synonymous with political units) pass through distinct phases of boom (or explosive colonisation[17]), bust, and recovery. Belich doubts the role of exports in triggering booms considering improved transportation and imports of goods, capital and labour, along with a 'boom mentality' to be more important.[18] Come the bust, however, 'export rescue' was essential to service debts amassed in the previous phase. While during the boom 'newlands' shook off the shackles of their connections to the old countries, the need to export after the bust initiated a phase of 'recolonisation' restoring bonds with the old world, and the reconfiguration of the economy to staples.[19]

Whatever the degree to which growth was export-led, one critical feature of societies containing regions of recent settlement (with the partial exception of the United States) was the relative shallowness of their capital markets along with the relative scarcity of labour.[20] This is not to say that settler societies lacked internal capital markets or, by the late-nineteenth century, savings and resources of their own.[21] However they frequently ran against internal barriers which could only be overcome through the importation of capital, particularly the need to construct railways, mines, urban utilities, ports, and other forms of 'social overhead capital'.[22] The flow of overseas capital *required* for development was often augmented as excited investors sought a slice of the expected returns from the development of 'young countries'. As a result an estimated 53 per cent of the stock of British, French, and German overseas investment was placed in settler capitalist societies, of which three-quarters had flowed through Britain.[23]

Capital imports tended to play different roles in the economic, and political, life of settler societies at different points in the economic cycle.[24] At the start of an expansionary cycle (whatever its origins) local capital and labour often proved adequate. As expansion ran up against internal barriers, often as migrants began to arrive on the basis of rumours of good times, a settler society began to look overseas (chiefly to Britain) for capital – often (but not always) for large social overhead capital projects. Capital imports also fuelled booms through their effects on local credit. Borrowing overseas also prevented a shortage of credit on local money markets. Moreover, as capital raised in London frequently increased the London (or in the Canadian case, New York) holdings of financial institutions operating in the borrowing society, it also promoted an expansion of the money supply, further stimulating the economy.[25] In these ways, investment itself often came to drive growth. This borrowing amassed liabilities which had ultimately to be serviced through exports.[26] However, while the boom lasted, they were effectively met through further borrowing. These relationships became exposed when boom, for whatever reason, turned to bust. As confidence weakened, interest rates would rise, and often credit overseas dried up entirely. The money supply contracted with overseas balances, and the full force of external liabilities became apparent. Then debt service became a strain, sometimes a major problem. In the age of the gold standard, this had to be tackled through domestic deflation and a reduction of imports. This point of crisis is the moment at which Cain and Hopkins argue that the 'rules of the game' bit hardest.[27] In the longer term, as Belich points out, expanding exports eased the pain.[28] Typically the cycle took about 15 to 20 years from start to finish.

Both Australia and Canada had broadly similar economic relations to the wider world. Both were relatively small open settler capitalist economies heavily reliant on overseas trade, investment, and migration. However the timings of their development differed, placing them at varying points on the cycle outlined above in the late-1890s and 1900s, the period covered by this book. There were also important institutional contrasts between them, particularly in the structure of finance and business, and in the role of the state. In the next two sections, the course of events and particularly shifting patterns of capital formation in the two dominions are examined in turn.

Australian development and capital formation, 1861–1914

Britain's Australian colonies were classic nineteenth-century settler capitalist economies. The tiny penal colony founded at Botany Bay in 1788 had, by the mid-nineteenth century become six colonies, occupied in 1850 by 389,000 Europeans.[29] The white population grew dramatically in the subsequent decade as gold discoveries attracted fortune-seeking migrants. From 1852, gold periodically joined wool as a major export from the budding settler societies.[30] Population and output continued to expand in the 1860s, and, as Graph 1.1, shows the 1870s and 1880s.[31]

The growth in population and output was not evenly spread during this 'long boom'. In particular, Western Australia did not experience

Graph 1.1 Australian and Canadian GDP, GDP per capita, and Population, 1870–1914

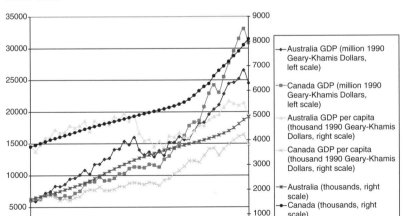

Source: A. Maddison, *Monitoring the World Economy, 1820–1992* (Paris, 1995), Table C-16a, Table A-13a.

the dramatic growth seen further east (especially in Victoria and New South Wales) prior to the 1890s.[32] This highlights an important feature of Australian development in the nineteenth century: the compartmentalised nature of the continent's economy. While there were some connections, each colony primarily functioned as a distinct entity with a port capital serving as the point of contact with a separate interior.[33] The lack of integration explains the bizarre fact that late-nineteenth century Australia possessed three separate railway gauges: the level of intercolonial integration did not justify standardisation.[34] The emerging banking system – comprising a combination of Australian-owned and anglo-Australian banks – also reflected this segmentation and, until the 1890s, individual banks tended to concentrate their activities in one or two colonies.[35]

It is with this regionalism in mind that the sectoral composition of GDP, as estimated by Butlin and reflected in Tables 1.1 and 1.2, ought to be examined. During the 'long boom' primary production declined as a component of GDP (largely due to the falling importance of mining). The 'golden fleece' remained a steady contributor to an expanding total GDP. Primary production declined as a proportion of GDP in the 1880s, but still enjoyed high growth rates. Mining lagged behind until the late-1880s, when the development of the vast mining complex at Broken Hill in New South Wales began, as well as gold mining booms at Mount Morgan and Chartered Towers in Queensland.[36] As the tables show, manufacturing also expanded. By the 1880s, a full-scale boom was underway in eastern Australia, especially in Victoria. In part it was driven by growth in the pastoral sector, but also by increased demand for housing and other urban facilities as the children of the gold rush generation reached adulthood, and migration increased.[37] Hence, in the private sector, pastoral expansion was joined by construction which contributed increasingly to GDP in the 1880s – especially in 'Marvellous Melbourne', the epicentre of the boom.[38] By the 1880s a long period of growth had itself conditioned high expectations about the future prospects of the economy.[39] In this climate, and contrary to the prevailing orthodoxy in Britain, many banks (especially those owned in Australia) began lending on the security of land; joined by a number of urban finance and land companies.[40]

The 1870s and 1880s also saw an expansion of public undertakings reflected in their proportion of GDP, and in the annual growth figures. The 1870s and 1880s saw significant levels of public spending on railways, and other urban and rural utilities, often with borrowed money.[41] The state played an important role in supplying capital in Australia, particularly in

Table 1.1 Sectoral Composition of Australian GDP, Selected Five Yearly Averages, 1861–1914 (per cent)

Year	Pastoral	Agri-culture	Mining	Other Primary	Tot. Prim.	Manu-facturing	Con-struction	Public Busi-nesses	Govern-ment Services	Finance	Distri-bution	Other Services	House Rents
1861–1864	8.8	9.2	14.5	3.9	36.4	4.1	9.4	0.7	6.0	3.9	16.0	11.8	11.8
1865–1869	10.9	9.5	10.9	4.1	35.5	6.6	9.3	1.0	5.9	4.1	15.7	10.8	11.6
1870–1874	14.7	8.0	9.2	3.8	35.7	8.3	9.2	1.1	4.8	4.3	14.8	10.1	12.2
1875–1879	14.4	8.3	6.1	4.2	32.9	9.7	12.6	1.6	4.6	4.0	15.3	8.9	11.1
1880–1884	12.3	8.1	4.7	4	29.1	10.8	13.4	2.3	4.3	3.8	14.1	9.4	13.5
1885–1889	10.8	7.1	4.3	3.9	26.0	10.8	14.2	2.7	4.4	4.0	15.1	10.2	13.5
1890–1894	12.8	5.4	6.5	5	29.8	11	9.7	4.0	5.0	2.8	13.3	12.6	12.8
1895–1899	10.0	6.3	8.7	5.3	30.2	12.4	7.3	4.5	5.4	2.1	13.2	14.5	11.5
1900–1904	11.2	6.5	9.9	4.6	32.1	11.5	7.4	4.6	3.8	1.9	16.0	13.6	9.5
1905–1909	18.5	6.0	8.3	4.2	37.0	11.8	5.7	4.8	3.5	1.8	15.5	12.6	7.6
1910–1914	13.0	6.8	5.7	4.1	29.7	13.7	8.4	5.2	3.6	1.7	18.2	12.1	7.8
Av. 1861–1914	12.6	7.4	7.9	4.3	32.2	10.2	9.7	2.3	4.6	3.1	15.2	11.4	11.2

Calculated from: N. G. Butlin, *Australian Domestic Product, Investment, and Foreign Borrowing, 1861–1938/39* (Cambridge, 1962), pp. 9–10, Table 2.

Table 1.2 Australian Annual GDP Growth by Sectors, Selected Five Yearly Averages, 1862–1914 (per cent)

Year	Pastoral	Agri-culture	Mining	Other Primary	**Total Primary**	Manu-facturing	Con-struction	Public Busi-nesses	Govern-ment Services	Finance	GDP
1862–1864	17.6	0.2	-5.5	7.0	5.2	4.5	-3.8	-1.7	2.8	1.2	0.28
1865–1869	0.6	9.0	3.9	6.5	15.6	6.6	3.5	3.4	3.6	2.8	3.47
1870–1874	24.1	0.0	1.7	10.1	11.5	10.1	3.2	2.4	11.2	11.7	7.87
1875–1879	2.5	8.3	-6.0	0.9	6.7	6.6	1.8	5.3	-0.9	2.4	3.28
1880–1884	4.2	2.0	1.3	6.5	8.0	8.5	2.6	3.9	6.9	6.2	5.18
1885–1889	14.1	4.3	7.8	5.0	2.9	5.3	2.7	2.7	5.2	9.0	5.68
1890–1894	-2.6	-13.1	2.5	1.8	-5.5	-12.8	-1.0	-1.3	-16.4	-10.1	-6.60
1895–1899	-4.2	13.4	8.0	1.6	5.4	8.7	2.0	-1.3	2.8	13.4	4.21
1900–1904	26.3	3.8	1.8	0.4	0.7	-2.7	0.0	-1.9	3.3	9.9	4.23
1905–1909	3.6	16.8	-2.1	1.4	9.1	10.5	4.1	5.6	4.9	9.4	5.88
1910–1914	-2.6	-0.6	1.7	9.1	8.9	18.3	4.4	9.1	6.0	7.0	5.83
Av. 1862–1914	7.1	4.2	2.1	4.8	6.5	5.9	2.2	2.9	2.6	5.2	3.7

Calculated from: Butlin, *Australian Domestic Product*, 9–10, Table 2.

constructing and managing urban utilities, and, crucially, railways.[42] It also owned and ran a number of manufacturing enterprises, particularly those servicing the railways.[43] Noel Butlin described this tendency to state ownership, along with an interventionist approach to economic management, as 'colonial socialism'.[44] In part, John Hirst has claimed, this was a legacy of the large role of the state under the convict system.[45] Of course such legacies can be discarded. The public ownership of railways in particular was also promoted by the early difficulties facing private enterprise. Eastern Australia was unconducive to private rail construction. Markets there were scattered and demand initially limited by the light weight of wool (which could be transported cost-effectively by other means). Many Australian port-cities were surrounded by difficult terrain (especially Sydney, hemmed in by the Blue Mountains). This led to high entry costs, with little prospect of immediate returns on completion of a line. These conditions, because of the barriers they presented to private enterprise, favoured state ownership of railways, setting a precedent for other utilities.[46] Davis and Gallman have suggested that the states' superior access to the London capital market further accentuated this pattern.[47]

The contrast with other settler societies should not be overstated. As we shall see in the next section, the private companies constructing and running railways in Canada received significant levels of state support. Nonetheless, the direct role played by Australian governments in building and managing railways shaped patterns of business in the continent, and hence connections with London. In particular it meant that Australia lacked the concentrations of interconnected financial, railway, and industrial capital which – as we shall see – played a central role intermediating between London and the Canadian economy and state. The closest equivalent prior to the 1890s, the pastoral 'squattocracy' (large land owners who originally 'squatted' on crown lands), were decimated in the economic crisis of the 1890s. There were also concentrations in the mining industry, particularly Melbourne's Collins House Group but they lacked the scale and scope of the clusters of big businesses surrounding the Bank of Montreal or the Canadian Bank of Commerce. This helps explain W. D. Rubinstein's finding that New South Wales had an anomalously low propensity to produce millionaires compared to Britain, Canada, the US, or South Africa.[48]

Since the state in Australia generally constructed the railways, it tended to play a central role in capital formation, itself a major driver of the long boom.[49] Graph 1.2 shows Australian and Canadian capital formation as a proportion of national income. In the Australian case, it

Graph 1.2   Patterns of Capital Formation in Australia and Canada, 1861–1914

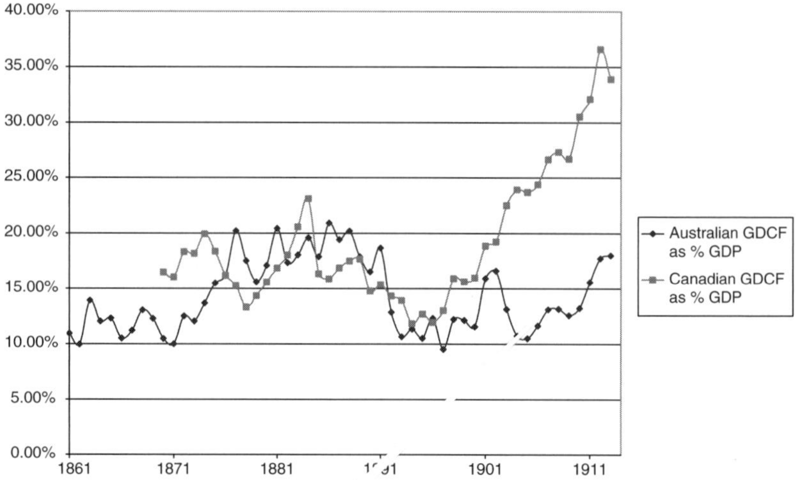

Calculated from: Butlin, *Australian Do .estic Product*, Table 1, 6; M. C. Urquhart, 'New Estimates of Gross National Produc' Canada, 1870–1927: Some Implications for Canadian Development' in S. L. Engerman .nd R. E. Gallman eds., *Long-Term Factors in American Economic Growth* (Chicago, 19′ ₂), 20–5, Table 2.4.

reveals high levels of capital formation especially during the long boom. After 1875 Gross Domestic Capital Formation (or GDCF) did not dip below 15 per cent of (an expanding) GDP until 1891. The composition of Australian GDCF can be seen on Tables 1.3 and 1.4. Unsurprisingly, the public sector played an important role, averaging 44 per cent of capital formation across the period. Its role tended to be proportionally greater from the 1890s onwards. Transport connections, and particularly rail-ways, were the most important single component of the public con-tribution, accounting for 24.4 per cent of total capital formation in the continent. In the private sector, pastoral and agricultural, and residential investment were the largest components of GDCF, the former playing (according to Butlin's estimates) a major role during the long boom, but falling from the early-1890s.[50]

The high levels of capital formation seen in the 1870s and 1880s relied heavily on imported capital (as Graph 1.4 below shows), creating a host of connections overseas. Almost all of this inward investment originated in Britain.[51] Graph 1.3 below shows the composition of British investment. Over the period as a whole, government borrow-ings dominated the export of British capital to Australia, particularly before the 1880s and in the 1900s. During the 1880s boom in eastern

Table 1.3 Australian Gross Public Capital Formation, 1861–1914 (£000 and per cent)

Period	Railways	Roads and Bridges	Water and Sewerage	Public Education	Other	Total Public Sector	TOTAL GDCF
1861–1864	21.6%	10.1%	0.99%	5.4%	2.1%	40.7%	34,878
1865–1869	14.7%	7.8%	5.03%	5.0%	1.2%	34.0%	39,694
1870–1874	13.5%	6.9%	1.97%	4.0%	2.0%	28.7%	50,713
1875–1879	16.2%	6.7%	1.16%	5.0%	1.2%	30.6%	102,000
1880–1884	22.6%	6.2%	2.44%	4.0%	1.4%	37.2%	135,950
1885–1889	22.2%	5.1%	3.10%	2.9%	1.6%	35.7%	175,228
1890–1894	25.3%	6.4%	4.15%	3.5%	1.7%	41.6%	115,542
1895–1899	25.0%	10.8%	5.53%	4.4%	4.3%	50.3%	83,848
1900–1904	21.3%	9.2%	5.26%	1.1%	4.4%	41.4%	135,100
1905–1909	18.9%	4.1%	4.37%	0.9%	6.9%	35.8%	153,208
1910–1914	25.9%	3.1%	5.21%	1.1%	9.4%	47.7%	285,727
Total	288,532	78,123	51,399	35,193	57,222	524,077	1,182,784
Total %	24.4%	6.6%	4.35%	3.0%	4.8%	44.3%	100.0%

Calculated from Butlin, *Australian Domestic Product*, 16–17, 24, Tables 4, 8.

Table 1.4 Australian Gross Private Capital Formation, 1861–1914 (£000 and per cent)

Period	Residential	Industrial	Commercial + Financial	Mining ~	Shipping	Pastoral and Agricultural	Total
1861–1864	38.4%	1.2%	3.4%	1.1%	0.3%	14.9%	59.3%
1865–1869	29.6%	11.7%	5.8%	3.2%	0.2%	15.4%	66.0%
1870–1874	28.1%	8.6%	6.9%	1.3%	0.9%	25.4%	71.3%
1875–1879	21.6%	5.8%	2.0%	1.0%	0.7%	38.2%	69.4%
1880–1884	27.1%	6.3%	5.0%	1.0%	0.3%	23.0%	62.8%
1885–1889	24.8%	4.5%	6.9%	1.2%	0.1%	26.8%	64.3%
1890–1894	23.3%	4.4%	5.1%	1.4%	0.1%	24.0%	58.4%
1895–1899 $	17.7%	4.8%	7.3%	3.8%	0.1%	16.0%	49.7%
1900–1904	20.6%	8.5%	6.6%	7.2%	4.7%	11.0%	58.6%
1905–1909	24.7%	8.6%	8.2%	6.1%	2.1%	14.5%	64.2%
1910–1914	21.2%	9.4%	8.0%	2.4%	1.7%	9.6%	52.3%
1861–1914 %	26.2%	7.8%	7.1%	3.2%	1.4%	20.9%	66.6%
Total	309,683	92,482	84,276	37,725	16,596	247,050	787,811

$ – Note Western Australian Residential and Mining Investment only included from 1897
~ – Until 1900 only gold mining machinery and plant are included.
Calculated from Butlin: *Australian Domestic Product*, 18–19, 24, Tables 5, 8.

Graph 1.3   Sectoral Composition of British Investment in Australia, 1865–1914

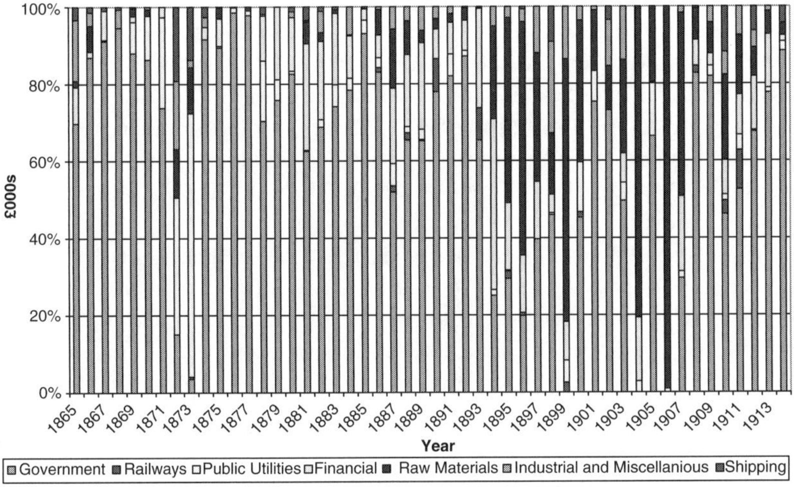

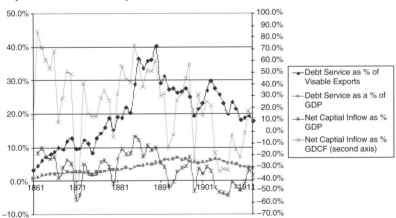

Source: *The Global Export of Capital from Great Britain, 1865–1914: A Statistical Survey* (Basingstoke, 1999), 72–82, Table 2.4.

Graph 1.4   Australian Capital Formation in the World Economy

Calculated from: Meredith and Dyster, *Australia in the International Economy*, p. 35, Table 2.7, Table 3.1, p. 42, Table 3.2, p. 50 and Butlin, *Australian Domestic Product*, Table 1, p. 6.

Australia, investment in financial companies (pastoral finance and real estate) played a large role; in the 1890s mining became significant. The relationships created by these patterns of inward investment are charted on Graph 1.4. With several dips prior to 1891, imported capital often accounted for over 20 per cent of capital formation, at times exceeding 60 per cent in the 1860s and 1880s. Capital formation during the long boom relied on British capital. Overseas debt charges grew from 0.9 per cent of GDP in 1861 to 5.9 per cent in 1891, or 3.2 and 29.5 per cent of visible exports.

The accumulated debt burden weighed heaviest just after the boom ended, and it is now possible to resume the narrative and examine economic developments in the period covered by this book. Australia's boom reached fever pitch in the late-1880s. Melbourne's property market became overheated and, after a restriction of credit by the Victorian banks, borrowed time as well as capital from British investors. The pastoral frontier, spurred by good prices, benign seasons, and sheer optimism moved on to marginal and less productive land. In the early-1890s, these forces unravelled. From 1890 a decline in wool prices shifted the terms of trade against Australia, raising the burden of debt service (in 1890 debt service just exceeded 40 per cent of visible exports), and reducing pastoral returns. In 1891 these troubles, combined with a new scepticism in London about settler societies in the wake of the 1890 Baring crisis curtailed the inflow of capital.[52] This finally undermined the property boom. It also placed colonial budgets under considerable strain, not least to service their debts, as revenues from import duties, rail freights, and land sales fell with the level of borrowing. Eastern Australian governments responded by reducing their expenditure. Thus, although many of the eastern Australia's economic problems were internal in origin, the cessation of capital imports helped to trigger and accentuate the growing crisis.[53] Matters became worse in May 1893 when 12 of eastern Australia's 18 note-issuing banks suspended payments. This debacle is at times blamed on withdrawals by alarmed Scottish depositors, but whatever their role, the banks' high levels of exposure to land and real estate (contravening more conservative British banking traditions), and the resultant high levels of illiquidity, lay at the root of the crisis.[54] The banking crisis further constrained credit and impeded exports, again weakening government revenues.[55] Even the weather conspired against eastern Australia. Poor rains from 1890 became a full drought from 1897 through to 1903, killing a quarter of Australia's sheep, and also curtailing wheat production and mining (which often used water in processing).[56] The resultant depression, the product of poor luck and poor judgement compounded, generated widespread unemployment, and left a political and economic legacy which, as we shall see, shaped Australian life down to 1914.[57]

From the late-1890s these economic woes were eased in several ways, both of which relied on new imports of British capital (as Graph 1.4 shows, excepting 1899, from 1894 until 1903 net capital importation resumed). Firstly many eastern Australian states – again under the influence of 'colonial socialism' – embarked on extensive public works programmes deliberately conceived to alleviate the depression.[58] As Table 1.3 shows, in 1895–1899 the public sector accounted for over half of Australian capital formation. Secondly, Western Australia – long excluded from the good times further east – boomed as gold was discovered in Coolgardie in 1892 and Kalgoorlie in 1893.[59] The gold itself boosted Australian exports, and the goldfields attracted fresh British capital. Intercolonial trade, and remittances from eastern migrants transfered a proportion of the benefits eastwards, easing the burden of debt service.[60]

Many of these palliatives proved temporary. The gold boom in Western Australia ended in the early-1900s with the industry, as we shall see, clouded in scandal in London. Equally from 1903 public borrowing in London became difficult (see Chapter 2, Graph 2.2).[61] Australian GDP began to recover nonetheless as exports expanded.[62] The end of the drought around the turn of the century began a restoration of the fortunes of the pastoral industry which, as Table 1.2 shows, grew dramatically from 1900 to 1904. By 1907 sheep numbers had returned to 1892 levels, and productivity gains meant that output already exceeded levels seen in the early-1890s.[63] Meanwhile other sectors became increasingly important. Agriculture and dairying expanded between 1905 and 1914 (see Table 1.1 and 1.2) assisted by the adoption of the drought resistant 'federation' variety of wheat, stump jumping ploughs, and refrigerated shipping.[64] Export earnings were boosted as the terms of trade, which swung against Australia in the 1890s, again became favourable.[65] Domestic manufacturing was stimulated both because these sectors required new equipment and more processing, and because the smaller farmers who tended to run them had a greater propensity to consume local products.[66] Construction also expanded from 1905 as the grandsons and granddaughters of the gold rush generation reached adulthood, and as immigration revived. All of these developments also prompted new growth in government businesses and services, especially the provision of further rural infrastructure – reflected in Table 1.1.[67]

Capital formation fell in the early years of the new century (and in 1900 capital imports still accounted for 25 per cent of new capital

Table 1.5 British Investment in Australia, Selected Totals, 1865–1914 (£mil and per cent)

	Government		(Private) Railways and Shipping	Public Utilities	Financial			Raw Materials		Industrial and Misc.
	Total	Colonial/ State Governments			Total	Finance, Land and Investment Companies	Banks and Discount Cos	Total	Mines	
Total by 1900	164.09	150.76	4.82	9.77	33.77	21.54	8.59	33.06	33.05	9.42
	64.4%	59.1%	1.9%	3.8%	13.2%	8.4%	3.4%	13.0%	13.0%	3.7%
1895–1899	13.40	13.40	1.19	0.37	6.67	2.10	1.47	22.52	22.52	4.13
	27.7%	27.7%	2.5%	0.8%	13.8%	4.3%	3.0%	46.6%	46.6%	8.6%
1900–1904	13.44	13.44	0.28	1.42	0.22	0.22	0.00	4.79	4.79	1.16
	63.1%	63.1%	1.3%	6.7%	1.0%	1.0%	0.0%	22.5%	22.5%	5.4%
1905–1909	13.71	13.71	0.10	0.62	1.26	0.13	1.05	5.80	4.94	0.43
	62.5%	62.5%	0.4%	2.8%	5.7%	0.6%	4.8%	26.5%	22.5%	2.0%
1910–1914	34.11	33.08	0.58	0.76	4.24	0.12	4.12	3.66	3.07	1.12
	73.8%	71.6%	3.7%	1.6%	9.2%	0.3%	8.9%	7.9%	6.6%	2.4%
Total 1895–1914	74.65	73.62	1.29	3.17	12.39	2.57	6.64	36.77	35.31	6.84
	54.2%	53.5%	2.4%	2.3%	9.0%	1.9%	4.8%	26.7%	25.6%	5.0%
Total 1900–1914	61.26	60.23	2.08	2.80	5.72	0.47	5.17	14.25	12.79	2.71
	68.5%	67.3%	2.3%	3.1%	6.4%	0.5%	5.8%	15.9%	14.3%	3.0%
Total 1865–1914	222.91	214.92	7.45	11.88	39.49	22.05	13.72	45.33	43.87	11.93
	65.8%	63.4%	2.2%	3.5%	11.6%	6.5%	4.0%	13.4%	12.9%	3.5%

Calculated from Stone, *Global Export*, 78–88, Table 4.

formation), and remained well below levels seen in the 1870s and 1880s (see Graph 1.2). Much of the Australian recovery and attendant diversification was possible without large-scale investment in new capital. Imported capital played little role after 1903, indeed from 1904 to 1911 Australia repaid debts overseas (as Graph 1.3 shows, in these years net capital inflow was negative). As exports recovered, debt service as a proportion of exports and of GDP gradually fell (see Graph 1.4). This did not mean that Australia had left London's embrace. Debts still had to be serviced or renewed. From the late-1900s demands for capital again grew, as construction expanded, and new rural infrastructure (irrigation, double tracked railways, and new branch lines) became (or came to be thought) necessary.[68] Table 1.3 charts the increase in capital formation by the public sector. From 1911, net overseas borrowing resumed, and in 1912, accounted for 18 per cent of capital formation – still much lower as a proportion of GDCF than in earlier decades. This was largely the result of renewed borrowing in London by the Australian states, as Table 1.5 shows.

Overall, the Australian economy experienced a long expansion from the 1860s culminating in a boom in the 1880s. Exports contributed to this role, as did the rising population, government railway construction, and the housing demands of the decedents of the gold rush generation. Capital formation was very high as a proportion of GDP in the boom, and imported capital (almost exclusively raised in Britain) significantly supplemented domestic sources. The boom gave way to a bust in the early 1890s, and the resultant legacy of debt deepened the pain. The depression was, though, ameliorated by further imports of capital by colonial governments and Western Australian gold mines. These palliatives gave way, from the early 1900s, to a recovery driven by exports with capital formation funded domestically and some debt paid off. This proved a temporary interlude and capital imports resumed just prior to the First World War. It was against this shifting backdrop that the politics of finance took place in Australia in the late-1890s and 1900s. In particular, the political and economic legacies of past debt often loomed large even as new borrowing waned.

Canadian development and capital formation, 1870–1914

British North America's economic trajectory presented several contrasts to the Australian colonies. Parts had been integrated into the global economy since the sixteenth century.[69] In the early-nineteenth century, the economies of the maritime colonies, central Canada, and the far west remained regionalised. Nonetheless, from the late-eighteenth century

a powerful cluster of anglophone (mainly Scottish) merchants and financiers based in Montreal dominated an integrated transatlantic and transcontinental trading system, a 'commercial empire, of the St Lawrence',
founded on fur trading activities that stretched through the river's drainage
basin deep into the continental interior, and well south of the modern
border with the United States.[70] In the early-nineteenth century, the unification of the rival Hudson's Bay and North West Companies consolidated
this fur trading elite, and from its foundation in 1917, the Bank of Montreal
occupied its financial apex.[71] By the mid-nineteenth century, Toronto
began to emerge as a rival centre. It too developed a mercantile elite devoted
to long distance trade. The Bank of Upper Canada and, from 1867 and after
that bank's failure, the Canadian Bank of Commerce, provided a focal point
for Torontonian finance.[72] Thus central Canada, unlike Australia, entered
the second half of the nineteenth century possessing several powerful
clusters of business institutions, with transcontinental aspirations.

These commercial empires frequently competed with their expanding
southern neighbour for migrants and the trade of the continental interior.
Unlike the Mississippi, the St Lawrence was not an easy river to navigate.
Improvements were required to remain competitive, first canal-building in
the 1830s and 1840s, and then, in the 1850s, the Grand Trunk Railway
from Montreal to Toronto – which enjoyed support from the recently
united Province of Canada, and attracted British capital.[73] Until the 1840s
the Laurentine system had been assisted by preferences in the British
market on Canadian timber and wheat. Britain's adoption of free trade
ended this advantage. The railway programme of the 1850s was, in part, a
response to the ending of the British preference.[74] A further response came
in the 1854 'reciprocity treaty' conceding freer entry to Canadian produce
into the United States.[75]

The abrogation of this treaty in 1865 ushered in a new era in British
North American political economy which was to last until 1914. The perceived need for a new market to make up for the supposedly lost trade was
one force driving the formation of the Dominion of Canada in 1867.[76] The
economic fortunes of the Maritimes, British Columbia, and the prairies
were, henceforth, to be welded to those of the central Canadian provinces
by central government action.[77] This project in transcontinental national-
building had a number of elements. Firstly, a measure of protection had
been adopted by the old province of Canada in 1859, and the new federal
government extended this to the new Dominion.[78] Tariff barriers were
further increased by prime minister John A. Macdonald in 1878 as a major
component of a 'national policy' which came to be seen as a means to
secure a separate economic and political fate on the North American

continent.[79] Secondly, from 1872, a federal land act allowed settlers access to land on easy terms in the west, which had to be populated if it was to provide a market for central Canadian industry, and if the projected nation was to become a reality. Finally, a national economy required unifying transport links. As a result railway construction formed a further plank of the national policy. In the 1870s a state-owned line linked central Canada and the Maritimes (its route was heavily influenced by strategic considerations, and it rarely generated profits as a result). A second line was to cross the prairies to British Columbia. In the early-1870s the proposal was mired in controversy, but in 1881 it was begun by a syndicate of Canadians and Americans. Completed in 1885 (and drawing heavily on British capital), the Canadian Pacific Railway (CPR) relied heavily on state support, receiving 250 million acres of land, $25 million in cash, and 700 miles of already completed lines.[80]

In this the CPR exemplified a common, and long established pattern in Canadian economic life whereby governments sought to, 'stimulate and direct the course of economic development ... by lending the authority and financial resources of the state to certain private business corporations which have become the "chosen instruments"... for the furtherance of national economic policy'.[81] This pattern had been in place at least since the first wave of canal-building in the mid-nineteenth century. The result in central Canada was a close alliance between the deeply intertwined upper echelons of finance and business in Montreal and Toronto, and policymakers in Ottawa.[82] Canadian politicians were not necessarily less interventionist than their 'colonial socialist' antipodean counterparts. They did, however, choose a different method of intervention: allying with business rather than replacing it.[83]

This method reinforced the power and integration of the Montreal's and Toronto's mercantile-financial elites. The Bank of Montreal enjoyed a close alliance with the Canadian Pacific Railway and the Conservatives, while the Canadian Bank of Commerce backed Canada's Liberals and supported rival routes west.[84] The power of these two banks was compounded by close links to many urban utilities (often built by contractors who had worked on the CPR), and with the commanding heights of an increasingly concentrated industrial sector.[85] Thus, in late-nineteenth and early-twentieth century Canada, finance capitalists were a powerful force. As we shall see, the projects of this group depended on access to British capital, and they maintained close connections in the City as a result. Thus, the differing distribution of responsibility between the Canadian state and big business moulded relations with the City, and hence its impact on Canadian politics, a point we return to in Chapter 2.

The path of economic development in late-nineteenth and early-twentieth century Canada has proved controversial. Traditionally it was argued that, in the absence of a staple, the economy stalled after the abrogation of reciprocity, and then changed up several gears from 1896 with the development of the wheat production on the prairies.[86] Since the 1960s a gradualist school argued that this account overlooked important developments in manufacturing in the intervening three decades, and that in any case per capita growth had not accelerated dramatically from 1896.[87] Urquhart's recent national income estimates have restored the notion that 1896 was a turning point (See Graph 1.1 above and Table 1.6 below). Altman has shown that even per capita GNP grew at 4.5 per cent per year between 1896 and 1913, compared to 1.5 per cent from 1877 to 1896.[88] Despite this, one recent econometric analysis has suggested that the underlying (i.e. non-cyclical) rate of growth per capita did not shift in 1896.[89] This may be so, although such statistical wizardry takes us far from contemporary experiences and perceptions, something which becomes abundantly clear in subsequent chapters.

The 1896–1914 boom's association with wheat has been questioned rather more successfully. As Table 1.6 shows, agriculture grew less rapidly than many other large sectors (sectors comprising more than 5 per cent of GDP) including construction, transportation, and manufacturing. It has been argued that population increase (from 1901, for the first time since 1861, Canada experienced *net* immigration), urbanisation, and capital formation, played a greater role than wheat exports in stimulating growth.[90] As far as primary products did contribute, mining and forestry also played a role and their production expanded at a faster rate. Between 1895 and 1899, mining was the fastest expanding sector, driven not least by the development of goldfields in the Kootenays and Yukon.[91] Even so, expectations of future returns from prairie agricultural development provided a major rationale for the rapid construction of railways and towns in the west. Consequently, central Canadian manufacturing's expansion also came in part from demands (for construction materials and consumer goods) generated ultimately by the expectations as well as the realities of western expansion.

Either way, capital formation played a starring role during the 'great boom', contributing more to the growth in national income than exports.[92] From 1905 GDCF exceeded levels seen in the mid-1880s as a proportion of national income, peaking at 37 per cent of GDP in 1912 (see Graph 1.2). The absolute figures from 1905 to 1914 dwarfed earlier totals. As Table 1.8 shows, the pattern of capital formation during the boom followed earlier

Table 1.6 Canadian Annual GDP Growth by Sectors, Selected Five Yearly Averages, 1870–1914 (per cent)

Year	Agri-culture	Mining	Misc. Prim.	Total Prim.	Manu-facturing	Con-struction	Transport and Com-munications	Electric Light and Power	Finance	Govern-ment and Educa-tion	Other	GDP, (New Basis)
1870–1874	0.5	8.5	9.8	1.3	6.0	8.3	0.2		3.9	10.6	11.9	5.0
1875–1879	0.9	3.8	-3.3	0.6	-3.8	-11.2	-1.8		-1.2	0.7	-2.3	-3.3
1880–1884	2.4	2.5	7.2	2.8	9.5	17.2	8.1		9.4	4.3	56.3	8.2
1885–1889	-0.2	11.4	3.3	0.6	3.5	-0.4	3.8		6.6	3.0	5.6	2.5
1890–1894	0.3	7.7	1.6	2.3	-1.4	-8.1	3.3	7.3	3.2	2.5	0.4	0.1
1895–1899	-1.1	4.9	1.7	-0.5	-4.2	-5.9	-0.6	7.1	4.3	1.5	-1.2	-1.6
1900–1904	7.1	3.1	4.0	6.1	7.5	28.0	9.6	26.1	8.4	8.4	7.0	7.8
1905–1909	8.0	7.4	6.2	7.5	10.7	15.6	10.9	11.5	9.2	8.9	11.5	9.3
1910–1914	4.3	8.2	3.2	4.5	2.4	8.3	11.6	17.6	9.6	15.2	6.3	6.1
Av. 1870–1895	0.9	5.0	3.9	1.3	3.0	1.5	3.1	7.1	5.2	4.1	13.2	2.4
Av. 1896–1913	7.3	10.8	4.7	7.1	8.0	15.4	11.3	16.0	10.9	8.2	9.1	8.4
Av. 1870–1913	3.3	7.4	4.1	3.5	4.6	6.7	6.2	14.4	7.2	6.2	11.0	4.6

Note: Misc. Primary includes Forestry, Hunting, Fishing, and Public Resource Royalties.
Calculated from Urquhart, 'New Estimates', 11–15, Table 2.1.

Table 1.7 Sectoral Composition of Canadian GDP, Selected Five Yearly Averages, 1870–1914 (per cent)

Year	Agriculture	Mining	Misc. Primary	Total Primary Products	Manufacturing	Construction	Transport and Communications	Electric Light and Power	Finance	Government and Education	Other
1870–1874	41.8	1.2	3.2	39.3	23.6	6.1	5.3		2.1	4.0	19.6
1875–1879	34.9	1.3	3.4	39.6	21.7	5.0	5.0		2.1	5.3	21.3
1880–1884	35.0	1.1	3.4	39.5	24.8	5.5	5.5		2.4	4.8	17.5
1885–1890	28.6	1.4	3.6	33.6	24.4	5.1	5.8		2.9	5.2	22.9
1890–1894	27.2	2.0	3.6	32.8	24.4	4.0	6.4	0.2	3.1	5.2	24.0
1895–1899	26.0	3.4	3.8	33.2	22.5	3.3	7.0	0.2	3.8	5.5	24.5
1900–1904	24.5	4.3	3.1	31.9	22.3	4.7	7.3	0.3	4.3	4.9	24.2
1905–1909	23.0	3.2	2.6	28.8	23.3	6.7	8.1	0.5	4.4	4.8	23.5
1910–1914	20.7	3.1	2.3	26.1	21.1	8.3	9.4	0.7	4.5	5.7	24.2
1870–1914	26.0	2.8	3.0	31.4	22.7	6.1	7.5	0.3	3.8	5.2	23.1

Note: Misc Primary includes Forestry, Hunting, Fishing, and Public Resource Royalties.
Calculated from Urquhart, 'New Estimates', 11–15, Table 2.1.

Table 1.8 Capital Formation in Canada, 1870–1914 (per cent)

Years	Total Manufacturing	Railway and Telegraph	Other Business	Housing Construction	Total Private	Government	Grand total $ mil
1870–1874	7.78%	29.60%	17.10%	38.92%	93.39%	6.61%	317.6
1875–1879	9.17%	19.26%	21.76%	33.13%	83.33%	7.04%	328.1
1880–1884	15.21%	41.20%	19.82%	15.87%	92.10%	5.68%	501.0
1885–1889	13.63%	25.27%	21.59%	30.85%	91.34%	6.18%	489.5
1890–1894	12.66%	13.49%	27.26%	37.08%	90.48%	6.45%	468.5
1895–1899	17.87%	9.45%	27.26%	18.88%	78.76%	5.75%	625.1
1900–1904	20.81%	12.78%	40.37%	17.36%	91.31%	5.59%	1060.3
1905–1909	16.49%	20.26%	33.75%	20.55%	91.05%	6.19%	2031.4
1910–1914	17.52%	18.90%	32.21%	19.46%	88.09%	6.71%	3671.1
Total 1896–1913	17.84%	17.92%	34.45%	20.06%	90.27%	6.22%	6509.4
Total 1870–1913	16.51%	19.49%	30.81%	21.81%	88.98%	6.32%	100%
Total $mil	1567.5	1850.3	2924.8	2070.6	8446.3	823.6	9492.6

Calculated From Urquhart, 'New Estimates', 16–17, Table 2.2.

precedents, despite dramatically increased volumes. During the boom, the private sector accounted for most capital formation, with housing, manufacturing, and transportation the largest single items. The latter is unsurprising. Two new transcontinental railways, the Grand Trunk Pacific and the Canadian Northern Railway were constructed during the boom, as well as numerous branch lines and other improvements.[93]

Graph 1.5 shows the role played by outside capital, and its impacts. Capital imports played an important role in Canadian capital formation through the late-nineteenth century, rarely contributing less than 30 per cent of GDCF, levels regained in the later years of the great boom (by which point absolute levels of capital formation were far higher). From 1903 net capital imports never contributed less than a quarter of GDCF – topping 50 per cent in 1911 and 1912. From 1904 they were never less than 10 per cent of GDP. The cost of debt service as a proportion of GDP had grown steadily since 1870, but declined in the early years of the boom (as national income expanded) before rising to just over 5 per cent in 1914. As a proportion of exports, debt service fell from a peak of 31 per cent in 1891 to about 20 per cent in 1902–1903 before rising thereafter.

While Australia did not have easy access to an alternative source of overseas capital, Canada could potentially look to the US as well as Britain. A permeable border and the proximity of New York (which

Graph 1.5   Overseas Capital and Capital Formation in Canada

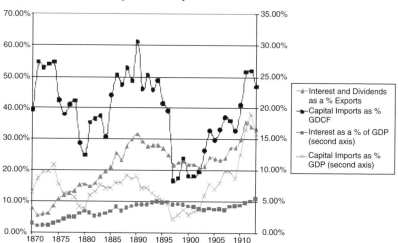

Calculated from: Urquhart, 'New Estimates', pp. 20–25, Table 2.4.

actually lay on one of the quickest routes to London from Montreal and Toronto) facilitated Canadian access to American capital. Canadian banks tended to invest their money at call in New York.[94] Despite these continental connections, Britain supplied the vast majority of Canadian capital imports. In 1900 accumulated British capital accounted for an estimated 85 per cent of all foreign capital in Canada, while the US supplied just 14 per cent.[95] Britain had lost some ground to the Americans by 1913, its proportion of accumulated capital slipping to 75 per cent (compared to 21 per cent), albeit of a much increased total (over the same period the total stock of foreign holdings increased by 204 per cent). Table 1.9 shows the flow of capital into Canada in the intervening period. Although the US supplied more capital from 1900 to 1903, Britain regained its lead thereafter and supplied at least twice as much capital annually as the US, this despite the US becoming a major exporter of capital from the turn of the new century with Canada the main beneficiary. British and US investments also differed in type. American capital tended to be

Table 1.9   Foreign Investment in Canada, 1900–1914 ($ mil)

Year	Britain	United States	Other Countries
1900	10.1	17.9	3.7
1901	15.1	18.3	3.7
1902	11.9	23.4	7.0
1903	28.9	22.1	3.7
1904	29.5	25.8	6.6
1905	76.4	32.5	3.7
1906	68.5	29.6	7.2
1907	65.2	26.0	3.8
1908	181.4	32.8	7.9
1909	212.7	36.2	4.5
1910	218.5	72.6	22.1
1911	244.4	76.2	27.8
1912	214.8	81.7	24.6
1913	375.7	134.2	36.0
Total	1753.1	629.3	162.3
%	68.89%	24.73%	6.38%

Calculated from: J. Viner, *Canada's Balance of International Indebtedness, 1900–1913*. (Cambridge, 1924), 31–2, 95, 102–3, 105–6, Tables II, III, XXVI, XXIX, XXX, XXXI.

concentrated in branch-plant extensions of US-based industries and in the extractive and manufacturing sectors.[96] British capital tended to take the form of equities, often without conceding control, with transportation and governments receiving most finance.

Thus, despite a growing US presence, Britain remained the main source of inward (especially portfolio) investment in Canada in the early-twentieth century. The composition of British investment is reflected on Graph 1.6 and Table 1.10. Investment in Canada was dominated by governments and railways, and since a good deal of Canadian government borrowing was also used for infrastructure, the contrast with Australia comes not in the uses to which British money were put, but in the differing distribution of labour between the state and the private sector. Matters were complicated by the fact that Canadian railway bonds were often guaranteed by the federal or provincial governments (and just after confederation some had imperial government guarantees).

Beyond government and railways other sectors could prove significant at particular junctures. Raw materials played an important role in the 1890s (almost entirely taken up by mines, and at a time when the aggregate inflow of capital was low). In the early-1880s, and after 1905, finance played an important role, particularly investments in finance and land companies. These either purchased property and brought it to

Graph 1.6   Sectoral Composition of British Investment in Canada, 1865–1914

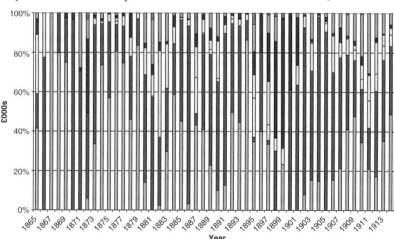

Source: Stone, *Global Export*, 52–62, Table 2.

Table 1.10 British Investment in Canada, Selected Totals, 1865–1914 (£mil and per cent)

	Government		Railways and Shipping	Public Utilities	Financial			Raw Materials		Industrial and Misc.
	Total	Fed./ Prov. Governments			Total	Finance, Land and Investment Cos.	Banks and Discount Cos.	Total	Mines	Total
Total by 1900	51.97 *39.9%*	41.10 *31.6%*	52.95 *40.7%*	2.57 *2.0%*	7.75 *6.0%*	5.22 *4.0%*	1.05 *0.8%*	9.52 *7.3%*	9.24 *7.1%*	5.35 *4.1%*
1895–1899	3.35 *23.9%*	2.03 *14.5%*	2.04 *14.5%*	1.23 *8.7%*	1.34 *9.5%*	0.32 *2.2%*	0.00 *0.0%*	4.88 *34.7%*	4.63 *32.9%*	1.23 *8.7%*
1900–1904	1.53 *8.5%*	1.04 *5.8%*	13.16 *73.1%*	0.57 *3.1%*	0.24 *1.3%*	0.24 *1.3%*	0.00 *0.0%*	2.15 *11.9%*	2.15 *11.9%*	0.35 *2.0%*
1905–1909	23.88 *31.0%*	16.42 *21.3%*	37.28 *48.5%*	5.12 *6.7%*	1.50 *2.0%*	1.31 *1.7%*	0.17 *0.2%*	1.62 *2.1%*	1.52 *2.0%*	7.52 *9.8%*
1910–1914	62.26 *32.5%*	27.89 *14.6%*	66.20 *34.6%*	15.06 *7.9%*	16.24 *8.5%*	10.15 *5.3%*	0.94 *0.5%*	3.49 *1.8%*	3.30 *1.7%*	28.33 *14.8%*
1895–1914	91.02 *30.3%*	47.38 *15.8%*	118.69 *39.5%*	21.97 *7.3%*	19.32 *6.4%*	12.01 *4.0%*	1.11 *0.4%*	12.13 *4.0%*	11.58 *3.9%*	37.43 *12.5%*
1900–1914	87.67 *30.6%*	45.34 *15.8%*	116.65 *40.7%*	20.74 *7.2%*	17.99 *6.3%*	11.70 *4.1%*	1.11 *0.4%*	7.25 *2.5%*	6.96 *2.4%*	36.21 *12.6%*
1865–1914	139.64 *33.9%*	86.44 *21.0%*	167.11 *40.5%*	23.29 *5.6%*	25.74 *6.2%*	16.92 *4.1%*	2.16 *0.5%*	15.19 *3.7%*	6.96 *1.7%*	41.55 *10.1%*

Source: Stone, *Global Export*, 52–62, Table 2.

the point of production, or supplied mortgages in urban areas. Both forms were often concentrated in the Canadian west. Utilities and manufacturing also played an important role after 1905, especially in comparison with Australia. This again reflected the differing role of the state in providing utilities (it tended to act as regulator not supplier) and the more advanced state of Canadian industry.

Conclusion

Australian and Canadian economic development in the late-nineteenth and early-twentieth centuries took place in a global context. Whether or not, as a crude reading of staples thesis might suggest, exports drove development and determined the character of society, they played important roles at particular junctures. At times (as in Australia after 1896) they did drive the economic expansion. Moreover, much capital formation and urban development originated in the forward and backward linkages from exports. These economies were also characterised by high levels of capital formation. Often this was heavily reliant largely on British investment. These imports often came when 'lumpy' projects such as railways (whose full returns would only be fully realised on completion) were being undertaken. Given this clear need to import capital, exports played a crucial role in servicing debts – especially once investment booms ceased – even if they were not always driving growth.

In this the Australian and Canadian economies were similar, but in other ways they differed. Firstly in the period covered by this book, 1896–1914, they were at different stages of their economic cycles. Australia had experienced long growth facilitated by imported capital until the early nineties. Subsequently it moved through a sharp depression, ameliorated by the rapid development of mining in Western Australia, and, from about 1904, into a recovery facilitated by export-led growth, rural diversification, and which saw overseas debt being repaid. Just before the war, though, capital imports resumed, as construction responded to revived immigration and the demographic echoes of the 1850s gold rushes, and the Australian states responded to demands for further rural capital formation. Canada, by contrast, had experienced less rapid growth in the first three decades of confederation. In 1896 its fortunes changed and the Canadian economy entered a period of growth based on primary production, on manufacturing, particularly on population expansion, on sheer optimism, and also on investment. Canada drew in large volumes of British capital.

As well as these differences in timing, there were also important differences in the role played by the state and business. In particular, while large-scale capital projects in Canada tended to be undertaken by a central Canadian business elite with state support, in Australia the state constructed railways and other utilities itself. This had several important repercussions, charted in subsequent chapters. Firstly it shaped the patterns of borrowing from Britain, with the public sector accounting for a higher proportion of Australia's total. Secondly, Canadian big business had much deeper ties to the City, and a much more powerful role intermediating between the City and Canada politically as well as economically. Although Canada and Australia both remained dependent on British capital in important ways, their different cyclical positions, division of labour between state and business, and degree of integration between business and finance all shaped their relationships with the capital market. The export of British capital, and the networks linking Australia and Canada to the City are the subject of the next chapter.

2
Australian and Canadian Borrowing in the Edwardian City

In 1913 an American financial writer observed, 'As Great Britain is a country where there is never any difficulty about raising capital for the creation or extension of business, it is natural that new countries where capital is scarce and credit scarcer should turn to London'.[1] The need for capital, and the necessity of managing existing debts, drew Australians and Canadians to the London capital market. In order to understand the impact of these relationships, it is necessary to look in more detail at the operation of finance in the Square Mile. This chapter first considers the functioning of the City. It then examines the institutions, individuals, and practices involved in organising Australian and Canadian borrowing. The two dominions possessed very different connections in the Square Mile.

The City and the organisation of overseas investment

Between 1870 and 1914 Britain lent an estimated 5.2 per cent of GNP overseas, compared to 2 to 3 per cent for France, and less than 2 per cent for Germany.[2] Indeed, according to one estimate, Britain may have been responsible for 75 per cent of all global capital movements in 1900, and more than 40 per cent in 1913.[3] The flow of capital overseas was subject to 'long swings', with peaks in 1872, 1890, and 1913, and troughs in 1878 and 1901 (see Graph 2.1).[4] With the exception of the United States, British investors tended to concentrate on particular regions for relatively short periods.[5] As Graphs 2.2 and 2.3 show, investors' largesse was conferred on Australia in the 1880s and on Canada after 1900.[6] By 1901, Australia had received four-fifths of all the capital it was to receive between 1865 and 1914, Canada only a third.

Graph 2.1 Net British Investment Overseas, 1870–1914

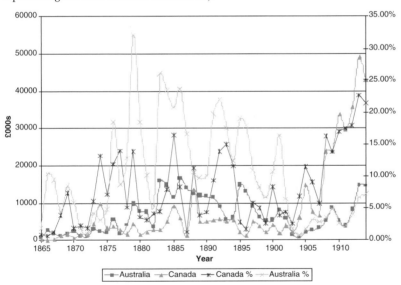

Source: C. H. Feinstein, *National Income, Expenditure and Output of the United Kingdom, 1855–1965* (Cambridge, 1972), 3, 15, Tables 10, 37–8.

Graph 2.2 British Investment in Australia and Canada, 1865–1914 (total and as a percentage of total overseas investment)

Source: Stone, *Global Export*, 52–62, 68–78, Tables 2 and 4.

Not all the capital exported from Britain in the late-nineteenth century flowed though the City. Migrants rarely left without some capital in hand, and individuals or companies at times purchased assets overseas directly.[7] Some outflows bypassed London. In the 1880s banks operating

Graph 2.3   Cumulative Total British Investment in Australia and Canada, 1865–1914

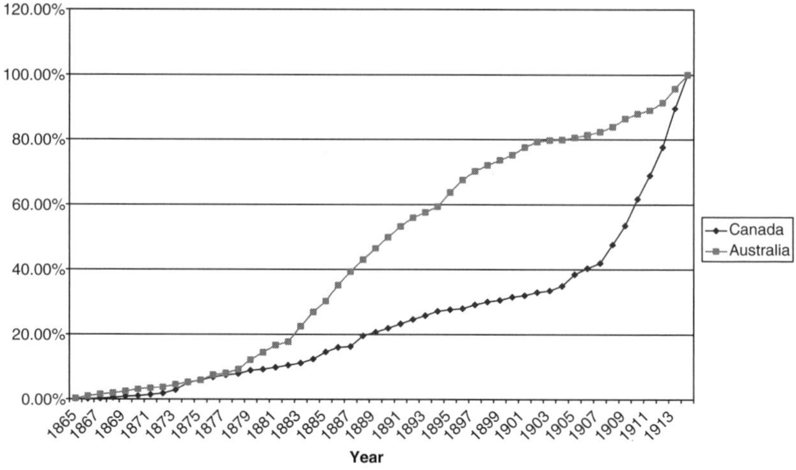

Source: Stone, *Global Export*, 52–62, 68–78, Tables 2 and 4.

in Australia accepted deposits in Britain, especially Scotland. J. D. Bailey estimated that Scottish solicitors selling to their clients accounted for a total of 40 per cent of British investment in Australia in the late-1880s.[8] Provincial stock exchanges, especially Liverpool and Edinburgh also handled overseas flotations. However, as Ranald Michie has argued, such activities were increasingly aligned with, rather than competing against, a London-dominated system. No one has challenged the view that the Square Mile was the primary channel overseas for British investment, as well as acting as a significant conduit for continental capital.[9]

The concentration of global finance in the City was intimately connected to its other functions as a global service centre. It remained an important port, although increasingly the handling of physical goods shifted towards Britain's west coast, particularly to Glasgow and Liverpool. More importantly, London organised much of the world's trade. Its merchants arranged for the purchase, transportation, and sale of goods, while various commodity exchanges cleared large amounts of global output. Insurance companies protected against losses and, by the turn of the twentieth century, futures markets guarded against fluctuating prices.[10] All these activities rested on up-to-date and detailed information. The Square Mile lay at the hub of a global communications network encompassing shipping lines, rail/sea routes to the continent, and the international telegraphic network.[11]

London's global commercial dominance also rested on the City's markets for short-term credit (the money market). One key credit device, 'the bill on London', lubricated world trade. These overcame major problem facing international merchants: that goods had to be purchased long before funds from their sale were realised. For a long time this had meant purchasing had tied up a large amount of merchants' capital. Bills removed this barrier by allowing merchants to borrow to finance their purchases, and hence to trade on much smaller capitals. To obtain funds a merchant would offer bills to the money market, sold at a slight discount (less than the amount finally repaid after a short period, often 90 days) which generated a small return for the purchaser. The bills were guaranteed by an acceptance house (a merchant bank) who judged that merchant's credit based on specialised knowledge of particular markets and regions. The merchant bank's reputation for sound judgement underpinned confidence in the bill.[12] Bills could be traded on the money market, organised by discount houses. As a readily realisable investment generating a small return, they were attractive investments for banks' reserve funds.[13] By 1900, funds flowed to the London money market from across the globe.[14] Indeed, the supply of funds exceeded the demands of trade, leading to the rise of the 'finance bill' which funded dealings in stocks and shares. In 1909, an estimated 90 per cent of purchases on the capital market relied on such credit, and by 1913, of £350 million bills outstanding in London, 60 per cent were finance bills. This linked movements in the stock market closely to the money market. Cheap money enabled brokers and jobbers to purchase more existing and new shares in anticipation of demand. Dear money had the opposite effect.[15]

Flows of information and the availability of short-term finance helped make London a leading market for long-term capital. Organising new issues of securities required a number of skills. It was necessary from the press, prices, and private information to judge the potential demand for the proposed issue. Then prospectuses might need to be prepared; advertising arranged; professional and other networks tapped; provisions made for subsequent payments of dividends; a company formed and registered; a board recruited combining various business and professional skills; and a listing secured on the Stock Exchange to increase marketability. For less savoury issues, journalists might be bribed with cash or shares; aristocratic 'guinea pig' directors recruited to lend an air of respectability; and a syndicate formed to conduct operations in the stock market. A range of groups could be involved in the process: bankers, stockbrokers, solicitors, industry specialists (such as engineers), accountants, 'guinea pigs', journalists, and underwriters (of whom more below). Unsurprisingly, in 1907 one prominent financial writer (H. Lowenfeld of the *Financial Review of Reviews*) estimated that the average issue cost £10,000 to arrange.[16]

A shifting group of financiers organised such issues. Banks played an important role. Merchant banks, exploiting the information on regions generated by the acceptance business and their wide client base, accounted for about a sizeable proportion of the issue market, and at times they lay behind the activities of other issuers.[17] The emerging 'big-beasts' of British banking, the joint-stock banks, played an increasing role in organising loans from the 1890s. British-owned 'overseas banks' (which exported the principles of joint-stock banking), and foreign-owned and colonial banks also participated at times. Investment trusts (companies formed to manage a body of capital), looser 'investment groups' surrounding merchants, stockbrokers and jobbers, and individual promoters (of whom Ernest Cassel was only the most stellar) also organised flotations of securities.[18] Often different issuers co-operated, and they drew on a range of services, something reflected in clusters of interlocking directorships between financial institutions, and between the companies they financed.[19]

The London Stock Exchange and its less formalised offshoots, where existing securities were traded, had close links to the new issue market. The Stock Exchange dealt in a vast range of securities. Few new issues lacked direct or indirect precedents. The state of the market for directly or indirectly linked securities acted as a benchmark for the terms of a new issue (especially its price).[20] Success depended on offering something that seemed a good deal either to investors or brokers, and this could only be judged in relation to comparable stocks on the market. Stockbrokers (who sold securities to investing public) and jobbers (who sold to other brokers) were well placed to make these judgements. As a result, they often became involved in new issues, buying new securities in anticipation of demand, as long as finance was available through the money market.[21]

Stockbrokers' knowledge of the markets also led many to become important members of underwriting syndicates. Underwriters insured issues against failure by forming a syndicate who, for a fee (normally ½ to 2 per cent), would agree to purchase a certain proportion of the stock should the issue fail to attract investors. Successful underwriting required a shrewd idea of investors' willingness to take up an issue, since the more securities the underwriter had to purchase, the lower his profit margins.[22] The practice had emerged in the 1870s, and occasionally caused controversy. Many borrowers resented the fees, while some in the City (notably the Rothschilds) thought the practice encouraged unscrupulous or reckless issuing. However by the turn of the century the business (especially in foreign and colonial government loans) increasingly attracted banks, insurance houses, and stockbrokers.[23]

All of these financiers (bankers, diversifying merchants, stockbrokers, jobbers, or individual promoters) tapped a shifting range of investors by a variety of methods. Much investment took place through what Ranald Michie has described as an informal 'social web' that linked financiers and possible investors based on personal or professional connections.[24] By the twentieth century, public appeals supplemented these private contacts. Circulars were sent in the mail, and according to one Edwardian writer, P. Tovey, 'In these days of the so called "small" investor, there are few persons who have not had the experience of finding on their breakfast table the familiar long envelope containing a "prospectus"'.[25] Press advertising could also attract investors. £94,000 of a £410,000 issue of bonds by Canadian Steel Foundries in 1911 came through direct responses to press advertising (50 per cent from the *Daily Mail*, 16 per cent from the *Daily Telegraph*, and 11 per cent from *The Times*).[26] The importance of these activities ought not to be exaggerated. When, in 1909, the South Australian government considered raising capital by issuing circulars to prospective investors, one banker observed:

> The business of private investors, Trustees and others in the United Kingdom is carried out almost entirely through their respective stockbrokers. ... The first thing an investor does, on receiving a notice, ... is to write to or see his stockbroker, who enquires in the usual quarters and finds the new loan is not known of or is being worked in an irregular way, antagonistic to brokers' interests, and... promptly condemns it.[27]

Many investors remained wary of appeals which did not come through the 'usual channels'.

The composition of Britain's investing classes remains unclear. Davis and Huttenback's study of the shareholdings of 260 defunct British-registered companies suggested that investors overseas and in the empire were concentrated in the south-east of England (especially London) and that Britain's 'elites' were particularly likely to invest in the empire.[28] This echoes J. D. Bailey's earlier finding that 40–50 per cent of Australian government securities issued in the 1880s and 1890s were bought by 'gentlemen and esquires', and that 80 per cent of these issues were held in the South of England (especially London).[29] Such figures have limitations. Firstly, many aristocrats from other parts of the United Kingdom owned a

London property and gave that address on share registers, while other holdings from elsewhere in the UK were often registered with London-based banks (both points of course confirm London's importance as a conduit for overseas investment).[30] Secondly, Davis and Huttenback's sample in particular overlooks two important categories of investment: government securities, and railways and other private companies registered overseas.[31] Since different types of investment attracted different classes of investors, there is no reason to expect that defunct British-registered companies would be typical.[32] Thirdly, they give no indication of changing patterns of investment over time. Combining the second two objections, their sample overlooks the increasing importance for colonial governments of institutional investors.[33] In 1909 T. A. Coghlan, the agent-general of New South Wales, observed that as private investors sought higher returns in foreign government and commercial stocks, his state had become increasingly dependent on insurance and other public companies to purchase its stocks.[34]

At times it was not even clear to financiers or borrowers who exactly invested in their securities. In 1903 the Australian state of Victoria needed to renew a loan for £5 million which had been issued as bearer bonds (meaning payment was made on presentation of a coupon). The Victorian government wished to contact existing bondholders to encourage them to exchange their old stocks for the new issue, and asked the London and Westminster Bank to make arrangements. The bank responded that this was impossible since their coupons were normally presented by bankers on their behalf. These bondholders could only be reached through their bankers.[35] This separation of borrower and lender seemingly placed a good deal of power in the hands of financiers. H. Lowenfeld thought investors in joint stock companies willingly submitted to the virtual 'despotism' of company directors; J. A. Hobson compared investors to a 'capitalist proletariat' subordinated to financiers primarily interested in speculative gain.[36] Nonetheless, the power of financiers can be exaggerated. Their ability to raise capital depended ultimately on the willingness of investors to invest, however misplaced and deluded that willingness may at times have been. They were interlocutors, ultimately reliant on the views of 'investors' or 'the market': views they might manipulate, but could not determine. Critically though, the financier not the investor was a borrower's chief point of contact.

The City lay at the confluence of the largest set of tributaries to the great flow of overseas investment – tributaries which stretched beyond London and the South East across the rest of Britain, and into continental

Europe. This financial dominance rested on its central role in world commerce, its location at the hub of a dense communications system, its credit markets, and the sheer accumulation of contacts with those possessing capital, and those requiring it. Borrowing was organised by a vast range of institutions, and every borrower possessed a unique set of connections in London. The final two sections of this chapter chart the groups organising British investments in Australia and Canada between 1896 and 1914.

Australia in the City

Australian borrowing was dominated by the public sector. By far the largest amounts were raised by the individual colonies (or states as they became after federation in 1901). Little was raised by municipal or other public bodies, and, the Commonwealth government (formed in 1901) did not borrow before 1914.[37] The states' dominance in the capital market reflected the fact that they retained most responsibility for public works policy. Table 2.1 shows the net new borrowings by the Australian states. Borrowing had boomed in the 1880s, especially by the populous eastern states. From 1890, Western Australian activity expanded dramatically following the concession of responsible government which finally lifted barriers to the London capital market.[38] After 1896 Victoria repaid debt on a large scale, while New South Wales and Western Australia were the leading borrowers. While the Western Australians were 'catching up', New South Wales' heavy borrowing around the turn of the century originated in an attempt to alleviate the effects of the depression through public works.[39] New borrowing by all states, except Victoria and Tasmania, revived just before the War.

New borrowing was only one element of the Australian states' financial relations with the City. As we saw in Chapter 1, by 1900 Australia, or at least eastern Australia, had a considerable burden of debt to manage. As of 30 June 1901, the states had a total of £203,518,272 outstanding, of which 86 per cent had been floated in London.[40] Managing these vast liabilities drew attention to London just as much as the desire for new capital. Most Australian state debt had been issued for a fixed period. Between 1901 and 1914, £48 million had to be renewed: £16 million by New South Wales, and £18 million by Victoria.[41] Although they are often disregarded by economic historians interested in fresh transfers of capital, renewals created financial problems which bound the states to the London capital market. Few had sinking funds or were able to pay off their debts in full from current revenues. As a result either some arrangement had to

Table 2.1 Net Capital Subscribed in London for Securities Sold by Australian Public Bodies, 1870–1914 (£mil)

	New South Wales	Victoria	Queensland	South Australia	Tasmania	Western Australia	Corp.	Total
1870–1874	234	2915	846	595	70	0	64	4724
1875–1879	4363	5857	4301	3993	283	196	232	19225
1880–1884	11568	7667	6970	8422	1487	393	1877	38384
1885–1889	19428	10775	8097	4996	1994	579	3847	49716
1890–1894	7556	7603	5340	858	1897	1858	2636	27748
1895–1899	1386	522	1725	525	-165	5599	-74	9518
1900–1904	9691	254	3288	684	314	3427	-339	17319
1905–1909	2109	-5578	1938	-3827	387	5327	-55	301
1910–1914	13412	165	9080	3684	466	7204	407	34418
Total 1865–1914	69747	30180	41585	19930	6733	24583	8595	201353
Total 1896–1914	24576	-4637	14761	1117	914	20788	-51	57468

Source: B. Attard, 'New Estimates of Australian Public Borrowing and Capital Raised in London, 1849–1914', *Australian Economic History Review*, 47 (2007), 176, Appendix 2.

Table 2.2 Australian Loans Due for Repayment or Renewal, 1901–1914 (£100,000s)

	New South Wales	Victoria	Queensland	South Australia	Western Australia	Tasmania	Totals
1901		30.00					30.00
1902	4.09					1.67	5.7
1903	10.04			0.65	3.15	1.69	15.52
1904	0.58	54.57		0.63		0.25	56.02
1905	9.04			0.73	0.17	1.77	11.71
1906	2.25			0.38		2.34	4.96
1907		40.00		10.38		0.26	50.64
1908	28.66	20.00		19.51		3.44	71.60
1909	2.84			31.23		1.14	35.21
1910	28.64			0.60	13.34	0.21	42.79
1911				0.68		10.25	10.93
1912	75.83			0.85		0.01	76.69
1913		40.00	14.67	0.00		5.47	60.13
1914				0.35		8.00	8.35
Total	161.96	184.57	14.67	65.97	16.67	36.50	480.34

Source: T. A. Coghlan, *A Statistical Account of the Seven Colonies of Australasia, 1901–1902* (Sydney, 1902), 1023.

be made with existing borrowers or else fresh loans raised. Renewals were hard to postpone, irrespective of the state of the market. Although temporary loans or accommodation from bankers might be available, this was costly.[42] Local borrowing met some of these debts; those of Victoria in particular.[43] Most was renewed in London. Outstanding debts linked the states and their politics to London just as much as the desire for fresh capital.

Early borrowings by the then colonies had been handled by Australian banks, but in the 1880s the business became concentrated in the hands of the Bank of England, and the London and Westminster Bank (a leading joint-stock bank). The move owed much to the desire to capitalise (literally) on the prestige and connections of these institutions.[44] In 1900, the Bank of England issued for New South Wales and Queensland; the London and Westminster for Victoria and Western Australia. South Australia and Tasmania issued through their agents-general, the latter with the London and Westminster's support. The Bank of England charged $\frac{1}{2}$ per cent for issuing, the London and Westminster $\frac{1}{4}$ per cent, and both also charged varying sums for managing existing stocks. In the early 1900s the better terms offered by the London and Westminster secured it New South Wales' business.[45]

From the turn of the century, all Australian states (with the partial exception of South Australia) routinely had their issues underwritten. Two firms organised this underwriting: Robert Nivison if the issue was through the London and Westminster Bank; Marshall Mullens and Co. (who cooperated closely with Nivison) if through the Bank of England. Nivison had moved to London from Scotland in the 1870s, working for the London and Westminster before joining the Stock Exchange in 1881. By the 1890s, he had amassed a vast network of contacts enabling him to judge demand for colonial stocks. Nivison first organised underwriting for a loan by Queensland in 1893, and by the 1900s he had become the dominant figure in the market for colonial stocks.[46] This move was controversial in Australia. Underwriting fees were thought to raise the cost of issuing, as was underwriters' preferred practice of issuing at a fixed price rather than asking investors to offer tenders on or above a minimum. Nivison and T. J. Russell (country manager of the London and Westminster Bank) argued that without underwriting loans would have had to be issued at lower prices to ensure success, wiping out any potential savings, and that tendering had been dominated by professional speculators who placed large bids a shade above the minimum, deterring the 'public' from participating.[47]

At times the states did explore other channels of issue. In 1901 the Victorian agent-general considered issuing in Paris; in 1906 New South

Wales' agent-general, T. A. Coghlan, examined (and rejected) the possibility of attracting German capital.[48] Other groups in London courted the states' business. In 1903 a group led by one Mr Webster engaged in discussions with Victoria.[49] In 1910 the Victorian government proposed that the state's ten leading British and Australian-owned banks float Victorian loans, a move opposed by the British-owned Union Bank of Australia both on practical grounds, and because it would expose participating banks to political pressures.[50] Other methods of issue were also examined. In 1909 Coghlan considered adopting the Australian practice of selling stocks 'over the counter' or of placing blocks of stocks with brokers. The Union Bank warned that investors would be put off by their brokers.[51] In 1913, Coghlan sought a deal with Norton Griffith, an engineering firm, to finance the construction of the Sydney Harbour Bridge.[52] However, only South Australia actually executed an attempted escape from the 'London Ring'. In 1908 the state engaged the pastoral finance company Elder, Smith and Co. to arrange for Lloyds Bank to issue a renewal loan in London. Nivison opposed the move and arranged a boycott by the underwriters. Cowed, Lloyds backed out. The loan had to be taken up by the Bank of Adelaide, which repurchased Nivison's support for an extra ½ per cent above his normal fees. The issue was not a success and of £2 million offered, £1,380,000 was left with the underwriters (with £550,000 taken up by existing bondholders and only £70,000 fresh money offered).[53] The radical Sydney *Bulletin* commented, 'Australia can't apparently borrow without saying "please Mr Nivison"'.[54]

Given the proportion of investment in Australia which flowed to the states, this was almost literally true. Yet there were private interests in the City which could prove significant, especially mines, pastoral finance companies, and anglo-Australian banks. They often either produced or serviced the primary product industries which dominated Australia's exports and hence its ability to meet obligations to bondholders. Furthermore, the clusters of individuals in London involved in these sectors were important commentators on Australian affairs.

Of the new capital flowing into the Australian *private* sector from 1896 to 1914, almost all was invested in mining, which accounted for 46 per cent of total British investment in the late-1890s, and a quarter from 1900 to 1914. The sector was characterised by large numbers of mines often bound together by interlocking directorships reflecting the activities of particular promoters. A. R. Hall found that the 1915 edition of the *Stock Exchange Official Intelligence* listed 91 mining companies operating in Australia formed between 1896 and 1914 (64 per cent were registered in Britain) and this only counts the survivors in a sector where many companies had short lifespans.[55]

The market for mining shares was subject to violent swings. The discovery of gold at Coolgardie and Kalgoorlie in Western Australia in 1892 and 1893 triggered a full-scale gold rush, and shares soon proved popular on a London market already excited by South African 'Kaffirs'. A large range of promoters became involved but two operated on a particularly large scale. Horatio Bottomley and Whittaker Wright wove complex webs of interlocking mining companies, using productive and unproductive mines as bargaining chips to attract investors. Wright's individual mines were subsumed into larger holding companies: London and Globe Finance, and the British America Corporation (which acted as an umbrella for his interests in British Columbia where another gold rush centred on the Kootenays).[56] Bottomley's empire collapsed under a 'bear attack' in 1900 and Wright's suffered a similar fate in 1901. Wright himself fled for the US, later poisoning himself in custody. The exposure of fraudulent practice by another promoter, Frank Gardener (an American engineer and chairman of the Great Boulder Proprietary Mine), in 1903 embroiled the industry in further scandal.[57]

In the wake of these collapses, new groupings emerged in the Australian mining market. Within 'Westralian' gold mining, a key cluster surrounded the Oxford-educated stockbroker, F. A. Govett, who from 1896 acquired large stakes in many of Wright's most productive mines. He subsequently orchestrated shareholders' opposition to Wright, acquiring control of much of Wright's empire. To manage these acquisitions, he employed the services of the engineering firm Berwick, Moreing and Company, who sent the young American engineer Herbert Hoover (later US President) to Western Australia.[58] Govett and Berwick Moreing became a powerful force within the sector. Another important figure was Lionel Robinson, a stockbroker who worked in Melbourne and Adelaide before transferring to London in 1899, joined in 1900 by another Adelaide stockbroker, William Clark. Both enjoyed close links with the Melbourne-based financier W. L. Baillieu. Robinson attracted British capital to Australian mining, especially to the emerging base metals mining complex at Broken Hill in New South Wales. By the end of the 1900s, the interests of Robinson, Clark, and Baillieu came into close alliance with those of Govett, Berwick Moreing, and Hoover through shared interests at Broken Hill, particularly the Zinc Corporation which processed tailings.[59] However, in contrast to the consolidated mining finance houses controlling South African gold mining, these two groupings never dominated a sector characterised by a shifting myriad of players.

Between 1865 and 1914, Stone estimates that 6.5 per cent of British investment flowed into 'Finance, Land and Investment Companies'.[60] These undertook three main activities. Some were urban real estate companies providing mortgages; particularly during the late-1880s when British capital propped up the flagging Melbourne real estate market. Some were mining exploration companies, seeking or holding potentially mineraliferous lands.[61] Yet the most significant (in terms of longevity, and influence within the City) were pastoral finance companies. These had mostly been formed in the mid-nineteenth century to finance and organise Australia's wool trade. They came to provide a comprehensive range of commercial and financial services to rural communities.[62] By the turn of the twentieth century many had become significant land holders after large numbers of pastoralists defaulted on mortgages during the depression of the 1890s.[63] One major player, the Australian Mercantile Land and Finance Company (known as the Australian Mortgage Land and Finance Company until 1910) emerged when two Scottish entrepreneurs floated interests amassed in eastern Australia as a joint-stock company in London in 1863.[64] Others which had originally been run from Australia as private partnerships were re-incorporated in London in the 1870s and 1880s, attracted by the capital, credit, and commodity markets and assisted by Australia's popularity. The market's leading player, Dalgety and Co., was floated in London in 1884 after a long struggle between its founder, F. Dalgety, and its rising star, E. T. Doxat. Both moved to southern England, Dalgety to retire, Doxat to join the City's growing cadre of anglo-Australian financiers. By the 1900s Doxat was a key commentator on Australian affairs in London.[65] Beyond these firms, there were many lesser players. Often their directorates were vocal almost in inverse proportion to their size and profitability.

From the mid-nineteenth century, a number of British-owned joint-stock banks had been founded to operate in Australia. Leading players such as the Union Bank of Australia; the English, Scottish and Australian Bank; the London and Australia Bank; and the Bank of Australasia were among the continent's largest banks. They were not heavily involved in transferring capital to Australia and absorbed little British capital themselves (about 4 per cent of British investment in Australia between 1865 and 1914 was in banks). Rather they exported the principles of British joint-stock banking and provided currency and exchange services to the budding colonies.[66] In the wake of the 1893 banking crisis, share prices had tumbled, and many depositors found their deposits converted into equity.[67] Few of these banks wished to increase their capitalisations in our period, and they did not borrow significantly. Like the pastoral finance companies they were awaiting an economic recovery to boost transactions and profits. However their directors, along with the London representatives of leading Australian-owned banks, were important spokesmen on Australian affairs.

This survey by no means accounts for every interest in London. One highly anomalous example which features later in this book should be noted: the Midland Railway Company of Western Australia. The Midland was floated in 1890 to construct a line from Perth to Geraldton. It was one of a tiny number of private railways in Australia, and it (like many Canadian railways) relied on various forms of state support: a government grant of 3,500,000 acres of land, progressive guarantees of debentures through the 1890s totalling £1 million, and £60,000 cash. The railway may have been an oddity, but it was a powerful oddity. Its directorate, which included members of the Australian section of the London Chamber of Commerce, were well connected in the City and operated in tandem with many pastoral interests.[68] Its importance outweighed the very small amount of capital raised on its behalf.

This section has highlighted the main financial protagonists in London with interests in Australia. The London and Westminster Bank, in conjunction with Robert Nivison and Co. played a critical role in the dominant public sector. A number of large pastoral finance companies and anglo-Australian banks facilitated Australian commerce, especially the overseas trade which serviced bondholders' debts. They were joined by the shifting protagonists of the Australian mining sector. Beyond the mining market (where change was a constant) Australia's connections in the City altered little through the period.

Canadian finance in London

Compared with Australia, Canadian connections with the City were not only greater in volume, but also in fluidity, complexity, and interconnection. While various sectors of the Australian economy borrowed through distinct channels, this was not the case for Canada's more diverse portfolio. The pages of the 1915 edition of *Stock Exchange Yearbook* list over 59 organisations issuing Canadian stocks and shares between 1900 and 1914.[69] Even within particular industrial sectors (railway or industrial stocks for example) individual borrowers issued though a shifting range of organisations. In the attempt to explore Canadian finance in London, it is easier, therefore, to consider the role played by particular issuers or the financing of particular companies.

Canada's financial institutions played a much more important role in funnelling capital to Canada than their Australian counterparts. Jacob Viner estimated that the Bank of Montreal, Canada's oldest bank and pinnacle of Montreal finance, arranged about 50 per cent of all Canadian issues in London between 1900 and 1914. The 1915 *Stock Exchange Yearbook* lists £85,925,912 of nominal capital issued by the bank in 60 issues on behalf of 28 borrowers including the Dominion government, provinces, municipalities, industrial companies, utilities, and railways.[70] The bank had long held the accounts of the Canadian government. In 1892 its London office (established in 1870) won the right to issue the dominion government's loans in London, displacing the merchant banks Barings and Glyn, Mills, Currie and Co.[71] Despite this, Canada's loans still relied on the same section of the stock market as Australian ones, something reflected in the fact that in 1908 Canada began underwriting its loans through Robert Nivison.[72] The bank was also active in other markets. Even without the £51 million issued for the dominion, it would still have been a key player.[73] Its London manager, Frederick Williams-Taylor, believed that its concentration on conservative issues enhanced its reputation. Its prominence aroused the jealousy of the Rothschilds, Glyns, and the Scottish banks, but it enjoyed support in the City from the Bank of England, the National Provincial, London and Smiths, and London and Westminster banks, and, crucially, from Nivison.[74]

The Bank of Montreal's Toronto-based rival, the Canadian Bank of Commerce, sought to match its role. The bank acquired a London office in 1901 when it took over the British-owned Bank of British Columbia.[75] According to the *Stock Exchange Yearbook*, the bank made £13,274,531 of issues in London on behalf of ten organisations including provinces and municipalities in the west, components of the Canadian Northern Railway (CNR), and industrials.[76] It aspired to win the Dominion government's business from the Bank of Montreal.[77] The bank was closely associated with another Canadian institution which issued in London, Dominion Securities. It also bought Canadian borrowers in touch with British banks, and participated in underwriting syndicates.[78] Byron Edmund Walker (the bank's general manager from 1886 to 1907, then president until 1924) was well known in the City as an expert on Canadian economic conditions and Canadian banking.[79]

A range of British banking institutions also participated in the market for Canadian securities. Lloyds issued for Alberta and Edmonton; the Canadian Northern Railway (CNR); and a wide range of utility, pulp and paper, and manufacturing companies.[80] It and the Bank of Scotland also provided short-term credit to the CNR.[81] Another joint stock bank, Parr's, acted for a range of lumber, brewing, and manufacturing companies.[82] Equally, merchant banks obtained a slice of Canadian business. One, Brown, Shipley and Co., managed 12 issues, especially for the City of Vancouver and the British Columbian Telephone Company.[83] The Rothschilds handled the first issue of the Grand Trunk Pacific Railway, which launched the British-owned Grand Trunk's ambitions to construct a transcontinental line. The merchant bank's connection to the line came through the railway's chairman, Charles Rivers Wilson, a former diplomat, civil servant, and finance minister in Egypt who, as a foreign office official, had drawn the Rothschilds into Egyptian finance in 1876.[84] In the event, the issue was soured by a rival offering of Canadian Northern Railway bonds by another merchant bank, Speyers.[85] Lazards also played a key role issuing for the CNR. They had been courted by the railway's Canadian owners and promoters – William Mackenzie and Donald Mann – on the advice of the Canadian Bank of Commerce. In 1909 they took Lazards' leading light, Robert Kindersley, on a tour of Canada, and thereafter Kindersley and Lazards sought to monopolise the issuing of CNR stocks.[86]

The large-scale involvement of Lazards through to the Rothschilds' cameo reflected the booming market in Canadian railway stocks. Between 1865 and 1914 railways accounted for 40 per cent of British investment in Canada (and the amount of British money spent on railway construction was higher given that lines constructed by Canadian governments were also funded by borrowing). The vast majority of this investment was placed in three railway systems: The Canadian Pacific, Grand Trunk/ Grand Trunk Pacific, and Canadian Northern Railways. In the early twentieth century, the Canadian Northern Railway and Grand Trunk had ambitious programmes to construct new transcontinental railways while the Canadian Pacific expanded branches and doubled up its existing track. According to Williams-Taylor, between 1902 and 1912, of a total of £101,340,000 raised by Canadian railways, these three had received £40,300,000, £34,022,000, and £21,223,000 respectively.[87]

Each attracted capital in different ways. Originally the Canadian Pacific Railway (CPR) completed in 1885, was financed largely by shares, supplemented (as we have seen) by land, cash, and completed lines from the Canadian state. Between 1886 and 1896 the railway paid for a consolidation of its network (its mileage doubled) through debenture issues (fixed debts). From 1899, the railway's American manager, Thomas Shaughnessy (who then replaced his fellow countryman, William Van Horne), continued this expansion while converting the fixed debt into shares (also known as common stock).[88] Investors accepted this change in part because the shares became increasingly attractive. Their average price increased fivefold between 1896 and 1912, while dividends rose from 1.5 per cent in 1895 to 10 per cent in 1913.[89] The CPR issued shares privately, although they subsequently found their way onto stock exchanges in London, New York, Paris, and Berlin. In 1913 Shaughnessy estimated that 60 per cent of the shares were held in Britain, 23 per cent in North America, and 15 per cent on the continent (although control remained in the hands of the Canadian management).[90]

By contrast, the Grand Trunk Railway was far more deeply embedded in the City. The line had been founded in the 1850s to link Toronto and Quebec with the support of Barings and Glyn, Mills, Currie and Co. In 1913 it was reckoned to have over 60,000 shareholders, and just prior to his death on the Titanic, the railway's American manager – Charles Melville Hays – estimated that 70–90 per cent were British.[91] Unlike its rivals, final control of the line (and especially of its financing) rested with its well-connected London board, chaired between 1895 and 1909 by Charles Rivers Wilson. His deputy chairman from 1904 and eventual successor, Alfred Smithers, had been a stockbroker and was also chairman of the English and American Association of American Bondholders (EAAB hereafter).[92] Other prominent figures on the board included Lord Welby (a former civil servant, chairman of London county council, and member of the free trading Cobden Club) and Sir Felix Schuster (chairman of the Union of London and Smiths Bank and another prominent free trader).[93] From 1902 the railway embarked on an ambitious programme to construct a transcontinental line – the Grand Trunk Pacific Railway – with the support of Canada's Liberal government.[94] The prestige and contacts of the board were crucial in issuing the necessary bonds, as were frequent guarantees by the original Grand Trunk Company, and the Canadian government. The company issued through the Rothschilds, the Bank of Montreal, and privately, doubtless exploiting the boards' City connections.[95]

Canada's third transcontinental railway was a much newer arrival. The Canadian Northern Railway system expanded from its beginnings as a provincial line in Manitoba under the management of two former CPR contractors: Donald Mann and William Mackenzie. After the completion of the CPR, the pair had moved into utilities in Canada and the Caribbean before returning to railways in the late-1890s. The Canadian Northern Railway was incorporated in 1899.[96] Lacking connections in London, the pair found it hard to raise capital there until, in 1901, Manitoba agreed to guarantee an issue of bonds. William Mackenzie travelled to London and persuaded R. M. Horne-Payne, a partner in the merchant bank Speyers, to undertake the flotation. Horne-Payne's interest in Canada dated back at least to 1897 when he arranged the re-financing of the British Columbian Electric Railway, a large Vancouver-based utilities firm. He soon became a central figure in the floatation of CNR bonds in London, breaking with Speyers in the process.[97] In 1902, he founded the British Empire Trust Company (BETC) whose share-holdings were concentrated in Canadian Northern stocks, those of the British Columbian Electric Railway, and other utility, lands, and raw materials companies associated with Mackenzie. The BETC also acted as trustee, registrar, secretary, underwriter, and issuer for many of these companies.[98] Horne-Payne became a CNR director in 1913 and by 1914 sat on the boards of 13 other Mackenzie companies.[99] The CNR valued his services highly enough to move to ensure he did not act on behalf of any other Canadian railway.[100] According to D. B. Hanna, another CNR director, Horne-Payne's main skills were his 'great faith' in Canada, the capacity to impart confidence in underwriters, and the ability to reach and judge the resources of the small investor. Apparently he once returned from a motoring tour to Buxton convinced he could place at least £350,000 in the town.[101] Yet neither Horne-Payne's faith nor his motoring holidays could quench the CNR's thirst for capital, and, as we have seen, the Bank of Commerce and Lazards, along with Lloyds and the Bank of Scotland also became involved in raising capital on its behalf.[102]

Complex and shifting combinations of expatriate and British financiers played a role in other sectors. Mining was dominated by similar players to Western Australia. Whittaker Wright's British North America Corporation used Kootanay mines as bargaining chips just as much as Westralian ones.[103] American capital tended to rival British investment in this sector, although one of the key players on the emerging base metals complex at Sudbury was Mond Nickel which served the chemical industrialist Alfred Mond's smelting complex at Port Pirie in Wales, but was financed through Mond's connections in London.[104] However, after 1900, invest-ment in mining was only a small portion of total British investment in Canada.

We have already seen that many utilities, municipalities, manu-facturing, and finance and land companies issued through various British and Canadian banks. However other groups also marketed these stocks. Arthur Grenfell became the most prominent British player. Grenfell was the son of Pascoe du Pré Grenfell, a partner in the merchant bank Morton, Rose and Company which was reconstructed in 1898 as Chaplin, Milne, Grenfell and Co. Arthur Grenfell entered the City with the aid of his cousin, E. C. Grenfell (who in 1900 became manager of J. S. Morgan, the American financier J. P. Morgan's London operation). Initially he took an interest in Rhodesia, become a director of Willoughby's Consolidated Company in 1896. He acquired close links to Earl Grey, a director in Rhodes' British South African Company (a connection strengthened in 1907 when he married Grey's daughter). Grenfell became a partner in Chaplin, Milne, Grenfell in 1899 and around the turn of the century his interests were concentrated in mining in southern Africa and Australia.[105]

In 1904 Grey was appointed governor-general of Canada (a post he held until 1911) and this, along with Canada's economic expansion, diverted Grenfell's attentions to the dominion. In 1906 Grenfell founded the Canadian Agency to act as 'the shop in all Canadian matters'.[106] The agency possessed a network of about 2,000 clients and published weakly reports which carried 'considerable weight' according to one journalist specialising in Canadian finances.[107] In 1909 a rival described the firm as a 'very big buyer of Canadian securities' which occupied 'a very important place in the Canadian market'. Business came through contacts with Canadians made in London, through advertising in Toronto and Montreal, and through Grenfell's own tours of the dominion.[108] The agency handled 30 issues between 1906 and 1914 for two western provinces, seven western municipalities, four land companies, nine industrial companies and two railways, raising a total of £13,424,951.[109] It also dealt in the shares of other companies, building up a large stake in the Grand Trunk. It co-operated closely with Chaplin, Milne, Grenfell, and Co, which lent money against the agency's various securities, as did other brokers and bankers. Grenfell's partner and brother-in-law, Guy St Aubyn, was also partner in Robert Nivison and Co, leading Nivison to underwrite several municipal and industrial issues.[110] Dividends grew from £44,058 in 1907 to £401,223 in 1913, but from 1910 these depended on the increasing value placed on its shares.

In 1913 the market for Canadian real estate, industrial, and municipal shares collapsed, and the price of Canadian railway securities slipped as it became clear that, despite their gargantuan borrowings, the Grand Trunk Pacific and Canadian Northern Railway were close neither to completion nor profit. This eroded many of the agency's paper profits. Grenfell actually purchased an even larger holding in the Grand Trunk that year, perhaps to boost the price of its shares, although he claimed he wished to use the stake to reform the railway's management. In 1914 both the Canadian Agency and an important satellite, the South Alberta Land Company, went bankrupt. Chaplin, Milne, Grenfell's position became exposed, since the value of assets pledged as security by the agency did not cover its liabilities. The bank was rescued in May by other City institutions fearing that panic might spread.[111]

The Canadian Agency was only the most prominent exploiter of the increasingly feverish expectations of the Canadian west and of an emerging market for Canadian industrial stocks. For example, Ion Hamilton Benn's Western Canada Trust operated in much the same market.[112] These British financiers were joined by Canadian émigrés enjoying close links to the upper echelons of Montreal and Toronto finance. In 1906, the Canadian industrial financier James Dunn arrived in London, forming Dunn, Fischer, and Co which specialised in marketing Canadian-run South American utilities.[113] In 1908, E. R. Wood's Dominion Securities opened a London office, managed by E. R. Peacock. Another prominent Canadian industrial financier who moved to London was Max Aitken, better known as the press baron Lord Beaverbrook. Aitken's Royal Securities Corporation had been established in Halifax in 1903 and moved to Montreal in 1906. From then on Aitken sought to place bonds in London and, after becoming frustrated with the Canadian Agency and Western Canada Trust, established his own London office in 1910; Benn and Lord Northcliffe eased Aitken's entry into the City, and also into Unionist politics: Benn introduced Aitken to Andrew Bonar Law, and Aitken became an MP for Ashton-under-Lyme that December. Ten other Canadian industrial finance houses followed Aitken and established London offices between 1910 and 1912.[114]

This account has traced the leading players in Canadian finance in London in this period, although the sheer volume, complexity, and diversity of British investment in Canada make it impossible to offer a comprehensive picture. The range of channels through which capital flowed to Canada was striking, as was their fluidity. The boom in Canadian stocks stimulated the formation of new ties between the dominion and the City just as the lower level of investment in Australia also saw relatively stable connections. Most of these connections linked Canadian borrowers and intermediaries with London-based financiers, and ultimately British investors. The roles of British and expatriate issuers in London did not differ greatly, what varied was the location at which the domestic and the colonial fused. Thus, the prominent role of Canadians in raising capital in London did not, in itself, confer greater autonomy. Despite the role of the Bank of Montreal, Canadian government bonds (and many others besides) still relied on the goodwill of Robert Nivison and the colonial section of the Stock Exchange. However the dynamism of the Canadian market brought large numbers of important Canadians into close contact with London, particularly those associated with the twin peaks of Canadian finance: the Bank of Montreal and the Canadian Bank of Commerce. They had every incentive to keep the City happy and the capital flowing. As we shall see, few were more active in publically and privately lobbying to maintain credit than Canada's financial elites. If economics might lead us to suspect that financial crises might heighten the City's influence, business dynamics suggest that booms widened and strengthened the City's 'bridgehead' in a debtor nation.[115]

Conclusion

Investment took place through a complex web of personal and professional contacts, supplemented by the press. These capillaries largely converged in the City where financiers attempted to judge investors' capacity and willingness to absorb new offerings. Each borrowing nation possessed a unique set of connections in London, reflecting both the structure of its economy, and the historical accumulation of networks. Australia had a considerable legacy of borrowing and a relatively stable set of connections in the City. Government borrowing dominated, with mining the only other sector raising significant amounts of new capital in the period, although important interests also existed in pastoral finance and banking. Canada, by contrast, raised significant amounts of capital across a range of sectors (but especially railways and governments) organised through a shifting set of intermediaries. Expatriates perhaps played a more important role in Canada than Australia, but it would be false to divide colonial and British financiers too starkly. All financiers required connections with both the creditor and debtor nation and at some stage this normally meant co-operation with those operating in each context. What varied was the point of articulation between those whose connections were primarily British or colonial. An expatriate arranging borrowing in London performed essentially the same function as a British financier.

The diverse range of individuals and institutions acting for Canada and Australia raises an important question: in what sense could an institutionally divided City (with a considerable expatriate community) be said to formulate unified 'rules'? Two points must be made. Firstly, as far as some borrowers were concerned, control of the market was highly concentrated. Most significantly, Australian and Canadian government stocks came to rely on Robert Nivison to arrange underwriting. Secondly, financiers were ultimately interlocutors between borrowers and investors. Often they offered different routes to similar sets of investors. Financiers relied on the willingness of investors to place their money in their hands. They did not manufacture perceptions of political economy, but rather interpreted or second guessed those held by investors. Therefore, thirdly and crucially, what mattered more than institutional structures were the ideas prevalent in the City and amongst investors. Institutional division might be perfectly compatible with common perceptions of interest. This does not mean that the institutions and individuals anatomised in this chapter were unimportant. They helped formulate, interpret, and transmit City views overseas. The construction and content of these views is the subject of the next two chapters: having established the key players it is time to turn our attention directly to the 'rules of the game'.

Part II

The City, Political Economy, and Settler Societies

3
The Rules of the Game

The next two chapters shift attention from economics and institutions to consider how groups in the City thought about political economy. This chapter examines how groups in the City thought about investments, the information flows available to them, and the issues which attracted attention. The next chapter examines how the political and cultural structures of empire fed into these concerns.[1] Thus both chapters probe the 'rules of the game' by reconstructing discussions of Australian and Canadian political economy, and teasing out the assumptions underpinning those discussions. Only by establishing how the City understood political economy, and applied these understandings at particular junctures, can we delineate the politics of finance. In order to do this, it is necessary to show how the City produced these understandings of political economy. Unlike Robinson and Gallagher's relatively coherent 'Official Mind', patterns of thought in the City were rather more chaotic and, crucially, no institutional framework existed to ensure a single line on any one issue.[2] Groups in the City started from similar premises but only rarely spoke with one voice.

The 'unofficial' mind

Understandings of political economy in the Square Mile were not based on any general economic model. There was a prevailing distrust of abstraction. The young Keynes complained that financiers 'will not admit the feasibility of anything until it has been demonstrated by practical experience'.[3] This did not mean that such financiers had no sense of their interests. S. G. Checkland, who highlighted the late-Victorian City's inability to formulate a comprehensive model of the workings of the world economy, nonetheless found it abounded in 'agenda theory': powerful homespun arguments in response to particular events, based on practical rules of thumb.[4] The City was not mindless. It was empiricist and conservative; Burkean not Benthamite. While investors and financiers did not base their views on formalised economic models, there were assumptions underpinning them.

A certain inherent logic underlay investment. As contemporaries observed, the ideal investment would be completely secure, yield high returns, and be readily marketable at a higher price than purchase. These desires were incompatible and in practice a basic compromise between risks and returns lay at the core of investment. These trade-offs were well understood and investment writers recommended complex strategies for various categories of investors to construct portfolios with an appropriate balance of risk, returns, and capital growth.[5] Different types of borrower were expected to carry different levels of risk. National governments, whose security was 'the taxable wealth of the nation', were considered most secure.[6] Railways, if they linked areas with large populations or natural resources, were also thought to be relatively safe.[7] Municipal bonds, industrial shares or utilities could all be good investments, but their returns were much less certain. Mines and other new companies occupied the riskiest end of the market. If different forms of business activity were seen to have different levels of risk, so too were various regions of the world.[8]

Although certain axioms arose from the activity of investing, this does not mean that investment decisions were rational (especially when judged retrospectively). Financial writers frequently criticised the irrationality of many (especially small) investors. In 1909 the *Financial Times* thought it 'a common failing of the multitude, when any country, any department of industry, any individual even, is being boomed in the press, to rush to the crude conclusion that everything in connection with that country, or market, or individual, must necessarily be good'.[9] Yet such speculative exuberances did not in the main occur beyond the trade-off between risks and returns outlined above. Indeed, much depends on what is meant by speculation. The financial writer H. Lowenfeld distinguished 'gambling' from 'legitimate speculation' where money is 'staked on sound ventures with full knowledge of the risks incurred'.[10] Furthermore, even risky investments were underpinned by certain expectations, however poorly informed an investor might have been. A gold mine might turn out to have poor ore, and yield low dividends, but this did not make fraudulent practices acceptable. This is why many booms turned sour when such practices were exposed. Often these booms were based on clear (if wildly overoptimistic) assumptions about the prospects of a region, industry, or company; and hence on ideas about political economy.

In judging an investment's prospects, it was necessary to examine the broader economic and political conditions in a region. As Lowenfeld explained, 'constantly occurring events in politics, and commercial and social developments, work great changes in the position of even old established investments'.[11] A close watch was maintained on such events and developments through the telegraph and press, private correspondence, and overseas travel. This information was dissected in a number of forums. Much discussion took place in private in clubs, offices, and on the floor of the Stock Exchange, but a good deal took place in more public venues, at innumerable formal dinners, at company meetings, or at events arranged by organisations such as the Institute of Bankers or the London Chamber of Commerce. One deputy chairman of the Chamber thought it held, '[a] watching brief, putting it constantly on guard against injury which might threaten business interests'. [12] In this it joined organisations such as the Corporation of Foreign Bondholders, the English Association of American Bondholders, or the British Australasian Society, all of which specifically guarded investors' interests.

London possessed a vibrant financial press which played a central role in the formulation of City views. By the turn of the century, three specialised dailies – *The Financier*, the *Financial News*, and the *Financial Times* – circulated widely.[13] Their popularity led the general press to include a good deal of financial analysis, not least in the chase to maintain sales in the growing commuter market. Thus *The Times* or even the *Daily Mail* could be as much a part of the financial press as the more specialised titles. Weekly journals supplemented this daily diet, particularly *The Economist*, the *Statist*, and the *Investor's Review*. So too did more specialised titles focusing on particular regions or industries such as the *British Australasian*, the *Mining Journal*, or *Canada*.[14] All of this coverage was based on journalists' 'daily intercourse' with financiers, as one leading writer innocently put it.[15] In 1910, the editor of the *Financial News*, E. T. Powell, described the typical day of a City editor. This began with an examination of rival publications, notices, and correspondence. Often letters arrived from 'important financial houses' and were reproduced verbatim. The remainder of the day was taken up with a watch on prices and an exploration of any sudden movements, finishing with a trip to eavesdrop on evening conversations in Lombard Street.[16]

The resultant articles were not mere reflections of City views. At times they could be pursuing political agendas. For example, George Paish, editor of the *Statist*, wrote on the merits of capital export to defend Asquith's government against the charge that it was driving capital abroad through high taxation.[17] Material interests also distorted reportage. Advertising contracts with governments and companies in borrowing nations provided incentives for some papers to damped criticism.[18] Aggrieved financiers and investors sometimes paid to place hostile coverage in the press to pressurise governments and undermine competitors. Individual journalists and editors would sometimes 'prostitute their profession' (as *The Economist* angrily put it).[19] In 1898 the *Contemporary Review* estimated that City editors could be bought for between £100 and £5,000.[20] In the late 1890s Howard Marks, the editor of the *Financial News*, blackmailed companies with threats of poor publicity and puffed securities by augmenting their virtues or turning a blind eye to their failings.[21] However, by 1913, the *Economist* thought that 'blatant and open puff' had given way to more subtle strategies involving talking up regions and industries more broadly just prior to an associated share issue.[22]

The importance of such influences should not be exaggerating. Many titles were generally above such shady practices. In 1904 the Western Australian agent-general, Walter James, asked the managers of the Union of London and Smiths Bank, the London and Westminster Bank, and 'a big South African man' which papers carried most weight, and which were most reliable. He was told that while the *Financial Times* and *Financial News* were widely read, *The Economist*, the *Statist*, and *The Investor's Review* were all considered more dependable, as were the City articles in *The Times*, the *Standard*, and the *Daily Telegraph*.[23] Furthermore, the manipulation of the press tended not to challenge the fundamental assumptions underpinning investment (the rules), but rather sought to shape how those assumptions were applied in particular instances in order to augment or reduce share prices and the flow of investment.

A similar point ought to be borne in mind when considering another notable feature of the financial press: the extent to which coverage of Australia, Canada, and indeed other parts of the globe, was produced by overseas correspondents. Most of *The Economist's* regular Canadian and Australian coverage was written in Ottawa and Melbourne. Such correspondents were frequently anonymous, and many seem to have been important businessmen, journalists, or occasionally politicians. Australian political struggles often spilt over into the London press. The dominant political figure of the early years of federation, Alfred Deakin, wrote a column for the *Morning Post*.[24] As James observed, 'Not content with fighting out political differences on Commonwealth soil the Australian Correspondent too frequently carried the heat and animus of political controversy into the London press, and... expresses political opinions with a bitterness that injures Australia'.[25]

The significance of this must be carefully weighted. Colonial correspondents were generally chosen (and survived) because they echoed the values and assumptions of their London employers (and their audiences, including investors and financiers), and could be relied on to apply them to developments overseas (Deakin probably enjoyed exceptional latitude).[26] Their role, far from undermining the notion of London rules, confirms their pervasiveness. A writer in Ottawa or Melbourne could, reasonably accurately, predict the issues which would concern British financiers and investors, and then comment in familiar language. The fact that Australian politics in particular spilt into the London press reflected the expectation amongst some, especially on the Australian right, that the London capital markets might influence Australian governments. The goal was not to change how the City judged investments, but how it judged Australia.

The press played a crucial role in the construction and application of the 'rules of the game'. It was the main way in which information arrived and circulated in London. Material from the press, discussed in private and public forums around the City, helped to frame reactions to events. T. A. Coghlan complained: 'There is nothing so stupid that it will not find credence and when a statement... is made by the leading financial newspaper of London, backed up by the chairman of a large Australian Company at his annual meeting, and by many other responsible persons, it is not surprising that people who depend upon such sources for information accept it unquestioned'.[27] The press was also an important means by which City views were transmitted overseas. Leading titles circulated widely and had their opinions reproduced. Press clippings frequently accompanied correspondence sent from London.

Discussions in the City, verbal and written, applied shifting assumptions about investors' interests (or the interests of certain groups of investors) to events overseas. The remainder of this chapter follows discussions of Australia and Canada between about 1900 and 1914 to tease out the factors considered of particular interest to investors. For most of our period Canada emerged more favourably from these discussions than Australia. The sections that follow discuss in turn the City's views on property rights, defence, monetary stability, budgets and tariffs, immigration and the notion of the young country, and organised and politicised labour.

Rights of property

Investment ultimately transferred property overseas and nothing was more fundamental to investors' interests than the security of that property. Writing on Russia in September 1906, *The Economist* commented pessimistically that there was 'no inducement for British investors at the present moment to participate in the fortunes of any Russian enterprise' because the country was 'powerless to give adequate protection to life and property' and because companies faced 'legal restrictions of a kind unknown to English law', all of which had resulted in 'terrible losses' for investors.[28] As *The Economist*'s view of Russia implies, investors and financiers thought a state powerful enough to guarantee law and order was essential. So too was freedom from arbitrary state intervention which effectively confiscated property. Government bondholders feared defaults on debts or, worse, repudiation. Although a few commentators thought such actions to be virtually impossible, and certainly irrational, financial writers generally encouraged investors to contemplate a state's 'reputation for honourable dealing'.[29] Canadian and Australian government stocks were generally considered to be secure. One financial writer, W. R. Lawson, wryly observed that, 'many borrowing nations... prefer the cynical view of Sheridan, who, when asked if the thought of his debts never kept him awake at night, replied, "Why should they? It is my creditors that they should keep awake"'. Lawson continued, 'as a rule Colonial Governments have not been of Sheridan's sort. They have appreciated the inestimable value of good credit, and have done their best to maintain it'.[30] Not all commentators were so sanguine. Some worried just prior to the Great War that many Canadian municipalities had overextended their finances and might be forced to default.[31] Concerns were occasionally expressed that the more radical elements of the Australian Labor Party might favour default or repudiation in a crisis.[32] However, in the event there were few serious challenges to the interests of holders of public stocks.

Private companies did not always seem as secure, and those involved watched closely for interference in their concessions. Railways and utilities were particularly exposed to political pressures. They provided services consumed by large numbers of individuals and businesses, and frequently possessed virtual monopolies. This underlay the predictable and often high returns which attracted investors but also made them targets for popularly inspired regulation.[33] Companies feeling threatened in this way often alleged that their property rights were being violated. When, in 1913, Canada's railway commission proposed a reduction of rates on Canada's transcontinental railways, Alfred Smithers (chairman of the Grand Trunk Railway), wrote to the Canadian prime minister, Robert Laird Borden, to warn of the 'disastrous effect' the move would have on Canada's credit. He also reminded Borden that a Canadian court had earlier found a proposed reduction in rates on the White Pass and Yukon Railway to be a 'confiscation of property'.[34]

While Smithers kept matters behind closed doors, several companies sought to defend their property in the financial press, attempting to damage the credit of their host states by suggesting that their plight highlighted a risk to holders of government stocks. Two examples illustrate these contests, and the ideas underpinning them. First, in 1903 the Western Australian government passed a number of measures to regulate the Midland Railway Company of Western Australia. A competing steamer was subsidised, a mining bill altered its title to minerals found on its lands, and a rail traffic bill imposed regulation which one director thought amounted to 'a diplomatic way to confiscate the railway'.[35] After a failed appeal to the Colonial Office, the company secured the support of the editors of *The Economist*, the *Financial Times*, and the *Financial News*. Forty-two articles appeared in a wide range of papers late in 1903 all agreeing that the measures interfered with the railway's contract and hence its property rights.[36] *The Economist* warned that 'if this principle is upheld, investors are likely to fight shy of Western Australia'.[37] The *Investor's Review* concurred: 'the government of that money wasting and semi-bankrupt colony is engaged in attempting a confiscation of a particularly scandalous character'. It hoped that, 'the next time Western Australia comes to the London market for a loan it can be reminded that the display of honesty is the first essential to borrowing'.[38] The government dropped the rail traffic bill just after the new year. Both the directors of the company and the financial press congratulated themselves on a triumphant defence of property rights.[39]

A less successful campaign opposed the Ontario government's policy after 1905 of establishing public competition (through its Hydro-electric Commission) against private companies generating electricity at Niagara Falls. One firm, the Electrical Development Company, had many British bondholders. The contest came to a head in 1909 when the companies challenged the validity of a provincial law amending contracts between various municipalities and the Hydroelectric Commission in the courts. The provincial government, not wishing the legal actions to delay a popular policy, passed an act suspending proceedings. This provoked a storm in London (at least partially instigated by the Electrical Development Company).[40] W. R. Lawson published three articles in the *Financial Times* suggesting that this, and several other cases, meant that Magna Carta no longer operated in Ontario. 'King John', he snipped, 'would simply have declared that the courts of Ontario shall be "forever closed"'.[41] *The Financier* explained that 'there is no disguising the fact that the British investor will hesitate to place his money where such legislation is possible. The first consideration he has the right to expect is that adequate protection is afforded to his rights'.[42] *The Standard, The Statist, The Outlook, The Economist* and the *Investor's Review* concurred.[43] In August J. P. Whitney, the province's premier, sent a letter defending his actions to *The Economist*. To Whitney's disgust the paper accompanied with an editorial condemning Ontario's violation not only of 'Magna Carta' but also the 'Ten Commandments'.[44] The province refused to give way, and a campaign to have the legislation disallowed by the federal government failed.[45]

Such disputes seem to have remained – in the eyes of most investors – isolated incidents. Despite the occasional dire warning, neither Australia nor Canada was generally thought likely to disregard property rights more generally. Nonetheless, the powerful rhetoric surrounding the Midland Railway and Ontario Hydro disputes show the centrality of property rights to investors.

Defence

Few in the City agreed with the radical thinker, Norman Angell, that economic interdependence guaranteed peace and the security of capital.[46] Hence a state's military might and geopolitical situation affected its credit: Japan's victory in the Russo-Japanese War reduced the interest charged on its loans from 5 to 4 per cent.[47] Canada's and Australia's locations led to contrasting assessments of their vulnerability. Canada was only really exposed to invasion from the south, and by the turn of the century, an American invasion had become a remote possibility. The resolution of the Venezuelan and Alaskan boundary disputes in 1899 and 1903 removed the last points of friction between Britain and the US in North America. From then on, if not long before, the Munro Doctrine effectively added a further guarantee of Canadian security. Canada could not be seen as strategically vulnerable by any stretch of the imagination.[48] Australia, by contrast, was more exposed. The far-east was seen as particularly unstable, with Japan's rise and the possibility either of a similar revival in China, or of its collapse generating a new imperial imbroglio.[49] Although the 1902 Anglo-Japanese alliance may have reassured investors, the contrast between Australia and Canada remained telling.

Australian politicians were accused of exacerbating matters. The 'white Australia' policy (which restricted the immigration of non-whites) and the heated associated rhetoric were thought likely to provoke difficulties.[50] The Melbourne correspondent of *The Economist* predicted: 'A very important political consideration will probably present itself to investors. It is the growing determination of the "yellow" nations, Japan and China, to assert themselves abroad... If the Australian is disdainful of "colour" the Japanese is also resentful... An outburst of ill-feeling might be provoked at any moment'.[51] *The Times* also warned that a white Australia should be pursued with tact.[52]

In this instance *The Times* had imperial interests, rather than those of investors, in mind, but the two were intricately linked. As the 1908 *Canadian Annual Review* (a Canadian publication reflecting the views of the anglophone establishment) explained: 'Canadian credit [is] enhanced and conserved by the British power behind it and around it, acting as a guarantee of immunity from the dangers of aggression and giving to a part of the empire the strength of the whole'.[53] Similarly, *The Times* argued in 1900 that 'British command of the seas... renders Australia as safe from naval attack as the Isle of Wight'.[54] It pointed out in 1904 that Canada's £31,341,000 trade was also protected by the Royal Navy at no additional cost to the dominion. Argentina had to spend £920,000 on her Navy. The Australian colonies contributed more to their defence. In 1887 they agreed to contribute £37,000 to the British fleet, raised to £224,000 in 1897 and £240,000 in 1902. This covered barely a third of the costs of the Pacific fleet. Reliance on Britain for defence seemingly enabled resources to be devoted to 'social overhead capital' ('reproductive works' to use contemporary parlance).[55] As a result, *The Economist* argued that, 'if the relation of the colony and Mother-Country were exchanged for the relation between independent states... their growth might very well be at an end'.[56]

Given this, it might be expected that directing resources to defence expenditure would prove unpopular in the City. Yet the opposite was often the case. Australian, Canadian, and New Zealand contributions in the South African War were widely praised. In 1900, the president of the London Chamber of Commerce expressed relief that with 'war clouds' in China and 'great cause for anxiety in West Africa' that, 'the people of all parts of the Empire are anxious to share our imperial responsibilities by rallying around the flag in South Africa, and thus proclaiming to the world the solidity of the British Empire'.[57] *The Times*, *The Economist*, and chairmen at various company meetings all expressed similar views.[58]

Such praise partially reflected a broader attachment to empire in the City, often described as 'sentiment' by contemporaries, as well as fears about Britain's declining supremacy. These fears heightened in the wake of the war, and with the subsequent naval arms race with Germany. Slipping control of the seas caused particular concern since it underpinned the security of the 'strong box' of Europe and of the City's global trading networks.[59] In this context, dominion contributions supplemented the imperial insurance policy that guaranteed investments, not least in the dominions themselves. These calculations, as well as 'sentiment', coloured perceptions of the emerging defence policies of Australia and Canada. If Australia was seen to be more vulnerable and more likely to provoke its neighbours, by the late-Edwardian period it was also applauded for its defensive initiatives. By 1910, both parties there were committed to the construction of a navy, including dreadnoughts.[60] In the military sphere, transcontinental railways and compulsory training for the young equally suggested a commitment to security. *The Times* expressed the 'profoundest satisfaction' at these initiatives, and even praised the (rarely popular) Australian Labor party for a 'keenness in defence... much appreciated in this country'.[61]

Canada proved less 'keen'. Canadian politics required a tough balance to be struck between Ontario's imperial enthusiasm and ambivalence in Quebec. Wilfred Laurier had stoutly resisted Chamberlain's attempts to secure greater colonial defensive contributions and Canadian participation in the South African War had received lukewarm support from the government.[62] The dreadnought crisis split Canadian politics with anglophone reactions generally favouring assistance to Britain and most francophones continuing to fear imperial entanglement. Seeking a middle way, in 1910 Laurier proposed constructing a fleet of five cruisers and ten destroyers largely for coastal defence, a 'tin pot' force according to some critics.[63] In the September 1911 election, Borden defeated Laurier. In 1912 the new prime minister announced direct payments to Britain to fund naval construction.[64] The new policy proved controversial. As Borden's measure was filibustered by Liberal opponents in the Canadian Senate, Alfred Smithers put a brave face on matters, telling the English Association of American Bondholders that it was, 'a matter of great rejoicing throughout the empire that the great dominion has devoted so much of the time of her parliament to the earnest discussion of defence'.[65] The City followed the debates closely, but was divided on the best form for Canadian contributions to take. *The Economist* thought Laurier's approach had better conserved the spirit of self-government.[66] However, members of the Canadian Section of the London Chamber of Commerce telegraphed to inform Borden of their 'satisfaction' with his change of policy.[67] When the Senate finally rejected Borden's bill in mid-1913, the London *Globe* thought this (along with the collapse of the western Canadian land boom) had stolen the 'glamour' from Canadian stocks.[68]

Defence was closely watched in the City. It was one point where investors' calculations interacted with the formal political structures of empire, both because the latter underwrote dominion defence and because concerns about British supremacy more generally were important to the City's own broader interests and may also have moved more imperially-minded investors. These points are taken up in the next chapter.

Monetary stability

After secure property rights and defence, a stable monetary system was essential to investors. Much historiographical attention has focused on the gold standard. Cain and Hopkins emphasise that Britain's commitment to gold underpinned confidence in the all important bill market, while overseas the gold standard eliminated fluctuations in exchange rates which might erode dividends and profits.[69] There were of course other means to insulate investors against currency depreciation. Foreign governments could issue bonds denominated in sterling, transferring the risk of exchange fluctuations and inflation to taxpayers.[70] Nonetheless devices of this kind were often greeted with suspicion. India after 1898 adopted a gold exchange standard which used gold for external transactions while maintaining a silver currency internally (and hence conserving bullion). The system, as Keynes noted, was introduced against the advice of leading financiers including Sir John Lubbock (Lord Avebury), Samuel Montagu, and Alfred Rothschild who thought 'a gold standard without a gold standard seemed... an utter impossibility'.[71] Although a few in the City had advocated bimetallism (fixing the price of silver relative to gold), the gold standard was the preferred means to ensure exchange rate stability (and internal fiscal discipline).[72] The standard was not challenged in Canada or Australia (the latter, as a significant gold producer, had a disincentive to innovate) excepting the radical fringe of the Australian left.[73]

Other aspects of financial systems also attracted attention. The merits or otherwise of a country's banking system directly concerned those holding bank shares. It also affected virtually every other interest since the provision of adequate credit was essential for trade, not least the export trade which serviced debts. As we saw in Chapter 1, the 1893 crisis in Australian banking had disrupted trade, and the Australian banking system remained suspect for a long time thereafter. There were also occasional fears that the Australian left might introduce inauspicious reforms. For example, proposals for a paper currency backed by a compulsory contribution from the bank's gold reserves were described as a 'forced loan' by *The Economist*'s Melbourne correspondent.[74] In 1910 Labor did introduce a federal note issue exchangeable for gold in Melbourne, and, in the following year, established a state-owned central bank. Although

The Economist's Melbourne correspondent criticised the latter and thought the note issue to be a 'humiliation' and 'practically inconvertible', few in the City shared this assessment.[75] Meanwhile, Canadian banking shone, especially when contrasted with its American counterpart. Its system of transcontinental branches was considered more robust and better suited to the strain of financing the western harvest. The contrast was highlighted when the October 1907 crash on Wall Street saw the failure of a large number of American financial institutions. Their Canadian counterparts remained seemingly unscathed despite close links to New York, and still facilitated the export of a bumper crop from the west. The financial writer Charles Duguid praised Canadian banking's 'soundness and self-reliance'; *The Times* its 'wholesome restraint... on the overwhelming energies of [common to] the inhabitants of every new and fertile country'.[76] *The Economist* recommended the Canadian system to the United States.[77]

A financial system, it was thought, ought not to encourage excessive speculation. A reputation for illegitimate promotions could deter investment. In 1905 Thomas Blackwell, president of the London Chamber of Commerce, warned visiting delegates from the Canadian Manufacturing Association that 'terrible results had accrued to other colonies from reckless speculation and attempts to grow too rich too fast'.[78] Nonetheless, suspicions grew as Canadian flotations reached record levels and expanded to municipalities, land and finance, and industrial securities.[79] *The Economist* thought that western Canadian towns 'in their anxiety to "get big" quickly [were]... equipping themselves with roads, sewers, lighting and water plants and schools, on a too generous scale'.[80] R. M. Horne-Payne agreed that, 'the British investor has had his confidence in Canadian reliability shaken by witnessing a scramble for money by municipal bodies'.[81] In 1913 Canada's land boom collapsed and the allure of Canadian industrials waned.[82] Canada's borrowings declined markedly in 1914, and confidence was further strained by the failure of Arthur Grenfell's Canadian Agency. The strains on Canadian credit were eclipsed by the outbreak of war.

Thus investors and financiers kept close watch on a number of aspects of a country's monetary and financial systems. The gold standard underpinned payments to investors, and a robust banking system was also seen as crucial for economic development and hence debt service. The prevalence or otherwise of excessive speculation forcing up stock prices and increasing the volume of poor issues to investors was also important. If a market became suspected of possessing such tendencies, it was likely to be condemned and ultimately shunned, and the fiction of reliability was just as necessary to those unscrupulous parties exploiting investors' misplaced confidence as to *bona fide* propositions. Any measures which might reduce (or seem to reduce) these tendencies would reinforce that confidence.

Budgetary policy

Cain and Hopkins argue that British investors required colonial governments to adhere to a 'Gladstonian' budgetary orthodoxy composed of balanced budgets and a regime of low taxation.[83] This is broadly true but matters often became more complex in practice. Most investors had interests at stake in budgetary policy. Bondholders used the buoyancy of revenues and the details of expenditure to gauge whether debts could be serviced and further borrowings justified. Private enterprises often relied on infrastructure and other services provided by the state, while costs depended on the prevalent tax regime. Certain coincidences of interest existed between investors in the public and private sectors. Serious financial problems for governments might raise borrowing costs for private enterprise, and lead to increases in taxation or reduced expenditure in ways affecting their interests. Equally, since government debts ultimately had to be paid through export surpluses, the impact of taxation regimes on the fortunes of exporting industries affected the interests of government bondholders. Nonetheless, for the holder of government stocks the overall state of the public finances was the most immediate concern; for investors in the private sector individual items of expenditure or taxation tended to loom larger.

Since the early 1890s, the budgets of Australian governments were subjected to sustained criticism (fuelled by Australian commentary). The continent's most persistent British critic, A. J. Wilson of the *Investor's Review*, argued that the Australian states were bankrupt, something only masked by continuing borrowing and the fact that tariffs converted capital imports into current revenues.[84] Although few critics were quite as vociferous as Wilson, widespread suspicion was aroused around the turn of the century when many Australian states borrowed heavily in the London market (see Chapter 2). The problem lay in the purposes of this borrowing. The City preferred to finance 'reproductive' or 'remunerative' works: infrastructure projects which would generate additional revenues.[85] However, New South Wales and Victoria were accused of undertaking unremunerative public works to generate employment. In June 1903, the *Daily Mail*, another perennial critic, argued, 'until great economies are effected in the government and administration, and until the extravagant outlay on public works ceases, the prospects of the British investor cannot be considered roseate'.[86] A month later the underwriters of colonial loans temporarily halted borrowing. Although it was (and remains) unclear how far this was intended to be a shot across the bows of wayward colonial governments, some interpreted it as such.[87] In the mid-1900s, the states continued to find it difficult to borrow other than to renew loans, and their stocks remained low because the 'feeling' remained, as *The Economist* put it, that easy access to capital, 'had encouraged the states to indulge in lavish expenditure on unremunerative public works, which, if not checked, might lead to serious embarrassments in the future'.[88] As good seasons saw revenues recover, criticism of Australian states' finances abated. By 1913, Victoria was even held up to the British government as a paragon of fiscal virtue.[89]

Expenditures by the newly-formed Commonwealth government came in for similar criticism, in particular the provision of old age pensions, and proposals to construct two transcontinental railways and a new capital city (the scheme that eventually produced Canberra).[90] Some items divided the City. Take the proposed transcontinental railways from Adelaide west to Perth and north to Darwin. *The Economist* thought them unnecessary, but, in the wake of Lord Kitchener's inspection of Australian defences in 1909, *The Times* considered them to be strategic necessities.[91] This reflected the general tension we have noted between the desire for reproductive works and adequate (but unreproductive) defence. Divisions also emerged because some interests expected to benefit from schemes which might be thought unjustified in the round. A director of two tram companies in Perth and Kalgoorlie predicted (rather implausibly) that the proposed line from Adelaide westwards would transform these towns into the San Francisco and Chicago of Australia respectively.[92]

Canadian finances presented a marked contrast to those of Australian governments. Canada's economic boom caused Ottawa's purse to swell, and justified expanding expenditure. *The Times* commented in 1900, 'Canada, a young and imperfectly developed country, is committed to a large capital expenditure, to a great extent in reproductive works'.[93] In 1908 *The Economist*'s Ottawa correspondent reflected on the fact that in the previous 12 years the dominion's debt had increased from $258 to $275 million and expenditure from $37 to $50 million, concluding that 'the country has been making rapid progress and is well able to carry its burdens'.[94] Many items of increasing Canadian government expenditure facilitated certain investors' interests. For example the dominion spent heavily from 1904 on the National Transcontinental, the eastern component of the Grand Trunk Pacific Railway, and through bond guarantees, the Canadian government lent its credit to this scheme and to the Canadian Northern Railways.[95] Thus increased expenditure (and increased notional liabilities on the part of the government) served the interests of investors in these lines.

Most in the City expected budgets to balance (meaning current revenues to match current expenditure) and there was a strong preference for loans to be spent on 'reproductive' works. However the balance of interests of different groups could diverge, with particular items of taxation and expenditure preoccupying particular companies and investors in government stocks paying more attention to the overall budgetary and economic position. Interpreting these interests also led to divisions in practice, and they could be hard to reconcile with other 'rules' – for example the need for adequate defence.

Tariffs and protection

The City is generally regarded as a bastion of British adherence to free trade which facilitated London's commercial activities. Free trade was also important to its financial sector, since little restraint was placed on the imports which enabled debts to be serviced, although Cain and Hopkins have pointed out that the gold standard probably ultimately mattered more.[96] Attitudes in the Square Mile to tariff policy in the dominions has been less studied. Cain and Hopkins argue that colonial tariffs were necessary for revenue while protection encouraged import substitution augmenting the export surpluses required to service debts.[97] Elements of this case were recognised by contemporaries. Lord Brassey, a former governor of Victoria and president of the London Chamber of Commerce, observed that 'colonial government's revenues must be drawn from indirect taxation'.[98] This was not always thought ideal. A. J. Wilson warned: 'Were they to become Free Trade countries there is not a single one of them that would continue to pay the interest upon its public debt, simply because the inhabitants would not endure the direct taxation necessary for the money to be provided'.[99]

There were again differences of emphasis between investors in government bonds and in the private sector. In 1901 the Commonwealth was devising its first tariff. Pastoral finance and mining companies followed proceedings closely, fearing additional costs. E. T. Doxat told Dalgety and Co's AGM that 'All... hoped that the search for revenue would not lead to the undue increment in the cost of imports and for the possible benefit of a few, cause injury to the general community'.[100] In 1902, it became clear that higher duties would be placed on mining machinery. A delegation under the auspices of the London Chamber of Commerce (representing

£13 million of capital) presented a petition to the Western Australian agent-general, asserting that cheap equipment was 'essential' for the state's 'prosperous development'. 'The millions of English and foreign capital invested recently in Western Australia', it proceeded, 'was due in no small degree to the moderate taxation and reasonable conditions ruling at the time'.[101] The state government (which, as we shall see in Chapter 6, was keen to foster the mining industry) lobbied, unsuccessfully, against the move. When the tariff passed, one mining company chairman condemned it as 'almost prohibitive', adding that, 'The government appealed to this country for capital to develop the resources of the colony... they should at least protect the property in which British capital was invested'.[102] Thus while the case for revenue tariffs might be accepted in principle, who exactly should be taxed, and whether protection ought to be involved caused more division.

The City's attitudes to Canadian protectionism were equally complex. This became apparent in 1911 when the Laurier government announced reciprocal reductions (reciprocity) in tariffs on certain primary products agreed by the US and Canadian governments. The *Financial News* thought, 'no fiscal arrangement of modern times... has given occasion to such animated discussion in the City of London'.[103] Yet no consensus was reached on the implications for the Canadian economy. *The Statist* predicted reciprocity would, 'stimulate Canadian production so greatly and make even more strongly felt than now the need for railways and other means of developing the Dominion's resources, [hence, accentuating the] demand for British capital, and [benefiting] the British investor'.[104] Others suspected that the agreement would, ultimately, lead to the dismantling of the regime protecting Canadian industry and undermine the east-west orientation of Canada's economy: the foundations of many investments' fortunes.[105] Even those interested in Canada's transcontinental railways (which lay close to the heart of this debate) reached no consensus. R. M. Horne-Payne thought that reciprocity had 'checked... a great wave of enthusiastic sentiment in favour of Canada and all things Canadian' and predicted that the dominion would sacrifice privileged access to the London capital market.[106] Ferdinand Faithfull Begg (a stockbroker who dealt in Canadian Pacific stocks and treasurer of the London Chamber of Commerce) feared that the loss of the east-west haul would undermine Canada's railways.[107] Initially (and in private) Alfred Smithers agreed that this 'may be bad for the railways' although he mused that the loss of the long haul might 'be compensated for in time by the larger population and increased cultivation'.[108] However, he soon endorsed the agreement at a meeting of the English Association of American Bondholders. Smithers' fellow Grand Trunk director Lord Welby, a prominent free trader, also expressed vigorous support at the Cobden Club.[109]

Discussions of colonial tariffs were complicated by the debate in Britain about tariff reform. From May 1903 Joseph Chamberlain argued that Britain should abandon free trade and, after raising tariffs, grant trade preferences to the empire. In part this programme sought to bind the dominions closer to Britain.[110] As a result, colonial tariff policy was examined closely to test the plausibility of Chamberlain's schemes. Tariff reformers argued that the colonies had offered to lower duties on British manufactures in exchange for British preferences on primary products (an idea originating with the Canadian concessions of preferences to Britain in 1896). To refuse this 'colonial offer' would drive the empire apart. Free traders replied that the colonies would never sacrifice manufacturing and suggested that endless wrangling over tariffs would weaken not strengthen the empire.[111] The bitter debate often eclipsed calculations of interest, and may have shaped some investors' behaviour.

As a result when, in 1908, Alfred Deakin's government combined a raise in the level of protection in Australia with a British preference, the move was widely analysed in the context of the 'fiscal' debate.[112] Deakin had pushed the case for tariff reform forcefully at the 1907 Imperial Conference.[113] However, while earlier Canadian preferences had reduced overall barriers to British goods, Deakin's government increased them, and hence was less welcomed. *The Times* called the preference 'derisory' while *The Economist* argued that it demonstrated that colonial manufacturing would not be sacrificed for the benefit of British industry as tariff reformers suggested.[114] Few discussed investors' interests and, in contrast to the first Commonwealth tariff, many declined to comment. C. J. Hegan (often outspoken on other matters) of the English, Scottish and Australian Bank avoided the issue at the bank's AGM: 'The opinions, even of experts, differ so widely, and susceptibilities might so easily be aroused, that... I think it best to say nothing'.[115]

Reciprocity was also judged through the prism of tariff reform and the different conceptions of empire it invoked.[116] Free Traders, including contributors to *The Economist*, claimed that Canada was acting in her best economic interests. Obstructing these would only drive her from the imperial fold. Tariff reformers claimed that Britain's adherence to free trade was forcing Canada into the orbit of the United States.[117] Financiers, such as Charles Moreing, commented that 'sentiment' caused 'Canadian securities to sell so high in London'.[118] But given the availability of conflicting free trade and tariff reforming conceptions of empire, there was no more reason for 'sentiment' to produce a common line amongst investors and financiers than material calculations.

Tariffs could affect investors' interests, and received widespread attention in the City. Although it was generally accepted that revenue tariffs were necessary to service colonial debts, protection and the exact burden of these tariffs caused division. The tariff reform campaign eroded faith in free trade more generally and led, from 1903, to discussions of trade being refracted through the lens of British and imperial politics. In these circumstances free trade had ceased to be a rule of the game, not because of a broad consensus regarding revenue tariffs and protection but because the City was too divided by interest and ideology to formulate a clear line.

Young countries and immigration

The City widely recognised that settler societies (or 'young countries' as contemporaries often called them) receiving large numbers of immigrants possessed enhanced economic potential.[119] The dramatic growth of the United States in the nineteenth century conditioned these expectations, and they were extended to Canada, Argentina, and (less frequently) Australia in the early-twentieth century.[120] In 1913, Robert Brand (then working for Lazards) predicted that Canada's future growth would be 'at least as rapid, or more rapid than it has been in the last few years', adding that 'the best test would be to place opposite the present figures of Canadian manufactures corresponding figures from the United States to show the sort of size the former might attain...'.[121] In 1901 *The Times* predicted that Australia's 'commercial capacities' would expand and develop 'as those of the United States, so insignificant a hundred years ago, have expanded and developed'.[122] The widespread recognition of the young country as a special category could excuse apparent violations of the 'rules'. As two financial writers observed, while 'a portion' of many young countries' borrowings had been 'injudiciously expended' or even 'senselessly squandered' in 'youthful follies', 'it would be foolish to close one's eyes to the strong probability that these past extravagances will be wiped out by future developments'.[123]

Migration (and an expanding population more generally) was widely understood to be the motor of development in young countries, and excused high levels of borrowing. After finding that the Canadian government's per capita debt to be five times that of the US, *The Economist* reassured its readers not to be alarmed since, 'A young country like Canada, with unbounded natural resources, into which population is being rushed at the rate of 200,000 a year, can stand a strain that would break the back of an old world community'.[124] Here Canada and Australia's fortunes contrasted. While Canada absorbed increasing numbers of migrants, migration to Australia tailed off in the 1890s and 1900s, only reviving in 1907.[125] Figures published in 1905 found that between 1903 and 1905 Australia lost 6,000 people while Canada gained 260,000. According to *The Times*, 'the extraordinary progress made by Canada in the last few years has to a very great extent diverted the attention of the British public from Australia'.[126] *The Economist*'s Melbourne correspondent warned, 'For the investor in Australian securities… the outlook is not encouraging'.[127]

Australia was further damaged by the perception that, as one company chairman put it, 'The Australians, unlike the Canadians, had done their utmost… to keep emigrants out of the country'.[128] The Commonwealth's new regulations restricted entry to migrants travelling under contract. In a prominent case in 1903, these regulations prevented six hat makers from entering Australia. *The Times* thought this highlighted, 'the defects of a clause which our correspondent himself describes as most injurious to Australian credit'.[129] The Australian prime minister, Edmund Barton, entered the fray, pointing out in *The Economist* that America had long prospered with similar restrictions, continuing that, 'it is taking an extreme view to think that such a law, when understood, can really injure the credit or retard the progress of this continent'.[130]

Later in the decade, Australia renewed efforts to attract migrants. C. J. Hegan thought 'every well wisher of Australia' would welcome the change in attitude and the fact that 'determined efforts seem about to be undertaken to attract a desirable class of emigrant from this country by the offer of good farming land on easy terms of payment'.[131] The *Daily Mail* snidely remarked that, 'there is only too much reason to believe that the declarations published in England to the effect that Australia is now anxious for settlers and immigrants are only a means of influencing the British investor in Australia's favour'.[132]

Some policies designed to attract migrants, and ensure that they settled on the land rather than in towns, proved controversial. Many states and, from 1910 the Commonwealth government, pursued policies to promote 'closer settlement' of the country by agriculturalists, in the process 'busting up large estates'. The chairman of one anglo-Australian bank observed, in 1910 that these moves were 'of the first importance to all those interested in Australia from the financial or patriotic point of view'.[133] However E. T. Doxat of Dalgety and Co warned that heavy taxation to achieve these ends, 'would not tend to improve the opinion of the British public as to the dangers of the investment of capital in Australia'.[134] Equally compulsory repurchase of estates could be controversial. In 1908, the Peel River Company, which owned land in New South Wales, accused the state government of seeking to confiscate its property under such a scheme.[135] Immigration may have underpinned confidence in young countries, but measures to promote immigration could be opposed if they damaged other interests. The rules were bent for young countries, not broken.

Labour relations and anti-socialism

The behaviour of labour was watched extremely closely in the City. Powerful unions could, it was thought, raise labour costs and reduce the returns on investments. British experiences conditioned such fears. Lord Avebury told the Associated Chambers of Commerce of the United Kingdom in 1900 that, 'Strikes have tended to diminish the confidence which is felt by investors; they have driven a large amount of capital abroad'.[136] The rise of a more militant 'new unionism' in Britain, the Liberals' overturning of the Taff Vale and Osborne Judgements, and the emergence of the British Labour Party all strengthened such fears.[137] Nor was it simply seen as a British disease. The City noted with no degree of satisfaction that, in the words of Alfred Smithers, 'The unrest in labour circles does indeed seem to extend all over the world'.[138]

Labour relations in Canada and Australia presented a stark contrast. Canada tended to be seen in relatively benign terms. As W. R. Lawson put it, 'There is one ordeal common to civilised nations which Canada has not yet gone through... Labour and Capital have not yet begun their inevitable conflict'.[139] Ferdinand Faithfull Begg told the London Chamber of Commerce in December 1911 that in the dominion, 'Working men and men in a better position of life all agreed that the capitalist was as necessary as labour and ought to be protected. Coming from this country, after passing through recent events, that was a most delightful discovery'.[140] There were some dissenting voices. Charles Rivers Wilson and Alfred Smithers of the Grand Trunk Railway complained that 'combinations' were forcing up labour costs.[141] Nonetheless Smithers expected militancy would have limits since if 'no profit were left for capital' inward investment would cease and Canada's cities would be 'crowded with the unemployed'.[142] In general few in the City had great fears of Canadian trades unions.[143]

The situation in Australia was very different. After a trip to the Congress of the Chambers of Commerce of the Empire, held in Sydney in 1909 (of which more in Chapter 4) Albert Spicer, president of the London Chamber of Commerce, remarked that, 'a much stronger demarcation between the representatives of capital and the representatives of labour in

Australia than there was in this country'.[144] Unionisation was prevalent in every sector concerning British investors: mines, the pastoral industry, and the publicly-owned railways. In the year of Spicer's visit, strikes paralysed production on the coal mines of Newcastle, New South Wales (curtailing economic activity across the continent), while a wave of strikes also hit the Broken Hill mining complex. F. A. Govett commented, 'It is from this constant liability to such crises that the great difficulty arises in the enlistment of capital to Australian enterprise; the danger is too great, for literally one never knows what may be the insane policy which the labour men, without asking questions, will adopt'.[145] The *Australasian World* (a specialist London publication) thought that a recent issue of stock by New South Wales had been 'adverse[ly] affected by the labour troubles at Broken Hill'.[146] Labour legislation also contributed to the distrust of Australia. Voluntary arbitration was the City's preferred response to labour disputes.[147] State and federal governments in Australia progressively adopted various forms of compulsory arbitration or – in Victoria – wages boards.[148] Compulsory arbitration in particular was thought to maintain high wages in times of high unemployment while failing to prevent strikes when the economy recovered. As Govett observed, 'the principle of compulsory arbitration has been established, and when established, labour will now only accept an award when plainly it is in its favour'.[149]

Yet it was not only organised labour that worried the City; its emerging political power was regarded with even greater trepidation. Arthur Grenfell wrote of 'anxious times' in the City in 1906 due 'to the want of confidence which has been gradually growing up as a result of State Socialism'.[150] While Canada lacked a significant labour party, Labor's emergence in federal and state politics in Australia was watched with disquiet (and the many on the right in Australia placed a rich stream of alarming reports before the City). On the inauguration of the Commonwealth, *The Times* commented, 'The aggressive predominance of the Labour party is the most formidable rock ahead', but reassured its readers that, 'The people of these colonies, bought up in a sound school of self-government and inheriting the best traditions of the mother country, may be trusted to work out their own destiny in a manly spirit and with the practical sagacity that marks the British race'.[151] Others were not so sure. Labor's hand was frequently seen guiding unpopular measures. The 'excessive borrowings' of the states for public works were thought to be the 'consequence of the political pressure exercised by labour'. Other items of 'unnecessary' expenditure such as old age pensions were similarly seen to be Labor's doing.[152] The party was also thought to be behind hostility to immigration, compulsory arbitration, and taxes on absentee landlords. The musings of Labor's radical wing stoked fears of what the party might do in office. *The Economist's* Australian correspondents warned that Labor might repudiate debts, abandon the gold standard, and prove disloyal to the empire (which had implications for Australian defence as well as upsetting imperialist loyalties).[153]

These fears affected Australian dealings with the capital market. The Melbourne *Age's* London correspondent warned that 'public and private credit' was being damaged because, 'the governing and business classes here do not seem capable of believing that a Labour administration could in any circumstances have an other than adverse influence on national policy'.[154] In 1906 New South Wales' governor, Sir Harry Rawson, quizzed Robert Nivison and T. J. Russell of the London and Westminster Bank on why his state's stocks sold for lower prices than those of Natal. He reported their answer to the state's premier, Joseph Carruthers:

> In the minds of financiers there was dread that at any moment socialistic legislation might be passed in Australia which would damage the prospects of a loan about to be issued and the value of stocks already in existence. So long as that dread existed, so long would it be impossible that justice could be done to Australia... it was not so much what had already been done by legislation as what people thought was likely to be done. [Rawson's or Carruthers' underlining].[155]

This fear of politicised labour revealed a final concern: that groups unresponsive to its interests might obtain control. Many in the City had little faith that economic dependence, of itself, would automatically secure their interests.

Such fears, so commonly expressed, make it hard to see why lending to Australia revived after 1909. This becomes stranger still given that, in 1910, Andrew Fisher's Labor party became the first to win an overall majority in both houses of the Australian parliament. By then Labor was also in office in several other states, including New South Wales. As we shall see, one of the government's first acts was to introduce a graduated land tax to 'bust up large estates' in pursuit of closer settlement and to fund the naval programme. This provoked an outcry amongst pastoral interests, and concerted lobbying orchestrated through the London Chamber of Commerce. The move was widely expected to deter investment. Andrew Williamson told the meeting of the Australian Estates Company (a middle ranking player in pastoral finance) that 'serious damage' had been done to Australian credit. He claimed to know of 'two large and promising industrial propositions' which had tried to obtain capital in the last two months and had 'found the door absolutely closed owing to the misgiving which has been engendered here as to the labour party's treatment of capital and the state of industrial strife at present in Australia'.[156]

But the overall volume of capital flowing into Australian government stocks increased, and even investment in the private sector was higher in absolute terms (but not as a proportion of total investment in Australia) between 1910 and 1914 than in 1905–1909 (see Table 1.5). Investors' fears may have been tempered in several ways. The Labor party in office proved more moderate than expected in other fields, especially banking, and just as committed to Australia's defence. Indeed using the proceeds of the land tax for naval construction was in some ways *more* orthodox than paying for the fleet through borrowing (as Deakin's last government had proposed) given the widespread preference in the City that loans be devoted to 'reproductive works'. The perceived leftward drift of British politics may also have dulled sensitivities. Hartley Withers probably had Australia in mind when he observed that, 'fear of socialistic legislation at home had the humorous result of making British investors fear to touch consols, but rush eagerly to buy the securities of colonial governments which had gone much further in the direction of socialism than we had'.[157] As Canada's boom began to overheat Australia looked less risky. Finally, the revival of immigration may have renewed faith in Australia's potential as a young country. As George Reid, Australia's first high commissioner, joked over dinner at the London Chamber of Commerce: 'Young people in young countries could travel more rapidly than the older people in the older countries... the advantage of a young healthy patient was that the doctors could not very easily kill him (laughter)'.[158] Many investors reached the same conclusion.

Conclusion

This chapter has examined how groups in the City assessed risks to their investments, particularly the risks associated with the actions of states. Without such an assessment it is hard to draw out the connections between the City and politics overseas, nor gauge its influence. There was a constant flow of information through the City and the implications of developments overseas for the risks and returns on investments were continually watched. A number of aspects of political economy (broadly conceived) were linked to investors' interests. Robust property rights, strong defence, and a stable monetary system were all seen as desirable. Budgets were dissected frequently and there was a broad preference for balanced budgets with borrowing only for 'reproductive works', and as far as possible low taxation. This could give way to disagreements in practice. There were often varying opinions as to who, or what, ought to be taxed, and over the precise role of tariffs – especially protective tariffs. These divisions were accentuated by the tariff reform debate in Britain. Notions of the economic potential of 'young countries', if supported by evidence of high immigration, could lead to more optimistic assessments of investments' prospects, and attract capital. Equally evidence of labour militancy raising costs caused concern. Confidence could be further dampened by fears that groups unsympathetic to British investors ('socialists' in the Australian case) might obtain power and violate the City's interests. On all of these issues, conflicts could emerge between different interest groups, over particular interpretations of the implications of some measure, or of the relative importance of these various factors. For example, many interested in Australian finance after 1910 grappled with the question of whether worries about Australian socialism outweighed its prospects as a 'young country'.

All of this meant that even though the City agreed broadly in principle, unity over particular instances was rare. Only in extreme circumstances would financing become impossible as a result of violating a rule, because only in such circumstances would the City reach a unified and unambiguous view. Yet even in the absence of such conditions influence could be exerted. The shifting balance of judgements could strengthen or weaken stock prices and hence the costs of raising capital – there was always some incentive to placate the City. The constant cycle of interpretation also meant that shifting the City's assumptions could be hard but was not impossible. Moreover, it was far easier to affect how groups in the City interpreted particular instances. All this may have lessened the City's control on a 'relational' level, but also strengthened the structural links between colonial politics and perceptions in London. Australians and Canadians had certain privileges in their ability to access London, due directly or indirectly to their membership of the empire. The next chapter examines how understandings of empire in London interacted with the rules and their application; and also the participation of colonial representatives in the ongoing cycles of interpretation in the Square Mile.

4
Risk, Empire, and Britishness

In 1906 Robert Benson, chairman of the Merchant's Trust, told its annual meeting that the 'sentiment of the Mother Country predisposes the public to lend capital to our colonies at lower rates of interest and with less security than we exact from borrowers elsewhere'.[1] By 1914, Edgar Speyer, George Paish, and R. A. Lehfeldt had all estimated that empire governments could borrow for 1 per cent less than foreign governments.[2] This has been confirmed in recent studies and in large part reflects a perception (accurate or otherwise) that the empire was a less risky place to invest capital.[3] Why this perception existed has become the subject of recent debate. Niall Ferguson and Moritz Schularick have suggested that political control and the accompanying spread of virtuous institutions (from investors' – and Ferguson's – perspective at least) explains this 'empire effect'.[4] By contrast, Andrew Thompson and Gary Magee have argued that information asymmetries and dense social networks across the 'British world' eased the flow of investment, lowering interest rates in the process. They also suggest (without emphasising the point) that assumptions about race, shared Britishness, and loyalty to the empire all played a role in financiers' and investors' calculations.[5]

In probing these questions, there are dangers in placing too much weight on statistics. By way of example, it is worth noting the limitations of Fergusson and Schularick's sophisticated exercise in cliometrics, which tests the contributions of a range of different factors familiar to contemporaries in explaining differences in government bond prices.[6] Firstly, their data only tell us about the 'empire effect' with respect to government bond yields (and the balance of investment in the private and public sectors varied across the empire). Secondly in aggregating data from 1880 to 1914, variations in yields (and therefore shifting perceptions of risk) cannot be explored. Thirdly, there is a danger in assuming contemporary categorizations were stable or self-explanatory (a necessary assumption for statistical probing).

This is particularly important when considering the 'empire effect' in the dominions. The British debated the nature of their settlement empire, particularly the degree to which it was based on institutions or 'sentiment'.[7] Thus, any attempt to delineate the 'empire effect' needs to take account of the contested nature of empire as a contemporary category.

If we are to understand the 'empire effect' in the dominions, we need to explore the ways in which financiers and investors understood empire (in its various incarnations) and how these understandings interacted with perceptions of risk. Here the term empire is treated in two ways; reflecting the competing contemporary conceptions. Firstly empire is seen as a set of institutions connecting Britain and the dominions (not necessarily institutions through which control could be exerted). Secondly, it is seen as a cluster of ideas including shared imperial loyalty, and an interrelated political life. These were connected closely to (but distinct from) notions of 'Britishness'. This chapter explores the role of institutions, social networks, and culture in turn, showing that each served to persuade some investors that the dominions were less risky. Finally it considers the role of colonial representatives in managing their image in the City, showing how they played on the rules discussed in this and the last chapter, perceptions which they could not, ultimately overturn.

Institutions

Ferguson has argued that prior to 1914, the fact that 'even the major colonies of white settlement had been granted only a limited political autonomy', helps to explain the 'empire effect'.[8] It is true that the dominions were subject to some theoretical controls. The British government remained responsible for foreign and imperial policy. Westminster retained the right to legislate for the colonies (and its rubber stamp was required for constitutional changes). Governors and governor-generals could veto colonial legislation or else reserve it for consideration (and possible disallowance) in Whitehall.[9] Yet these powers were very rarely used in practice, and then only to maintain clear 'imperial' or diplomatic interests. Internal autonomy was hardly limited, and had been conceded on almost every matter of interest to investors and financiers. Most in the City would have recognised *The Economist*'s observation that the dominions were, 'for internal affairs almost independent republics'.[10]

The British government certainly did *not* use its remaining powers in the interests of British investors, not was it expected to. When, in 1906, Newfoundland imposed a tax on cable companies, an investor complained: 'Is the colonial minister likely to stand up against an act of a self-governing colony? If not, it would be better for the 7000 British investors to become an American company... They would then have a chance to have their interests looked after at Washington'.[11] Another illustration came in 1903. Faced with competition from a subsidised steamer, alteration of the rights to minerals discovered on its lands, and tighter regulation, the Midland Railway Company of Western Australia appealed to the Colonial Office, arguing that its treatment raised serious questions about the 'security for property in the State of Western Australia'. They were informed that the colonial secretary, 'will not accept the position of a court of appeal in cases in which individuals or corporations consider themselves aggrieved by the action of the legislatures of self-governing colonies'. Not giving up easily, the railway's directors replied that they did not ask for a departure from the 'your policy of abstention from interference in the domestic affairs of the great self-governing communities of the Empire' (thus confirming expectations of normal practice). Rather they claimed that their case had a 'special character' since the railway's contracts with the state had been signed while it was a crown colony, and that some of the measures violated the Western Australian constitution. The Colonial Office curtly told the company that it had recourse to the courts.[12]

Other formal institutional ties were thought to reduce risk even if they did not confer control (and more as we shall see in a subsequent section promoted valuable social connections). As we saw in Chapter 3, the strategic guarantee supplied by British arms was one important way in which membership of the empire was thought to reduce risk. The continued legal integration of the empire also reassured investors. The Judicial Committee of the Privy Council (JCPC) was the highest court of appeal in the empire (with some exceptions, one discussed below). It did not necessarily favour investors in its judgements. One former colonial secretary pointed out that the self-governing colonies had a perfect right to abolish appeals, but had little appetite to do so given the JCPC's, 'unbending probity'.[13] Nonetheless the JCPC's role offered certain safeguards – as long as colonial consent continued. It underpinned a system whereby English common law – especially commercial law – was extended automatically to the dominions (unless altered by statute). It also encouraged colonial statues to be formulated along British lines to ensure that precedent applied.[14] This promoted a legal uniformity conducive to business.[15] Equally often, the Privy Council upheld particular laws within different sections of the empire, but even then it did so in accordance with British interpretative traditions.[16] As a result, as one Canadian banker wrote to Wilfred Laurier in 1902, the JCPC 'has always been regarded as one of the chief safeguards of private rights and property'.[17] When Ontario considered limiting appeals in 1908, William Mackenzie of the Canadian Northern Railway warned the province not to 'interfere with the efforts of Canadians to get capital in England'.[18]

The importance of the JCPC was highlighted when the draft bill for Australian federation came to London for passage through parliament. The respective roles of the Privy Council and a proposed Australian High Court had been frequently discussed during the federation debates of the 1890s.[19] Although many wished to see the complete abolition of appeals, a compromise allowed appeals except in constitutional matters.[20] In May 1900 the draft constitution arrived in London for passage through Westminster, accompanied by Australian delegates. When introducing the bill into the Commons, Joseph Chamberlain proposed to retain the full appeal to the JCPC to defend one of the few unifying institutions of empire and the interests of 'banks and other large financial institutions'.[21] Opinion in London was divided over Chamberlain's move. *The Times* was supportive, arguing that the full appeal would prevent constitutional disputes (especially over states rights) causing a US style civil war. It also warned that 'capital from this country will flow less freely to Australia in the absence of the security provided'.[22] In contrast, several anglo-Australian banks (whose interests Chamberlain supposedly defended) thought the commercial advantages of federation too great to jeopardise.[23] *The Economist* also opposed the colonial secretary's move. It pointed out that the right of appeal had not prevented the American Revolution, did little to ease the Irish situation, and that, 'Spain did not keep her colonies because a great number of links bound them to the mother country'. It continued that the only 'valid link' between a 'free colony' and the mother country existed in 'the consciousness of both populations'.[24]

The Australian delegates exploited such sentiments to oppose Chamberlain. At a dinner held by the London Chamber of Commerce, Edmund Barton (then premier of New South Wales) played on the spirit of responsible government: 'If the people of Great Britain said that the Australians were entitled to formulate their own constitution for the purpose of self-government, they must also allow them to say what they meant when they framed that constitution'. J. R. Dickenson of Queensland warned against '[cooling] the ardour of Australians, who had voluntarily sent a not inconsiderable contribution to the battlefields of South Africa'.[25] Alfred Deakin thought this an effective line of attack in the year of the Khaki election.[26] In the end, a compromise was reached by which appeals were restricted in matters concerning states' rights but could, if consent were granted, be heard by the JCPC.[27] *The Times* was satisfied that the danger of constitutional conflict had been averted.[28]

The episode revealed that the right to appeal to the JCPC was considered an important safeguard for investors, but also that this right rested on colonial consent, while for many in the City 'loyalty' was worth more. Indeed many thought loyalty underpinned every institutional tie – including defence – and that any attempt to control the dominions would prove counter-productive. As the treasurer of the London Chamber of Commerce, Sir Fortesque Flannery, told a dinner in honour of the colonial leaders gathered for the 1907 Imperial Conference, the British had learned to 'recognise the right of the colonies to democratic government' by parliaments as 'free, as democratic, as powerful, and as representative as our own Imperial Parliament', a lesson which had begun 'in Boston harbour when the tea chests were overthrown'.[29] This is not to say that the JCPC or other institutions were unimportant, only to note that few thought their continuation rested on British control.

There is, however, one other possibility. If the British government was not expected to interfere in the dominions on the capital market's behalf, might it assist them in that market? It very occassionally guaranteed loans, normally justified by some broader imperial interest, although the practice became increasingly rare.[30] It also intervened through various acts regulating the issuing of colonial stocks, conferring some marginal advantages. The Colonial Stock Act of 1877 permitted self-governing colonies to issue inscribed stocks rather than bearer bonds, which attracted small investors as they provided greater security against loss, theft, or destruction. A further intervention came in 1900. Up until then holders of funds in trust could only invest in colonial government stocks if specifically empowered by their deeds of trust, otherwise they were restricted to a confined list of stocks. The New Zealand and Canadian High Commissions had campaigned for inclusion on this list in the 1880s and 1890s. In the context of colonial contributions to the South African War, resistance in the Treasury (which feared the move would raise its own borrowing costs) was overcome. The 1900 Colonial Stock Act admitted colonial government bonds to the trustee list, widening the pool of funds that the self-governing colonies could tap.[31] Admission required that colonies legislate to pay stockholders as required by a court in the United Kingdom; satisfy the Treasury that adequate funds would be available to make such payments; and 'place on record a formal expression of their opinion, that any colonial legislation which appear to alter any of the provisions affecting the stock to the injury of the stockholder, or to involve a departure from the original contract in regard to the stock,

would be disallowed'.[32] Ostensibly, these clauses offered additional commitments to property rights, and sound finance. The *Westminster
Gazette* and the *Empire Review* (wrongly) predicted that few colonies
would accept such additional controls.[33] In practice these terms
were largely technical and required only an 'opinion' to be expressed
that legislation affecting stockholders would be disallowed. There
was no additional legal safeguard: the dominions' (already clear)
commitment to avoiding defaults and repudiations was the real
guarantor.

This perhaps helps to explain why the act had little impact on the
dominions' borrowing costs. Nonetheless initial expectations were
high. The Canadian finance minister, W. S. Fielding, predicted in his
budget speech that the act would reduce the cost of loans by 2 per
cent, thus: 'the gain that we shall make by this assertion of the British
government in coming to the assistance of Canada will be in actual
cash be equal to every penny we spend for the sending of Canadian
soldiers to South Africa'.[34] Both *The Economist* and the *Australian
Insurance and Banking Record* thought Fielding's claims to be excessive.[35]
In 1933 A. J. Baster estimated that that the Act resulted in savings
of only $3/8$ of a percent.[36] Even so, trustee status may have maintained
an existing preference in a changing market in which colonial stocks
relied increasingly on institutional and trustee investors.[37] Australian
colonies were advised to adopt its terms, not least by Robert Nivison.[38]
The Canadian provinces and railways lobbied for inclusion and were
resisted by the Treasury, which was worried by rising yields on consols.[39]
The perceived connection between the act and better (or stable) rates of
interest was a force linking empire membership and the capital market
in the absence of wise cliometricians (or lawyers) to prove it had little
value.

The 1900 Act may also have reinforced a perception that the British
government would not allow the dominions to default, whatever the
statutory situation. In 1914, a correspondent asked the *Investor's Review*,
'Do you think it is likely that any of the colonies would default, or
that the British Government could possibly allow them to default?'[40]
A. J. Wilson replied that legally, 'it can never be too often repeated that
the British Government is not responsible for a shilling of any colonial
debt nor directly endorsed by it'. Since 1877 every colonial government prospectus had been required to carry a disclaimer to this effect.[41]
However Wilson continued that whatever the legal position, '[The
British Treasury] could hardly have evaded the moral liability even had
the colonial stocks been kept outside the trustee list'. Moreover, 'by

bringing their securities inside the trustee compound there is the danger that any default, or hint of default, by these insatiable borrowers might dangerously injure the credit of some of our banks and insurance companies [which would] have repercussions for the financial system too dire to contemplate'.[42] Some considered the dominions too big to fail.

Institutional factors did contribute to a perception that investment in the dominions was less risky, but these perceptions had little to do with direct political control. As well as the defence guarantee, the JCPC provided legal reassurance. The colonial stock acts gave (limited) preferences in the capital market, and in part as a result, some thought the British government likely to act to prevent a dominion government default (investors in private companies were on their own). Yet it was increasingly understood that, in the absence of coercion, these links depended on colonial consent. This depended in turn on a range of social and cultural factors, also which provided reassurances for investors in their own right.

Social connections and information flows

The empire helped generate and intensify the social and informational connections recently described by Magee and Thompson. Simon Potter has shown how from the 1880s news sharing arrangements and the career paths of journalists forged an 'imperial press system' dedicated to bringing dominion news before the investing and migrating public. The dominions themselves encouraged British publications to offer more, and more favourable coverage, particularly by offering lucrative advertising contracts. In the Edwardian period coverage of the settlement empire increased as a result. The *Standard* founded a sister paper, the *Standard of Empire*, and from 1909 the *Times* issued a dedicated Empire Day Supplement.[43] The politics of empire also facilitated the formation of anglo-dominion connections. Many politicians and journalists travelled to the dominions with imperial issues in mind, not least the tariff reform debate.[44] In 1908 Lord Milner visited Canada to rally support for Chamberlain's schemes. Enjoying free travel on the railways, he met leading businessmen and politicians.[45] The president of the Canadian Bank of Commerce, Byron Edmund Walker, eagerly organised a reception in Toronto and dispatched Milner back across the Atlantic 'very much impressed with regarding the bank' and anxious to meet its London manager. Knowing Milner was not universally popular in the City, Walker devoted similar attention to F. W. Hirst, editor of *The Economist*, who was following Milner preaching free trade, and to Lord Northcliffe, proprietor of the *Daily Mail*.[46]

The appointment of members of the British aristocracy as colonial governors and governors-general, who often had links in the City, created another important connection. Former governors often acted in the interests of their charges. In 1900 the former governor of Western Australia, Sir Gerald Smith, delivered a bullish speech at the Royal Colonial Institute as confidence in the state's mining industry waned.[47] In 1904 New South Wales' former governor, the Earl of Jersey, acted as agent-general for the state, negotiating loans. He later advised his successor, Timothy Coghlan.[48] Less savoury undertakings could also benefit from aristocrats' colonial connections. In the late-1890s, Lord Dufferin chaired a number of mining companies floated by the notorious Whittaker Wright. Dufferin had been a successful career diplomat, viceroy of India, and governor-general of Canada.[49] He was attracted to Wright's schemes by a salary of £10,000 a year and (or so he claimed) a desire to assist Canadian development.[50] When Wright's empire collapsed, *The Economist* thought it 'extremely unfortunate' that his role had been, 'to cover with a cloak of respectability the essentially speculative character of its transactions, and to inspire investors with a confidence in it which they may not otherwise have shown'.[51] One shareholder claimed he had 'invested in the company entirely on the strength of the chairman's name'.[52] Thus the episode highlighted the influence such ornamental 'guinea pigs' could exert. Empire eased access to such men: an 'empire effect' which had little to do with risk reduction.

The City possessed a significant expatriate business community and received large numbers of visiting colonial businessmen. In 1902 an Australian feminist visiting London complained, 'the sort of people who travel... what a disillusionment! Those who travel from Australia are the money-makers, the business people'.[53] Canadian businessmen were just as mobile. The chairman of the Canadian Northern Railway was a frequent transatlantic traveller, and in 1912 the Toronto *Mail and Globe* wrote, 'if there were a competition at the Olympic Games for ocean travellers... Canada might well have entered Sir William Mackenzie with a fair chance of winning first place'.[54]

These visits reflected the attractions of London as a business centre: they were not obviously generated by the empire. However the existence of the empire created additional reasons for inter-imperial travel, forging connections in the process. Major royal events, which from 1887 were normally accompanied by Colonial Conferences, drew politicians (and often businessmen) to London. After 1902 the conference (renamed the Imperial Conference in 1907) was made quadrennial.[55] Colonial politicians also travelled to discuss defence or other business with the imperial government. Visiting London thrust colonial politicians into an exhausting social whirlwind. While negotiating a loan in 1897, the Canadian finance minister, W. S. Fielding, wondered, 'where shall rest be found for the weary politician? Not in London, surely'. He continued:

> I have been here something over three weeks, and I have been on a continuous rush. I had a good many callers in connection with my immediate business of the loan but outside of that a large number of people either have business, or think they have business, with the Canadian government... If you add to these the visits of the newspaper men who swarmed about me and numerous social calls you will readily see that most of my time has been more than filled up.[56]

Empire (in both senses) also promoted links between businessmen. The London Chamber of Commerce organised a conference of businessmen: the Congress of Chambers of Commerce of the Empire (CCCE hereafter). This 'unofficial commercial parliament of the empire' first met in 1886, coinciding with the Colonial and Indian Exhibition, with further meetings in 1892, 1896, and 1900; thereafter it became triennial. It was normally held in London, but Montreal and Sydney played host in 1903 and 1909.[57] Chambers from cities across the empire could participate (along with leading politicians and other dignitaries), but proceedings were dominated by delegates from Britain and the dominions (especially Canadian boards of trade). It debated matters ranging from business technicalities through to political economy and imperial policy. In the Edwardian period preferential trade inevitably dominated and, equally inevitably, little agreement was reached.[58] How far the CCCE influenced policy even when it could agree is unclear. But this is to overlook much of its value which, as with so many conferences, lay in its associated social activities. The *Chamber of Commerce Journal* thought it, 'a unique opportunity... for the businessmen of the Empire to become acquainted with each other and appreciate the needs and aspirations of their fellow countrymen in distant lands'.[59] Canadians seized this opportunity. They often dominated debates; in 1906 the Western Australian agent-general bemoaned a 'Niagara like flow of Canadian eloquence' which he thought confirmed the 'Americanization' of Canadians.[60] The relocation of the conference to Montreal in 1903 was a deliberate attempt to promote the dominion – backed by a $15,000 grant from the Canadian government.[61] Canadian railway and steamship companies provided free travel to the visiting delegates, and the *Chamber of Commerce Journal* predicted the event would, 'give a fillip to the expansion of the agricultural and other resources of the country'. (In this instance the Eastern US also received a 'fillip' since the London delegation travelled via New York).[62]

By 1906, the Australians and South Africans also wished to host the congress. Sydney was chosen as the 1909 location, a proposal which ironically attracted the support of Canadians calculating that British delegates would take the 'all red route' to Australia across their dominion.[63] The Western Australian agent-general's secretary predicted the Sydney CCCE would bring, 'before the Public of the Country and Europe generally the natural wealth of our State, together with that of the rest of Australia'.[64] The visitors were wined, dined, and the Commonwealth won several powerful allies. These included Sir Albert Spicer, the Sydney CCCE's chairman and president of the London Chamber of Commerce, who wrote and spoke in the dominion's favour on his return.[65]

The empire acted to augment information flows and networks. This occurred because empire existed as a constitutional entity and as a set of ideals. It drew together politicians, businessmen, and London financers in ways which would not otherwise have happened. The foundation and continuation of the CCCE showed how business could be imagined in an imperial mould. A determination to increase the level of colonial news only made sense because many thought the empire mattered and needed to be preserved. Thus cultural factors underpinned pan-imperial social and informational connections as much as institutions.

Empire, Britishness, and investment

C. K. Hobson observed in 1914 that, 'A common language and kindred institutions place the British investor in a position of great advantage for investing in the British colonies and the United States'.[66] However, settlers in the dominions could draw upon common vocabularies and imageries of Britishness and imperialism unlikely to be acceptable to an American, or any other non-empire borrower. For example, in 1903, the Montreal Board of Trade held a banquet for visiting delegates of the CCCE. The hall was decked with Union Jacks and Maple Leaves; trophies representing the various components of the empire were displayed with the escutcheon of Britain in place of honour over the chairman; the menu was printed on a map of the British empire surrounded by British, Canadian, and other colonial arms; and 'God Save the King' was sung with gusto.[67] In the inevitable speeches the governor-general spoke of imperial progress and Wilfred Laurier toasted the empire. Lord Brassey, president of the London Chamber of Commerce, thought

'Everyone who came to the congress must have been deeply gratified by the loyal tone and strong imperial sentiments which marked the utterances of every speaker'.[68]

A vigorous showing at a colonial conference could lift a dominion's popularity. Chapter 5 shows how Laurier dazzled the City in 1897. Similarly, in 1907 Alfred Deakin's pursuit of pan-imperial preferential trade helped dispel fears of Australian disloyalty.[69] H. A. Gwynne thought Deakin had 'stirred the blood of even an old imperialist like myself'.[70] One Sir William Manning told a Melbourne audience that Deakin's performance, 'would have a beneficial effect on Australian finance.... Australia had demonstrated beyond doubt the utter worthlessness of much of the criticism to which she had been subjected by alleged financial authorities in some British newspapers'.[71]

Serving broader imperial goals was also used to court investors. Some were offered a share in the romance of the frontier.[72] In 1909 the chairman of the White Pass and Yukon Railway (which linked Skagway in Alaska with Whitehouse on the Yukon goldfields) told its AGM that their line was, 'eloquent testimony to the fact that the character which has made the British conquer still survives as strongly as ever in the hearts of this generation'.[73] Many less romantic investors probably agreed with Ferdinand Faithfull Begg that, 'If capital must go out of this country... let it go to countries where it would be used under the British flag in building up a nation which would stand by us in times of trouble'.[74] The CNR's financial wizard, R. M. Horne-Payne, promised that investors in the British Empire Trust Company would be, 'strengthening the Empire and strengthening it permanently by increasing intercourse and sympathy between its widely separate parts, and forming bonds of partnership between the older and younger countries that compose it'.[75] Horne-Payne was not the only promoter to use such rhetoric. In 1910 a correspondent to *The Economist* pointed out, 'high-flown phrases about the consolidation of the Empire used to be a favourite of promoters connected with wild-cat schemes connected with Rhodesia in the days before the South African War'.[76] The journal's Ottawa correspondent warned readers that patriotism was 'the last refuge of the Canadian promoter'.[77] Canadian railways frequently portrayed themselves as links of empire because they could both secure Britain's food supply and transport troops eastwards.[78] A. J. Wilson wrote sarcastically: 'The troops have but to be unshipped at some Atlantic or St Lawrence River port trundled across the continent by rail, and reshipped at Vancouver and lo! Our army may be slaying and being slain in China before a slow-moving Peninsular and Oriental fleet could have got as far as Hong Kong'.[79]

Notions of a shared imperialism were entwined with, but distinct from, ideas about a shared Britishness. As Peter Cain has recently shown, racial differences were expected to produce differing economic characteristics.[80] Trustworthiness, and hence confidence, depended in part on calculations undertaken through the prism of race. In 1910 the Mexican dictator Porfirio Diaz was overthrown. The company promoter Henry Osborne O'Haggen later recalled how the manager of a large engineering firm, S. Pearson, told him that, 'the problem with Mexico is the paucity of European inhabitants', advising, 'if you want to invest your money in South America, go to the Argentine; there the European population is large enough to have an influence. The great businesses, the banks, and the railroads are in the hands of Europeans, and the native population is of a different character to the semi-Indian Mexicans'.[81] This was certainly less intellectually taxing than assessing the complex political and socio-economic factors that made for stability or instability!

If a European population was seen to reduce risk, Britishness constituted an additional guarantee of probity, fair play, and constitutionalism. As Robert Benson explained to the Merchant's Trust, 'Blood is thicker than water, and we are naturally inclined to trust... the Scotch brain and bone which has built up and is continuing to build up Canada, rather, than the mixed Scandinavian, Teutonic, Slavonic and pure American brain which is building up the North-West prairies across the imaginary line which divides the two countries'.[82] Victoria's agent-general concluded a long re-iteration of the state's economic fundamentals against A. J. Wilson's persistent attacks, delivered at the Royal Colonial Institute (another venue only open to members of the empire), by remarking, 'Surely a country where 97 per cent are British, your flesh and blood, your language, and under one flag, is a safe spot to invest British capital'.[83] Bitter complaints were heard when such expectations were not met. In 1914, the Western Australian government began constructing a line in competition with the long-suffering Midland Railway Company. One shareholder complained, 'The action was absolutely what would have been expected from some South American Republics'. Andrew Williamson, the company's chairman, went one step further, regretting that, 'As Britishers they had been far too trustful of their Australian cousins and had not exacted for their capital that protection which was given in the republics he alluded to'.[84] Britishness was expected to be a guarantee of probity, even if such expectations were sometimes dashed.

This frequent emphasis on Britishness complicated City views on the use of non-white labour in 'young countries', an important issue in Australia and (at least) on Canada's Pacific coasts.[85] In 1901 the white Australia policy restricted non-white migration, and British Columbia also imposed restrictions. Some City interests bemoaned the loss of a source of supposedly cheap labour. Charles Rivers Wilson of the Grand Trunk Pacific regretted his railway's failure to obtain permission to use Chinese or Japanese coolies.[86] Climatic determinism led some to condemn the white Australia policy for 'virtually forbid[ing] the turning of the tropical parts of the continent to wealth producing pursuits'.[87] Nonetheless, if Britishness guaranteed economic probity (and was seen by some as inherently desirable) then restrictions on non-British (especially non-European) immigration could be considered to serve investors interests. In 1911 *The Economist* wrote that Canadian development rested on the 'quality and quantity of [the] yearly stream of new arrivals', and thought the dominion's English and Scottish intake to be of, 'very superior calibre and race to the South Europeans and Asiatics who are pouring into the United States'.[88] Similarly *The Times* acknowledged that the 'white Australia policy' was 'necessary to the existence of our race in Australia'.[89] One former South Australian premier warned the Associated Chambers of Commerce of the United Kingdom of the dangers of aggressive Asian expansion, arguing that the defence of 'civilisation' required the settlement of the empire with British emigrants. The conference agreed.[90] Financiers (and other businessmen) were torn between the capitalist desire to drive down labour costs and develop tropical estates, and the equally widespread equation of Britishness with security and probity, and whiteness with civilisation.

While it is difficult to gauge the overall significance of these cultural factors, it is clear that financiers and investors frequently discussed the shared imperialism and Britishness of the dominions and thought them relevant to their interests. Some considered these desirable ends in their own right, worthy of support. They intermeshed with the institutional and social forces discussed in earlier sections. The final section of this chapter looks at one particular social and institutional connection – the various official (and semi-official) colonial representatives in London, and shows how they manipulated all these forces, as well as the rules discussed in Chapter 3, in an effort to maintain credit.

Colonial representatives in the City

Edwardian Canada was represented in London by a high commissioner and the Australian states by agents-general. The Commonwealth also appointed a high commissioner in 1910.[91] These posts in part dealt with the Colonial Office, however most of their work lay in financial and commercial dealings with the City, and in promoting emigration. In 1905 Walter James argued that the offices of the Western Australian agent-general ought to be relocated to the City from Westminster since, 'a short experience shows that in the City one finds the men interested in our state and commonwealth', while the Colonial Office 'hardly affects us now-a-days'.[92] James' proposed relocation reflected the close watch colonial representatives kept on the City. A number of techniques and strategies existed to sway its opinions. Colonial representatives tended to combine the 'rules' and the languages of empire to attempt (not always successfully) to reassure financiers and investors of their probity and prospects.

Canada stole a march on Australia in its public relations exercises in the City. The election of Laurier's government and the concession of a preference on British goods helped start this trend. So too did the appointment in 1896 of the 76 year-old Lord Strathcona as high commissioner. Born Donald Smith in Forres (in north-east Scotland) in 1820, Strathcona emigrated to the North West Territories, rising rapidly through the Hudson's Bay Company. He became a leading figure in Canadian business, working closely with the Bank of Montreal before becoming the bank's president from 1887 to 1905. He was also a member of the Canadian Pacific Railway syndicate and an important figure in the Canadian Conservative party.[93] This Scottish embodiment of colonial social mobility proved an excellent operator in London. On his first official appearance, at the 1896 CCCE, the veteran journalist W. T. Stead wrote (seemingly in earnest) of the septuagenarian: 'In the vigour, the youthful freshness, that massive head crowned by glistening snows, I seemed to see the great Dominion of Canada incarnate, and in his language I heard the Canadian creed of hope, self-confidence and loyalty'.[94] Strathcona was rarely absent from events concerning Canada (or indeed the empire more generally).[95] These included the 'dominion day banquet' organised by the High Commission to celebrate confederation which frequently attracted leading City men. The 1896 gathering, held at the Royal Colonial Institute, was attended by 500–600 guests.[96] The high commissioner was also a prominent supporter of emigration; sponsored a regiment, Strathcona's Horse, to fight in South Africa; and was a vocal advocate of 'all-red' cable and shipping routes across the Pacific and of subsidised mails between Canada and Britain.[97] All this gave Canada prominence and assured Britain's pro-imperial investing classes of Canadian loyalty. As one Canadian commented in 1906, 'No other part of the Empire can hold such a place in British eyes as Canada, for no other colony has a Lord Strathcona'.[98]

Strathcona's High Commission kept a close watch on Canada's image in the British press. So too did leading Canadian bankers in London. Frederick Williams-Taylor, the London manager of the Bank of Montreal, thought, 'safeguarding the national credit of Canada [to be] one of the most important accepted duties and responsibilities of the Canadian banks with branch offices in London'.[99] Both the banks and the High Commission sought to secure favourable coverage of Canada in the British press. In 1896, Strathcona persuaded the *Daily Mail*'s proprietor, Alfred Harmsworth, to commission the journalist, Beckles Wilson, to tour the dominion. Wilson's series on 'Our Western Empire' helped dispel the image of Canada as cold and snowbound.[100] In 1903, B. E. Walker of the Canadian Bank of Commerce instructed his London manager to get *The Economist* to tone down adverse coverage.[101]

Through much of the Edwardian period Canada shone but the press was still avidly monitored. However, by 1912 the perception was spreading that Canada was over borrowing. Some thought it better not to respond since this would generate further criticism.[102] The Canadian government and Bank of Montreal disagreed and decided to answer the dominion's critics. In November 1912 Williams-Taylor presented a paper at the Royal Colonial Institute. Lord Strathcona acted as chair, and the Canadian trade minister (and former finance minister) George Foster acted as discussant.[103]

Williams-Taylor's defence illustrates how the tightly interlocking assumptions about the 'rules' and empire could be interlaced to defend credit. First, he reviewed investment in Canada, concluding that most had been placed in sound enterprises. Then he acknowledged that 'Canadian borrowers and their Anglo-Canadian associates needed to recognise... the absolute necessity of exercising discrimination and restraint', although he added that 'unsound Englishmen' were responsible for some of the worst excesses.[104] Finally, he concluded:

> Who is there to dispute the fact that Canada is a land of great natural resources... Do we not possess to a marked degree the three fundamental forms of wealth, viz. material wealth, wealth of labour and wealth of credit? Have we not a climate which has produced and is producing a hardy virile Northern people? Have we not a banking and currency system admirably adapted to the requirements of our country? Is it not the case that justice is obtainable throughout the Dominion, and that the laws of the land are administered in a manner comparing favourably with any other portion of the world? Have we not immunity from war, to say nothing of freedom from political,

social and seismic disturbances, and last but not least, does not the British flag float over our land?[105]

In the subsequent discussion, Foster added that in Canada railways 'had only to be built to become paying institutions' and that immigration continued apace.[106] Thus, and within the framework of the rules, Williams-Taylor and Foster re-iterated Canada's economic potential, its security of property, its financial stability, and its defence and probity within the empire. After the event Foster wrote to Robert Borden, the prime minister, that the paper 'has been very extensively circulated and, I think, has had a good effect'.[107]

This was not the end of the matter. As Canada's railways encountered financial difficulties and the land boom in the west faltered, Borden continued to be kept informed about the views of the London press. For instance, in 1913 a series of letters appeared in *The Economist* arguing that falling wheat and livestock prices spelt an end to Canadian prosperity and would make it hard for the dominion to service its debts.[108] Strathcona telegraphed Borden recommending that it would be better not to respond. Borden concurred and Strathcona wrote in acknowledgement, 'as the "Economist" is one of the leading financial journals here it was not a matter which could be passed over unconsidered'.[109] That an anonymous letter in *The Economist* was considered sufficient grounds to *cable* the prime minister of Canada shows the weight placed on the maintenance of credit in London.

As we have seen, Edwardian Australia generally suffered rather more at the hands of the London press than Canada. Prime Minister Alfred Deakin complained that, 'Of all the people in this world, the most harshly used and the most wickedly assailed abroad were those of Australia'.[110] Around the turn of the century, the agents-general tended to ignore criticisms. Victoria's representative, A. G. Dobson (along with Robert Nivison) thought, 'it would be absolutely suicidal to reply upon any points [which] might lead to a bitter controversy and to the dragging before the public of some matters which are really detrimental to Victoria in common with the other States'.[111] Similarly, the earl of Jersey advised New South Wales' premier Joseph Carruthers, 'Every now and then a writer under some colonial pseudonym dashes out a furious attack. It is generally a mistake to take notice of it'.[112] As attacks continued unabated, Australian politicians began to suspect that such inactivity was far from masterful. Hence many states began appointing more active agents-general such as Walter James (Western Australia, 1904–1906), J. W. Taverner (1904–1912), and Timothy Coghlan (1905–1918).

Coghlan, New South Wales' pioneering statistician and later author of a definitive economic history of Australia, was particularly vigorous in his confrontation of London critics. He arrived early in 1905 and instantly plunged himself into a vigorous campaign to refute inaccurate coverage in the London and provincial press. By April 1906 he claimed to have written over 50 letters to the press.[113] December 1905 saw a particularly bruising encounter with the *Mail*, long a vitriolic critic of Australian affairs. The *Mail* wrote an article alleging that New South Wales was trying to silence its correspondent and to obscure its 'poor progress due to the dominance of the Labour party, which had declared war on god, capital, and children'.[114] Coghlan wrote an irate response denying any pressure on the paper's Sydney correspondent, and exclaiming in frustration that, given space, he could:

> Prove... that socialism is not rampant in Australia, that the Labour party has not... declared war on God, children, or capital, that immigration is not discouraged, that the birth rate (though greatly reduced) is still at the same level as it is in this country, that the States are not burdened with debt, that the financial condition of the country is not unsatisfactory, and that so far from taxes being heavy, they are lighter than in almost any other English speaking country.[115]

This typifies Coghlan's approach, denying specific allegations but not the premises on which they were based. Some questioned Coghlan's tactics. B. R. Wise wrote to Deakin, 'Coghlan has again shown his inability to understand London ways... A personal call on Harmsworth instead of a "scoring" letter would have got the "Mail"'. Wise claimed to have tempered the *Pall Mall Gazette*'s coverage in this way. Actually Coghlan was not averse to acting behind the scenes.[116] In May 1905 he persuaded *The Standard* not to publish an anonymous attack arguing, 'Some courtesy is due to a great dependency of the Empire'.[117] In 1908 he finally secured a change in the *Daily Mail*'s Sydney Correspondent, something he described as his 'best day's work in London'.[118]

Nonetheless, denying specific allegations and applying pressure behind the scenes was not sufficient. In a report sent to Deakin by the agents-general, Walter James observed, 'our object should be to alter that condition of mind which accepts misrepresentation more readily than it listens to facts'. He continued, 'no other country has so much to gain from a sound public opinion which exerts a direct and immediate influence on all financial transactions... The prices of our loans depend upon the demand for our stock and on that point public opinion is decisive'.[119] The solution, in James' view, was to devote more resources to advertising. Due to Canada's promotional effort, 'her stocks are the most favoured and not only do very few adverse opinions obtain publication in the press but when they do they pass off unnoticed and disregarded'.[120] He wrote that had Australia advertised in the same way, 'we should have saved hundreds of thousands of pounds in our loans during the last 10 years'.[121]

From about 1905 the states increasingly devoted resources to publicity. For example, Western Australia began spending on newspaper advertising, splitting resources between cheaper provincial papers likely to be read by prospective migrants, and the London press read by capitalists.[122] In 1912 the state established a dinner along the lines of Canada's dominion day banquet, which (as the agent-general explained), 'forms an admirable focus for the state's affairs in London' and 'is also made the occasion for a review of the year's progress in the state which in its dissemination through the newspapers of the Kingdom is of high value…'.[123] The states co-operated at the Franco-British Exhibition of 1908. Victoria and New South Wales arranged a joint dinner to mark the occasion. When the Victorians withdrew to hold their own event, New South Wales followed suit so as not to be 'behind-hand in its courtesy'. The dinner was well attended by leading bankers, shippers and Colonial Office officials. According to Joseph Carruthers the event had 'a very beneficial effect so far as the esteem in which our state is held here is concerned'.[124]

Thus, by the time of the Sydney CCCE in 1909, there had already been a concerted Australian charm offensive. However the absence of a single representative of Strathcona's stature continued to be a problem. As Walter James perceptively explained:

> The public opinion of Great Britain deals with and alone comprehends Australia… When that opinion favours the Commonwealth each state benefits by the efforts of the others but when the current of public opinion moves in the opposite direction every adverse report from any one state prejudices each of the others.[125]

The problem was compounded by the tendency for the agent-generals to speak only for their own states. The *Sydney Morning Herald* complained of 'the harmful confusion which is wrought to the Commonwealth as a whole by the presence in London of various state agents-general, who speak only for their respective states and often in conflicting terms'.[126] One conservative bemoaned the contrast with 'the lordly manner in which the interests of the Dominion of Canada are represented'.[127]

In part, these continuing image problems prompted the federal government to establish the Australian High Commission in 1909.[128] As the first high commissioner, George Reid, recalled, 'one of the most important objects of my appointment was the spread of information... concerning Australia and the varied openings it affords, as a source of raw materials and food supplies, as an attractive home for the emigrant, and as a place for the investment of British capital'.[129] Reid quickly embraced this side of the job. Widespread newspaper coverage surrounded his arrival, or as the *Pall Mall Gazette* quipped, 'as many columns as Mottle and Van Roon invaded France with in 1870'.[130] On his first day in London met Alfred Spicer, and other leading City men in the morning, revealingly only visiting the Colonial Office after lunch.[131] A banquet was held in the Trocadero in his honour, attended by leading commercial men, financiers, and shippers.[132] Reid became a regular diner at City functions, and later wrote, 'in London a man of my position had to regard attendance at dinner or luncheon functions of a public or semi-public nature as a primary duty'.[133]

Reid probably enjoyed dining for Australia but used such occasions to reassure financiers and investors. For example, on the 123rd anniversary of Cook's landing at Botany Bay, Reid addressed the Chamber of Commerce. His speech emphasised Australia's agricultural and pastoral potential. He defended the white Australia policy, which ensured that Australia was a 'British country' without 'racial troubles'. He also defended Australia's debt, which had been devoted to railway construction in the spirit of 'an improving English landlord' rather than 'running away in the gutters of war'. He concluded by combining imperial loyalty, migration, and defence, arguing Australians were devoting their 'whole soul' to making the 'boys' of England, Wales, Scotland, and Ireland, 'not only as intelligent and as strong and as patriotic as they were, but prepared to take on an even greater burden in order that, whatever the strain in the human race for supremacy might be the British flag might still remain in front'.[134] Excepting such flourishes, little Reid said differed from earlier defences of Australia, although possibly his bonhomie won more converts than Coghlan's statistical barrage, and like William-Taylor he elided the fundamentals of political and cultural economy.

Colonial representatives tended not to contradict the shared assumptions which, the last chapter argued, constituted the rules of the game. Rather they either challenged points of detail (Australia's debts were reproductive and so not a cause for concern) or else suggested that, in the context of economic, political, and imperial fundamentals, particular problems (Canadian overborrowing, Australian socialism) were not significant. The attention devoted to image management by colonial representatives reveals the close structural ties between political and economic life in these dominions and London finance (as well as similar links with British migrants, traders and shippers). Their fluid blending of economics fundamentals and imperial loyalties reflects the degree to which the two intermingled in the way the City thought about investments. These were not desperate gambits. The dominions' representatives knew their audience, and told it what it wanted to hear.

Conclusion

Empire shaped the way many in the City thought about investment. The British government was not thought able or likely to act in the interests of investors, nor did it intervene in a significant way in the capital market on their behalf. Some expected it would not allow colonial governments – but not of course private enterprise – to falter in extremis. Other institutions did provide some reassurance. The JCPC guaranteed legal uniformity and fair play, and British arms helped secure the dominions from external threats. Institutional links also promoted social connections and information flows between Britain and the dominions which eased capital flows. Social connections were also augmented as an indirect effect of imperial politics, and because business activity was often imagined in an imperial mould. Institutional and social connections were nurtured by a shared vocabulary of Britishness and empire which boosted confidence that the dominions would remain members of the empire, played on 'imperial pieties', and increased expectations of probity.[135] Yet the significance of these 'empire effects' must be carefully qualified. Neither socio-cultural nor institutional factors circumvented the 'rules of the game', rather they strengthened expectations of adherence to those rules. Robert Benson, quoted earlier explaining that 'sentiment' generated preferential terms in the capital market, also thought (without noting the contradiction) that, 'colonial borrowers should understand that they must offer as good security and as high a rate of interest as other nationalities do'.[136] Nor could image management – presenting occurrences in the colonies in the best possible light – overcome pressure to act in accordance with the rules. At best it created elbow room. If empire and Britishness promoted sanguine expectations, these expectations had ultimately to be met. It is the impact of the capital market's expectations on Australian and Canadian politics which are examined in Part III of this book.

Part III
The Politics of Finance

5
Canadian Politics and London Finance, 1896–1914

At the start of this book, we saw how economic growth in settler societies depended – at certain junctures at least – on imports of British capital, generating links with the London capital market. The 'rules of the financial game' were examined in the middle section of this book. This final section explores how the need to borrow and the assumptions surrounding debt manifested themselves in Canadian and Australian political life. The form and influence of this politics of finance depended on a number of local variables: on the point at which a colony found itself on the economic cycle; on the institutions mediating borrowing or receiving capital, and their relationships with political parties; and on the degree of consensus on the importance of importing capital and maintaining credit. When the economy did not require British capital; when links with the City became less dense; or when the need to borrow was questioned by powerful groups, the influence of the City would be curtailed – although even in such circumstances (as we shall see) the politics of finance continued in modified form.

This chapter examines the Canadian experience of the politics of finance from 1896 to 1914: from the election of the Liberals, led by Wilfred Laurier, through their defeat in the 1911 election by the Conservatives under Robert Laird Borden, and on to the outbreak of war.[1] The period saw Canada boom economically, absorbing ever increasing volumes of British capital until, just prior to the war, credit became strained. First, the chapter reconstructs Canadian attitudes to borrowing, showing a virtual consensus that credit was essentially for economic and national development. Even so maintaining credit had to fit with (federal and provincial) political aspirations, and when the two clashed risks could be taken with credit, as a brief excursion into the controversy surrounding Ontario's hydro-electric policy shows. The remainder of the chapter follows federal politics.

A second section shows the close attention paid by both Laurier's and Borden's governments to the views of the City, and the ways this shaped budgetary policy. Then (and in a third section) we see how Laurier's Liberals, having revived (or benefited from the revival of) Canadian credit, used it to back politically conceived railway projects which bound electoral success, development, and popularity in London together, and bequeathed a financial legacy Borden's Conservatives could not escape. Finally (and backtracking a little) the chapter examines the operation of the politics of finance in the 1911 election; one dominated (outside Quebec) by the issue of Canadian-American reciprocity. As Chapter 3 showed, the City was both divided on, and keenly interested, in the outcome. The section reveals that even in these circumstances, the politics of finance continued to operate even if it did not decisively shape events.

Canadian financiers and the maintenance of Canada's credit

As we saw in Chapter 2, by the late-nineteenth century control of Canadian finance was concentrated in clusters of financial institutions, industries, utilities, and railways centred on the Bank of Montreal and the Canadian Bank of Commerce. By 1910, $16 billion of assets were controlled from St George's Street, Montreal, and King Street, Toronto.[2] The implications of this concentration of money power were debated by contemporaries. In 1913, H. R. Emerson drew the Canadian parliament's attention to the fact that 128 leading Canadian companies were controlled by just 28 directors. They constituted a 'powerful monopoly... the directive forces of practically all of Canada's economic life.[3] The *Canadian Annual Review* dismissed Emerson's claims: 'There were too many rivals in policy, finance, transportation in the list to make such a thing as organised action amongst them feasible. What common ground... had the C.P.R and C.N.R financial interests, or those of Lord Strathcona and Senator Cox?'[4] Toronto tended to support the Liberals, Montreal and the Canadian Pacific Railway (CPR) the Conservatives, although the Bank of Montreal's role as banker to the federal government tempered its attitude. Yet divisions between the two cities can be overdrawn. There were frequent instances of co-operation between Montreal and Toronto, for example in Latin American utilities or lobbying on revisions to banking legislation.[5] Ironically given its comments in 1913, the *Canadian Annual Review* itself drew sponsorship from both cities, almost functioning as an official organ for the financial elite.[6]

Montreal's and Toronto's financial elites invariably argued in public statements and private lobbying that Canada's economic and national development depended on imported capital. Most politicians and a large section of the press agreed. Railways especially were understood to bind the dominion into a single nation, enabling its vast landmass to be settled and developed.[7] In 1914, O. D. Skelton reviewed half a century of Canadian 'progress':

> The two oceans had been linked in triple bands of steel. The waste places had been filled, and prosperity brought to the native-born and the swarming immigrants alike. The farmer had fought a good fight, against nature's caprice and market forces beyond his sway, and won. The miner and the lumber-man had mapped out the new world's riches over wide areas and had brought their development to a fever pitch. The fisherman, if not always keeping pace, had yet a notable haul to show. The manufacturer had developed enterprise and energy in the effort to give Canada an all-round development. National unity had wonderfully grown.[8]

All this, Skelton argued, had only been possible through, 'the co-operation of foreign capital and foreign enterprise with the faith and energy of [Canada's] native sons'.[9]

This dependence on imported capital became increasingly apparent at the start of the twentieth century. The proportion of US investment increased in this period, and the relative contributions of British and American investment were discussed in Canada. Lord Strathcona observed in 1909, 'One hears more of American capital than British, for the reason that our cousins from the United States... go to the country themselves and look after the business in which they are interested, and obtain much publicity'.[10] Canadian financiers certainly watched for openings on Wall Street; in 1914 E. R. Wood of Dominion Securities wrote optimistically of the prospects of an expanding US market for Canadian railway bonds.[11] Nonetheless, Canadian business elites often found borrowing in Britain more attractive. American direct investments challenged their hegemony in the dominion while British portfolio investment kept control in Canadian hands.[12] This may explain why the Canadian Manufacturers Association placed measures, 'to direct British investment and immigration to the colonies' top of a list of items it wished Laurier to pursue at the 1902 colonial conference.[13]

Those Canadians pointing out the attractions of borrowing in Britain largely made virtue of necessity. As we saw in Chapter 1, Britain remained far and away the main source of inward investment in the dominion. The scale of Canada's dependence on the City became more apparent during the Laurier years. From 1905 E. R. Wood and F. W. Field (a journalist at Montreal's *Monetary Times* – Canada's leading financial journal) began publishing separate estimates of the volumes of capital invested in the dominion. Wood consistently found between 70 and 90 per cent of investment in Canadian bonds (including domestic investment) came from Britain.[14] In 1914 Field estimated that of $1,462,483,453 raised since 1905, 85 per cent came from Britain.[15] Seven years earlier, Wood observed that, '[in] the United States... the interest return from local investments is more favourable... than that from Canadian securities of the same class'. As a result, Britain would continue to be Canada's 'chief banker' at least in the near future.[16] On another occasion he wrote that it was, 'obvious... that for great permanent investments... we must apply to the world's financial centre'.[17]

This perceived need for British capital led Canadian financiers to emphasise repeatedly the need to maintain credit. As B. E. Walker (general manager and then president of the Canadian Bank of Commerce) remarked in 1907, 'We are a borrowing country, and we cannot be reminded of that too often'.[18] In 1904 George Cox (president of the same bank until 1907) contrasted Canada's prosperity with Australia's drought and South Africa's post-war depression, continuing:

> Whether our credit will be aided by the contrast we present both in prosperity and in the extent of our demands on the money market, or not, this much is clear – that it should be, and that we should do as little as possible to impair the high standing to which we are justifiably entitled at the present time.[19]

Wood reached similar conclusions, 'we must meet the British investor not merely with the good faith to which his confidence and enterprise entitle him, but with such abundant good faith as shall keep our financial reputation second to none'.[20] When the first edition of Field's *Capital Investments in Canada* was published in 1911, the *Toronto Globe* wrote, 'The lesson of this dependence upon British capital is the need of keeping Canadian credit above suspicion', comments echoed in other newspapers across the dominion.[21]

Canada's leading financial groups saw themselves as guardians of credit, displaying what R. T. Naylor later called a 'paranoid obsession' with the Square Mile.[22] The management of Canada's financial system, particularly unpopular restrictions of credit by the banks, were justified through the need to attract British capital in the national interest. In

1907 Canadian bankers got early word of the financial crisis that eventually hit Wall Street (where their short-term reserves were held) in the autumn of the year. Harvest time saw the greatest demand for credit (since the harvest had to be gathered and transported prior to the crop realising its value on world markets). Thus the Canadian banking system was particularly vulnerable to autumn crises.[23] As a result the banks restrained credit – especially in the west – earlier in the year and, with further assistance from the federal government and permission to issue notes temporarily without the backing of gold, financed the harvest.[24] However the restriction of credit arrested western progress and the banks were accused of withdrawing funds from the western economy to invest in New York (which in one sense they did – to build up reserves).[25] In response, Walker argued that the pause had demonstrated the stability of Canadian banking system, checked speculation, and thus helped 'sustain the high credit Canada enjoys in Great Britain'. He reminded his audience that without this credit, 'we cannot build a third continental railroad in addition to providing for the growth of older railroad systems; we cannot take care of an enormous and unprecedented inflow of immigrants, and we cannot build up new towns and cities by the hundred'.[26]

The next crisis was internally generated. Canada had suffered in the 1850s and 1880s from the collapse of railway and land booms souring credit, while cautionary parallels could be drawn from Australia, Argentina, the US, and Britain.[27] As Wood put it, 'A securities market like any other market can be spoiled by dishonesty. The magnitude of our needs shows that to spoil it would be a national calamity and would put back the dial of progress for a generation'.[28] However, as Canadian offerings reached new heights in the half decade prior to the First World War, suspicions of excessive borrowing and speculation increased in Britain.[29] George Drummond, president of the Bank of Montreal warned that, 'only by prudence in the taking and granting of credits, and the avoidance of wild-cat ventures and exploitations of the high reputation Canada enjoys on the London money market, can we reasonably anticipate a continuance of the prosperity we now enjoy'.[30] However, other than cautioning promoters not to 'kill the goose that laid the golden egg', there was little that Canadian bankers could do to restrain promotions beyond warning *caveat emptor*.[31] They had more control over the overheating real estate market in the Canadian west, which had begun drawing in significant amounts of British capital. In 1913, the banks again restricted credit in the west, refusing to lend against real estate and to over-ambitious municipalities. Again the action aroused protest against a check to development, and again the banks were accused of draining the west to invest in New York. The *Canadian Annual Review* responded that 'Speculation had been rife and was obviously reaching its limit, while the sharp tone of the occasional London comment showed signs of the strain at the resources of Canada's capital, credit and financial development'.[32] Thus restrictions in credit by the banks in 1907 and 1913 were justified (and probably motivated at least in part) through references to the opinions of the London capital market, evoking the long established connection between credit there and national development in defence against populist criticisms.

Arguments based on maintaining credit were equally likely to be deployed in interventions in political decision-making, public and private. In both contexts Canadian financiers repeatedly re-iterated that, in the words of George Drummond, 'it is very important... that nothing should be done in Canada by injurious legislation... to stop this flow of capital'.[33] Two incidents (both involving Ontario) illustrate financiers' potential influence and its limitations. In 1901, under pressure from the Toronto Board of Trade, the Ontario government imposed licence fees on the export of nickel matte (unprocessed nickel). Large nickel mines had been established at Sudbury, and the fees sought to recoup development costs and encourage processing in the province. The measure was opposed by the American-owned International Nickel Company and the British-owned Mond Nickel Company; part of the Brunner Mond industrial conglomerate floated in September 1900 to supply its Swansea smelters.[34] E. S. Clouston, general manager of the Bank of Montreal, warned the prime minister that if the measure went ahead, 'The inevitable result... will be the closing of the doors to the flow of English capital'. He continued, 'if it is known in the London markets that after investing very largely in this country, [Mond's] property was practically confiscated by the Ontario Legislature, it will have a very serious effect on future English enterprise here'.[35] Laurier replied that he considered this 'a very serious matter', and, although he was not prepared to recommend disallowance (on grounds of provincial autonomy), added that, 'the bill is one which I certainly do not like'.[36] After a meeting between Laurier and George Ross, Ontario's Liberal premier, on 8 May 1901 the licence fee was quietly dropped.[37]

In the second incident, intervention behind the scenes was coupled with public protests, to less effect. Against the backdrop of a widely supported popular campaign led by the cigar manufacturer Adam Beck, in 1905 Ross's Conservative successor, J. P. Whitney, began sponsoring the development of public distribution (and later generation) of hydroelectric power at Niagara Falls.[38] The establishment of public competition was seen to violate private property rights, not least (as we have seen), in the City.

In 1908, and with Beck's populist campaign in mind, B. E. Walker warned Canadian Club audiences in Halifax and Toronto of the 'dangers of democracy'.[39] In Halifax he explained that the bases of Canada's credit were her 'natural resources', 'the agricultural and pastoral basis of industrial life', and a 'love of law and order'. The west's development meant, 'we shall need to sell our securities abroad in increasing amounts, and it must be plain to every thinking man that we shall obtain money or fail to obtain it in proportion to the maintenance of our high credit'. It was also 'plain that our credit depends on the opinion held regarding us by the lender or investor in our securities', opinions formed through bankers' and lawyers' advice, and press coverage. He proceeded to warn, 'if any country is *supposed* to be filled with agitators who are opposed to capitalists and to corporations generally, and if the politicians in such a country are *supposed* to be listening... *whether the integrity of contract is violated or not*, it is not likely that such a country will obtain capital' (my italics).[40] Walker concluded that it would be a 'national shame' to sacrifice credit which would halt the development of the west, and urged Canadians to 'gravely realise their responsibility for our national enterprise'.[41] Thus Walker tied the need to maintain property rights in the face of popular pressures (and to be seen to do so, even in the face of ill-founded or unreasonable criticism) to national development.

The issue came to a head in 1909, when Ontario suspended court actions brought by aggrieved hydroelectric companies, and (as we saw in Chapter 3) criticism in the City reached a peak. With Whitney's government intransigent (despite warnings from Frederick Williams-Taylor that the City thought 'your government has gone too far') attempts were made to persuade Laurier to disallow Ontario's legislation in order to defend Canadian credit and hence national wellbeing (the latter theoretically allowed by the constitution).[42] Walker wrote a (barely legible) letter warning that, 'There can be no stronger evidence of alarm at what shows a willingness to go astray with the soundness of contract than that we [find] in our [...] financial friends'.[43] Wood too called for Ontario's legislation to be disallowed to 'save the credit of the Dominion' from 'as much as a suspicion that our governments will break faith with investors'. He reminded Laurier that for 'the wealth of this country' to be developed, 'our great transportation and other enterprises must be financed by British and foreign capital'.[44] The federal government received a barrage of correspondence to this effect.[45] Yet in the end it did not obstruct Ontario. The attorney-general ruled there were no constitutional grounds to intervene.[46] Moreover, Laurier was reluctant to oppose a popular policy in Ontario, and to violate provincial autonomy – a key Liberal principle dear to many in Quebec.[47] The risk of alienating opinion in the Canada's two largest provinces made meddling in the affair difficult for Laurier, whatever the risks to credit.

These two instances illustrate the extent to which leading financiers made the maintenance of credit a lynch pin of opposition to unfavourable policies in public and in private – in the process drawing on contacts and information from London, and showing an effortless familiarity with the rules. They deployed the vocabulary of property rights, and in the case of the hydroelectric commission, anti-socialism, repeatedly, and with an easy fluency. Yet in that case, the attempt to apply pressure on the dominion government proved unsuccessful. Even then, credit was used as a trump card, although it did not win the trick. While these examples focus on Ontario, the remainder of this chapter follows the connections between the City and the federal government's budgetary, railway, and tariff policies.[48] It reveals that the City – frequently through the mediation of Canada's financial elites – was a constant factor in federal decision-making, inter-meshing with domestic political forces that could augment or curtail its influence.

Credit and budgetary policy

Canadian budgetary policy was consistently formulated with the Square Mile in mind. Federal politicians eagerly sought information on the City and its reactions to their financial management. In 1900 (the year in which Canada's tariff preference on British goods was raised to 33 per cent, on which more below) Canada's deputy minister of finance, J. M. Courtney, cabled the High Commission: 'pray send all clippings relating to the budget quickly'.[49] After being sent summarised coverage from *The Times, Standard, Financial News, Westminster Gazette,* and *Bullionist,* he replied specifically asking whether *The Times* had speci-fically referred to a forthcoming loan. (It had not).[50] Craving accurate information, Canada's minister of finance, W. S. Fielding, even complained about the quality of press cuttings sent by Streets clipping service.[51] Fielding was a frequent visitor to London, normally overseeing loan flotations personally. His Conservative successor, W.T. White (a formerly Liberal financier from Toronto who defected to the Conservatives over reciprocity) visited London in 1912 to investigate Canadian credit. In 1913 he requested that the Bank of Montreal's London Manager write privately on any important matter *in addition* to sending his weekly reports to the finance department. The High Commission had already been informed that he was 'very desirous of keeping in touch with the English press'.[52] We have already seen that anonymous letters in *The*

Economist found their way to Borden's desk. All this reflects the close attention paid to the views of the City.

This attention originated in the links between credit and a range of policies. Investors' goodwill was obviously necessary when undertaking large construction projects. Even after the completion of the CPR in the late 1880s, the need for further infrastructure remained a central plank of the Conservative's electoral platform. 'What veins and arteries are to the human body' their 1896 manifesto declared, 'so are railways and water lines to a country'. In the same period, the Liberals emphasised (as their 1893 manifesto put it) the need for 'the strictest economy in the administration of the government of the country' (which implied a curtailment in public works).[53] This did not make the Liberals any less interested in London. As Table 5.1 below shows, when they came to office, debt service consumed a quarter of all federal expenditure.[54] Refloating debt at a lower rate of interest could result in savings, but this depended on strong credit.

Thus, when the Liberal party returned to office in 1896, improving Canada's image in Britain was as an important priority. Strathcona was confirmed as high commissioner and Fielding's 1897 budget announced a 25 per cent reduction in tariffs on British goods (raised to 33 per cent in 1900).[55] This measure had its roots in domestic politics. The Conservatives had supported a preference only if Britain made similar concessions (which required an improbable departure from free trade). For Laurier's Liberals, a unilateral move had numerous attractions: it offered a means to retaliate against the US Dingley Tariff which raised US protection to an average of almost 50 per cent; it offered the prospects of lowering supply costs for primary producers, especially in the developing west; and seized the banner of imperial loyalty from the Conservatives (helpful in much of anglophone Canada). It also asserted Canadian autonomy (popular in Quebec) both because the move had not been initiated by Britain, and also because it required the amendment of British treaties with Belgium and Germany – thus subtly eroding Britain's continued dominance of foreign policy.[56]

Even if the preference emerged from domestic political circumstances, Fielding and Laurier were keen to exploit positive British reactions, including those of the City. The move appealed to a broad spectrum of opinion. *The Times* applauded Canadian loyalty attributing this to Britain's concession of political and fiscal liberty.[57] Rudyard Kipling's 'Our Lady of the Snows' picked up on these themes; a rare occasion when tariff policy has inspired verse, however insipid. (Some Canadians feared the emphasis on snow would deter migrants).[58] The move heartened many imperial federationists

Table 5.1 Canadian Federal Government Expenditure and Revenue, 1896–1913 ($mil and per cent)

Year*	Total Revenue	Expenditure								
		Total	Defence		Transport and Communication		Economic Development		Public Debt	
	$mil	$mil	$mil	%	$mil	%	$mil	%	$mil	%
1896	38	42	3	7.1	14	33.3	2	4.8	11	26.2
1897	41	44	2	4.5	16	36.4	3	6.8	11	25.0
1898	47	52	3	5.8	20	38.5	5	9.6	11	21.2
1899	51	52	4	7.7	19	36.5	5	9.6	11	21.2
1900	53	57	3	5.3	24	42.1	5	8.8	11	19.3
1901	58	62	3	4.8	25	40.3	9	14.5	11	17.7
1902	69	59	3	5.1	23	39.0	8	13.6	11	18.6
1903	71	72	4	5.6	26	36.1	9	12.5	11	15.3
1904	71	79	4	5.1	34	43.0	12	15.2	11	13.9
1905	80	82	6	7.3	36	43.9	12	14.6	11	13.4
1906	68	66	4	6.1	30	45.5	9	13.6	7	10.6
1907	96	133	7	5.3	73	54.9	19	14.3	12	9.0
1908	86	115	6	6.1	54	47.0	18	15.7	13	11.3
1909	102	119	9	5.0	61	51.3	16	13.4	13	10.9
1910	118	135	10	6.7	63	46.7	19	14.1	12	8.9
1911	136	142	11	7.0	69	48.6	18	12.7	13	9.2
1912	169	183	14	6.0	91	49.7	35	19.1	13	7.1
1913	163	188	14	7.4	79	42.0	43	22.9	16	8.5
Total	1517	1682	110	6.5	757	45.0	247	14.7	209	12.4

*In 1907 the Fiscal Year's end was changed from 30 June to 31 March so the 1906 figures are for nine months only.
Source: Leacy, Historical Statistics..., H18, H19-34.

as a step in the right direction in the year Chamberlain sought an imperial zollverein at the colonial conference.[59] Conversely, free traders applauded a first step towards full Canadian free trade; the Cobden Club awarded Laurier a medal.[60] Others drew satisfaction from the fact that the move had been advocated by a French Canadian.[61] The cumulative effect, as the *Toronto Globe*'s London correspondent reported, was that 'everywhere Canada and Canadians are spoken of in enthusiastic terms'.[62] This goodwill was reinforced when Laurier visited to attend Queen Victoria's Diamond Jubilee in 1897 and the accompanying colonial conference. The prime minister stormed London society (into which he was introduced by the press baron, Alfred Harmsworth), speaking eloquently at formal dinners and at the conference itself (where he resisted Chamberlain's moves for more formalised imperial integration).[63] According to a High Commission official, 'Laurier has made a most pronounced and distinguished mark in London. It is perfectly wonderful what a hold he has upon the people here. His praises seem to be in the mouth (sic) of everyone'.[64]

The effects on the City were tested in October 1897 when Fielding arrived to place a large loan.[65] £2 million was offered with a nominal interest rate of 2.5 per cent and a minimum tender of £91 – the first time a colony had offered such a low rate of nominal interest. £4,205,460 was tendered and the full sum raised at an average price of £91 10s 5d. The London and Canadian press thought the loan a success; Harmsworth believed it would 'do more to strengthen the dominion here than the preferential tariff'.[66] This popularity continued, and in 1902 Fielding boasted that Canadian credit rivalled that of the mother country.[67] In their early years in power, Laurier and Fielding were keen to nurture (and be seen to nurture) Canadian credit, capitalising on the preference. Little wonder the Department of Finance observed the effects in London of raising the preference to 33 per cent so assiduously.

Subsequently the department continued its vigilant watch on the capital market. Memoranda from the department and its minister transferred the Square Mile's ebbs and flows to the spending ministries. In 1900, Fielding circulated a notice to his colleagues predicting that the South African War would restrict credit, and urged 'the uttermost caution in the preparation of the main estimates'.[68] A similar memorandum in 1901 concluded, 'So far our government has had a prosperous condition of finances, and I am very anxious that we shall not spoil our record in that respect'.[69] In 1905 Fielding urged his colleagues not to yield to pressures to increase expenditure, as 'any advantage... would be more than counterbalanced by the effect upon us all of a mad financial statement at the end of the year'. He 'trusted that his colleagues felt a "warm interest" in the maintenance of our high public credit and the continuance of the satisfactory financial record of past years'.[70] Clearly many of his fellow ministers showed insufficient warmth and in October, with Laurier's support, all departmental expenditure required Fielding's personal authorisation while works would be slowed or stopped.[71]

Any respite gained was temporary. In 1908 a finance department circular estimated that current expenditure would exceed revenue by $1 million, and warned that if the government paid, 'generally for services which the investors regard should be met out of ordinary revenue, the rate of interest will inevitably be enhanced'. With renewals and new borrowing totalling $227,750,000 expected in the next few years, as well as a number of possible issues of guaranteed railway bonds, this was clearly undesirable. The report darkly predicted that the 'agitation against colonial borrowing' might turn on Canada and, 'lead to the absolute failure to secure the monies needed'. It concluded that it was imperative that expenditure be cut 'down to the lowest possible point compatible with the public interest rather than borrow for current expenditure'.[72]

The report's warning soon became all too real. In January 1909 the Canadian government needed to float £6 million of 3¾ per cent stocks in London to cover maturing loans and to fund rail construction.[73] When negotiations began in late-1908, E. S. Clouston (general manager of the Bank of Montreal) wrote to Laurier warning that the market was weak, partly because Fielding had placed many small loans in the past year, but also due to falling revenues, increasing expenditure, and because, 'knowledge that the total liability incurred on account of the transcontinental railway is much in excess of the original estimates [had] created a very unfavourable impression in the minds of many English financiers'. Clouston concluded that the loan would require the 'backing of some house of worldwide reputation', and sought 'assurance' that no new loan or guarantee bonds be issued for three years, while dictating that, 'your present ordinary expenditure must be reduced'.[74] Laurier rather supinely replied, 'almost everything you suggest must be done', promising the restriction on borrowing and guaranteed loans, and that expenditure would be 'curtailed' along with a 'stop [on] all new works'.[75] With these assurances, Robert Nivison agreed to arrange underwriting for the issue. While in London Fielding also won over F. W. Hirst – editor of *The Economist* – by agreeing to issue bonds of a lower denomination designed to appeal to the small investor.[76]

Despite these efforts, 59 per cent of the loan remained with the underwriters. Clouston thought this a good result (given competition from the Indian government), one only obtained, 'by the understanding that you will make a public declaration that the government are committed to a policy of retrenchment... and that no new or costly public works will be undertaken'.[77] Later in the year Laurier forwarded the latest Canadian estimates showing cuts. Only the militia had been excepted because, 'to completely suppress the annual drill of the militia... would have created a bad impression, not only in this country, but also in England'.[78] Even this small act of defiance was justified within the framework of the 'rules'! As Table 5.1 shows, the deficit was halved as a proportion of revenue from 1908 to 1909, although expanding revenues rather than falling expenditure largely accounted for the change.

After gaining office in September 1911, Borden's Conservatives were no less attentive to the capital market. We have already seen that Borden, and W. T. White maintained a close touch with City opinion. In his second budget speech in 1913, White devoted considerable attention to relations with London, boasting how 'in a period of great financial stringency', the government had, 'been able to reduce so substantially the debt of the Dominion, thus diminishing our interest charges and still further enhancing the high value of our securities'.[79] He concluded that while it was:

> Too much to hope that we shall always be able out of revenue to meet capital expenditure of great undertakings of a permanent character, the advantages of which endure for the benefit of generations to come... it would nevertheless seem a wise policy that in times of abounding prosperity we should conserve our credit and establish as close an equilibrium as may be possible.[80]

This was an implicit criticism of his predecessors. The Borden government faced the consequences of large liabilities in Britain amassed in the later years of Laurier's government, when expenditure (especially on transportation) had increased rapidly (see Table 6.1), particularly due to the costs of constructing two new transcontinental railways. This loosening of Liberal purse strings reflected changing economic and political realities, particularly the repercussions of the rapid settlement of the west. It is to these policies, which again entwined Canadian politics and credit, that we now turn.

Railways and politics

From the early-1900s railways returned to the fore in Canadian political life. The Conservatives never abandoned a commitment to transport expansion, but in 1896 economy and reductions in taxation – along with educational issues and provincial rights – were the Liberals' priorities. To understand how railway construction re-ascended to the political agenda and became a central strand of Liberal policy, it is necessary to sketch developments in western Canada. The Canadian Pacific Railway, the embodiment of Macdonald's 'national policy' was completed in 1885. As well as lavish state subsidies, the line enjoyed a monopoly (enshrined in law until 1888) through to the mid-1890s.[81] The CPR was not popular. Farmers and merchants complained of high freights and goods damaged in transit. The allegedly harsh terms of the 'fiefdom' were thought to retard immigration and development. The anger in the west was encapsulated in one apocryphal story which told of a farmer who, on returning home to find that his daughter had lost her virginity to a railwayman, threw his hat to the ground, stamped on it, and cried out 'Goddam the CPR!'.[82] Laurier's government was sensitive to such discontents (except perhaps those concerning the sexual activities of CPR employees) as Clifford Sifton, minister for immigration, began a systematic campaign to accelerate settlement: a policy which, if successful, was expected to increase the political importance of the west.[83] In 1897 Laurier secured a reduction in the CPR's freights in exchange for cash subsidies for the construction of a line through Crowsnest Pass in the Rockies.[84] This set a pattern of financial assistance in exchange for politically useful concessions which later marked Laurier's railways policy.

As the population of the west grew, so too did its harvests. As a result rail capacity as well as freight rates became a pressing issue. Settlement was only practical within a relatively short distance of a railway and hence access to global markets: continued growth needed new lines. Moreover, the wheat crop tended to be exported eastwards through the Great Lakes region, subsequently travelling on up the St Lawrence or crossing the eastern United States on its journey to the Atlantic. The early onset of the Canadian winter meant that it was essential either to secure passage before ice made these routes treacherous if not impassable, or to store the grain until the thaw. The result was a hectic rush in which farmers paid (or felt they paid) high prices for transport and storage facilities.[85] Greater capacity, it was thought, would resolve all of these problems.

As these pressures grew more acute, transportation became a pressing issue in federal politics. In 1902, when Fielding's budget speech boasted of the rehabilitation of Canadian credit, the Conservative E. B. Osler (also a director of the CPR) criticised the Liberals for failing to take, 'a single step towards relieving the pressure in the North West caused by the lack of facilities for bringing the grain east'.[86] Many wished to see competition established to the CPR, and, from 1896 Manitoba had been supporting William Mackenzie's and Donald Mann's embryonic Canadian Northern Railway.[87] The Liberals' allies in Torontonian finance also wished to see a competitor to the Montreal-aligned CPR. In November 1902 George Cox headed a list of petitioners to Laurier arguing that it was 'desirable' to construct a second trans-continental railway, 'without any unnecessary delay... in order that additional facilities may be provided for the large growing business of the North West which might, otherwise, find its outlet through American channels'.[88] By the end of 1902, it was clear to Laurier that the west had not been won at Crowsnest Pass. A new strategy was required to secure the prairies and hold Toronto.

How though was this to be achieved? Cox and his allies favoured a second transcontinental railway, but the key question was who would construct and own the line.[89] A purely publicly-owned railway was scarcely considered by the Liberals. The longest state-owned line in Canada, the Intercolonial linking Quebec and the Maritimes, was not a financial success (routed with strategic considerations in mind, it was not originally intended to be).[90] Hence, a private partner would be necessary – in accordance with normal practice in Canada – and two contenders emerged. Firstly there was the Canadian Northern Railway (CNR), run by the relatively unknown figures of Mackenzie and Mann. Secondly, the British-owned Grand Trunk (which linked Toronto to Quebec City) became interested after its American manager, Charles Melville Hays, per-suaded its chairman, Charles Rivers Wilson, in 1902 that the line required its own connection to the expanding western market.[91] With the CNR developing from Manitoba, and the Grand Trunk established in central Canada, a merger would have been the most economical means to create a new transcontinental. Laurier's government initially sought this but the main players were unable to agree and rather than pick one, the govern-ment supported both lines.[92] Given the lukewarm support of Grand Trunk shareholders, it is likely without the dominion's backing, that the railway would have backed down.[93] Laurier's sponsorship of the CNR and the Grand Trunk was to saddle Canada with excessive rail capacity (espe-cially beyond the prairies) and large liabilities in London.[94]

Political considerations explain why then did Laurier risked straining credit by supporting both lines. Laurier needed a scheme bold enough to offer tangible benefits to (and hence rally Liberal support in) every province and striking enough to live up to expectations that, in his own words, the twentieth century would be 'Canada's century'. A project on this scale would require British capital, hence the scheme had to command the support of the London capital market. Mackenzie and Mann then lacked the stature (in Canada as well as Britain) to be plausible partners. Many in 1902 doubted their commitment to constructing a lasting transcontinental and at that point they had only floated one issue successfully in London, that with a guarantee from Manitoba.[95] Yet the CNR could not be ignored. It was already becoming a force in the west, and railways had considerable political influence (particularly through their employees' votes).[96] Moreover, it had close links to the Canadian Bank of Commerce, a key Liberal ally. Mackenzie and Mann could not be dropped but they lacked the stature in the City to deliver the political tool Laurier required.

An alliance with the Grand Trunk therefore became attractive. It was well connected in London and able to secure financial support for a grand scheme while reassuring the dominion's creditors of its merits. This, it seemed, would allow what Laurier later called 'a work of national character' to be undertaken without sacrificing Canada's carefully nurtured credit.[97] Such calculations animated Laurier and Fielding as they negotiated a joint project with the Grand Trunk management. As Hays noted, 'One point the premier keeps re-iterating is the desirability of our having associated with us as director, some strong financial name on your side, such as a member of the house of Rothschild, or Barings, or someone who would carry equal weight'.[98] In 1905 (after the scheme had been announced) Fielding and Rivers Wilson persuaded the Rothschilds to float the first issue of Grand Trunk Pacific bonds; their goodwill in part secured by an offer to settle 2000–3000 Jewish refugees on the Lake Superior section of the line.[99]

The competing demands of finance and politics shaped the details of the 'National Transcontinental' scheme. The Grand Trunk sought to enter the prairies, and wanted government support especially in the construction of a line across the unproductive and unpopulated stretch north of the Great Lakes (where the Jews were to be settled). The Liberals wanted a project that would generate economic and electoral benefits in every province. As a result, and after long negotiations, it was agreed that the Grand Trunk would found a new company, the Grand Trunk Pacific, which would lay a line from Winnipeg across the Prairies and then the Rockies to Prince Rupert in British Columbia. This would be supported by bond guarantees, and subsidies for the costs of the mountain section. The government would construct a line – the National Transcontinental – east from Winnipeg, across the Canadian Shield and Northern Quebec, to Moncton in New Brunswick, which would then be leased to the Grand Trunk Pacific.[100]

This was a project which Laurier could portray as 'national', necessitated by Canada's rapid development, while also benefiting every province. It enabled Laurier to wax lyrical as he unveiled the scheme to the Canadian parliament:

> To those who urge upon us a policy of to-morrow and to-morrow and to-morrow; to those who tell us, Wait, wait, wait; to those who advise us to pause, to consider, to reflect, to calculate and to inquire, our answer is: No, this is a time for action. The flood tide is upon us that leads on to fortune; if we let it pass, the voyage of our national life, bright as it is today, will be bound in the shallows...[101]

He continued that the prairies, 'which for countless ages have been roamed over by the wild herds of the bison, or by scarcely less wild red men, are now invaded from all sides by the white race'. It was the government's 'duty' to ensure that 'the products of these settlers may find an exit to the ocean at the least possible cost, and... likewise a market may be found... for those who toil in the forests, in the fields, in the mines, in the shops of the older provinces.[102] He then outlined in considerable detail the specific benefits elsewhere: the maritimes would gain a quicker route east and traffic for their ports; settlement and minerals would be opened in northern Quebec, in northern Ontario, and the Rockies; and a new shorter route from Europe to the Far East would through Prince Rupert capture further trade for Canada.[103] He concluded that just as 'railways had been the great agency of the last century' and the Grand Trunk, Intercolonial and CPR had made confederation more than a 'paper union', so the new line would be 'another link in that chain of union'. For that reason alone, 'it would be worth all the sacrifices and far more than we are called on to make'.[104]

The Liberals' move left the Conservatives in an awkward position. They had long demanded greater transport investment. Robert Laird Borden, recently appointed leader, criticised the details of the scheme, and advocated a hybrid alternative based on publically-owned railways and waterways. The complexity of Borden's proposals lessened their political currency, while advocating the public ownership alienated the CPR, a powerful Conservative ally.[105] It was Laurier's former minister for railways, A. G. Blair (who had resigned over the issue) who offered the most cogent critique, focusing in part on the repercussions for Canadian credit. Cast in the role of Cassandra, he predicted that adding $120 million to Canada's financial obligations through bond guarantees (which Laurier portrayed as a notional cost) would be impossible without 'startling financial men on the other side'. The Australian colonies, he argued, 'No doubt moved by influences similar to those which are now moving this government, added to their obligations to such an extent that they practically destroyed their credit'.[106] Despite these warnings the bill passed the Commons in September and the Senate in the following month.[107]

The political fruits of the scheme were tested in 1904 federal election. The *Canadian Annual Review* commented, 'The Grand Trunk Pacific not only bulked larger but unquestionably influenced more votes than any other matter'.[108] Laurier launched vigorous attacks on public-ownership of the railways, helping drive a wedge between the CPR and the Conservatives.[109] The Grand Trunk threw its weight behind the Liberals. For example, its allies produced a leaflet listing 30 reasons why the Grand Trunk Pacific was 'the people's road'. The pamphlet stressed that the new line would receive far less state support than the unpopular CPR had in the 1880s and that the scheme would 'induce the investment of thousands of millions of profitable capital in Canada'.[110] The Liberals were returned with an increased majority. Laurier wrote to Rivers Wilson that 'Our victory is so complete as to leave no doubt that our railway policy is extremely popular'.[111]

Railways remained central in Canadian politics thereafter. In 1907 Laurier told a Toronto audience that 'Transportation is now the question of questions'.[112] In the 1908 election the Liberals adopted the campaign slogan 'Let Laurier finish his work', referring to the National Transcontinental.[113] In 1910 he opened a tour of the west: 'What is our first need? Transportation. What is our second need? Transportation. What, I ask you gentlemen, is our third need? Transportation.'[114] Fielding's 1908 manifesto to his constituency of Shelburne and Queens in Nova Scotia shows how the politics of railways integrated national and local aspirations. The manifesto began by sketching the dominion's 'progress' and argued that it was 'essential' to the welfare of the country, 'that much attention and liberal financial assistance should be given to the development of the great west through the bringing of immigrants, the construction of railways, and the organization of new provinces'. Yet, lest Fielding's Nova Scotian constituents feel neglected, it continued to highlight the local manifestations of national transformation; especially that 'the railway which for which your fathers so long agitated has become an accepted fact'. It concluded, 'in the general policy of the country, and in all matters of particular concern to the constituency, the interests of the two counties had been well considered'.[115] This typifies the way the Liberals translated credit into an electoral weapon. No wonder Liberal politicians watched London's opinions carefully.

This political and financial alchemy became increasingly strained. Relations between the government and the Grand Trunk quickly became tense. In 1905 they clashed over whether the proceeds of guaranteed bond issues should be held by London or Canadian banks (the latter, favoured by the government, eventually prevailed).[116] In 1906 Rivers Wilson complained that duties on imported steel were raising expenses; the duties were later dropped.[117] This related to a more fundamental problem: that the costs of the National Transcontinental, the Grand Trunk Pacific, and the Canadian Northern Railway were all spiralling.[118] This created disputes between the government, the CNR (which was also issuing guaranteed bonds in London), and the Grand Trunk over who would pay, and over the extent to which Canada's credit would or should be stretched by additional bond guarantees. The government (with the backing of the Bank of Montreal) wished to avoid excessive issuing and hence preserve credit while the railways, which would only fully pay once completed, pushed for further finance almost regardless. In 1909, having agreed (as we saw earlier) to a hiatus in the issuing of guaranteed bonds, the federal government had to loan the Grand Trunk Pacific $10,000,000 to prevent further flotations.[119] Meanwhile, the weakening of Canadian government stocks also led to a decline in the proceeds of guaranteed issues. The Grand Trunk claimed that the government had guaranteed not just the issues but that they would realise a minimum level of funds – a view supported by the Judicial Committee of the Privy Council (JCPC) on 16 November 1911.[120] As relations deteriorated, the Grand Trunk often warned Laurier that 'a disaster to Grand Trunk credit would have serious consequences both in London and Canada'.[121]

It was, however, Laurier's Conservative successors who had to deal with what George Foster called '[Laurier's] foolish and criminal railway blundering'.[122] By 1912 some £17 million of Canadian railway securities had been guaranteed by the dominion, along with £13,800,000 by the provinces.[123] A financial sword of Damocles hung over the Canadian government and many in London were growing concerned. In December 1911 Mackenzie issued £7 million of Canadian Northern guaranteed bonds, leading many in the City to wonder whether he anticipated a collapse in Canadian credit.[124] In 1912 the government tried to encourage the railways to show restraint. However the CNR and Grand Trunk Pacific were rushing to drive their last spikes and, as Alfred Smithers told Williams-Taylor, 'I wish to meet the government in every way, and do all in my power to sustain Canadian credit, but I must have that money'.[125]

In 1912 the Conservatives considered their response. By then they had long been advocating public ownership, and opposed to excessive rail construction. Given this, could the government allow the lines to go bankrupt – in which case the state could step in and pick them up at a bargain price? The new finance minister W. T. White thought so, as (unsurprisingly) did their CPR allies, Thomas Shaugnessy and E. B. Osler. Yet the bond guarantees could not be ignored, nor could the effects on Canadian credit. The Conservatives had their own capital projects in mind, particularly a line from Manitoba to Hudson's Bay which had helped woo parts of the west in the 1911 election. There were fears that the Canadian Bank of Commerce might be undermined if the Canadian Northern Railway failed.[126] With new borrowing looming, and national and provincial credit on the line, the City concluded, as Williams-Taylor informed White, 'that your government must stand behind both the Canadian Northern and the Grand Trunk Pacific'. The effect of this conclusion, he continued, was 'reassuring, as after all, it is said if our three great Railways, Banks, Provinces and Cities are safe, the credit of the Dominion cannot be seriously affected'.[127] Hence, Borden's government assisted the lines (while exacting certain concessions) as they struggled towards completion against the backdrop of a weakening capital market. In 1913 the government lent the Grand Trunk Pacific $15 million to prevent its collapse. The CNR too lobbied repeatedly for assistance and, in 1914, the government guaranteed $45 million of bonds in exchange for the cancellation of a $20 million debt to Mackenzie, Mann and Co (the CNR's contractors), and the concession of a 40 per cent holding of the line's common stock.[128] Only the coming of war finally tipped the lines into bankruptcy, allowing the government to take over – not without a bitter fight in the case of the Grand Trunk.[129] By then London's capacities to fund grandiose railway schemes had been dramatically curtailed.

Maintaining credit was a central priority for both Laurier's and Borden's governments. This was not an end in itself. Credit and debt were essential means to promote national and local economic development, while particular projects – especially railways – forged powerful alliances. The political as well as economic consequences of undermining credit were too difficult to contemplate. Yet London finance did not always occupy centre stage in decisions about Canadian political economy. The final section of this chapter examines the role of the City in Canadian discussions of reciprocity in 1911, an issue which, ultimately, precipitated Laurier's replacement by Borden. Despite being inflated into a debate about Canada's economic orientation and place within the empire, a divided City had little capacity to shape events. Even so, both sides of the Canadian debate paid attention to London's views in ways which reflected the structural connections between credit in Britain and Canadian political and economic life.

Reciprocity, 1911

Infrastructure was not the only issue concerning the nascent west. Laurier's government also sought markets for the prairies burgeoning output (and for other Canadian primary producers). Britain remained the main outlet for Canadian trade.[130] However securing as many customers as possible was essential to help to maintain prices as output increased, both to sustain western incomes, and to avoid a negative shift in the terms of trade raising debt service costs. This in part was why Canadians beyond Quebec tended to support Chamberlain's tariff reform proposals which would have enhanced access to the British market.[131] Canada also looked elsewhere, and in 1906 a new intermediary tariff offered concessions to any country willing to negotiate. In 1907 Fielding agreed mutual reductions with France; and with Germany and Italy the following year.[132]

Nonetheless the largest prize lay to the south. Past precedent weighed heavily on Canadian thinking. In 1854 reciprocal trade concessions with the US had ushered an era of economic prosperity (or so Canadians remembered).[133] This came to an abrupt halt when the protectionist north won the Civil War. Thereafter successive Conservative and Liberal governments in Ottawa had sought in vain to revive reciprocity. Even Macdonald left the door open to negotiations with the US. In 1892 a Conservative delegation had been rebuffed in Washington where agricultural and industrial protectionism remained ascendant. In 1897, when the Dingley Tariff raised average US duties to 47.5 per cent, Laurier made virtue of necessity and declared an end to 'pilgrimages to Washington'.[134] However, the new century saw shifts in the US position. Many business interests, such as J. J. Hill's Great Northern Railway, cast their eyes longingly on the booming market to the north. The powerful newspaper industry sought to reduce costs through enhanced access to Canada's seemingly inexhaustible supply of wood pulp. Complaints about the costs of urban living became widespread, and would only grow once the US became a net importer of foodstuffs. Cries for freer trade were galvanised when, in 1909, the Payne-Aldrich tariff raised protection to new heights.[135]

Despite Laurier's earlier bravado, Washington found Ottawa open to freer trade. It was becoming clear that railway construction was not sufficient to secure western support. During a tour of the prairies in

1910 Laurier heard numerous complaints about the higher costs for equipment and items of consumption and the lower prices paid for produce on the Canadian side of the border. In 1910 farmers laid 'siege' to the federal parliament in Ottawa in protest.[136] By then Fielding was deep in negotiations with the Taft administration. An agreement was reached to abolish or reduce tariffs on a range of primary products and agricultural implements while otherwise maintaining the protection of industrials unchanged on both sides of the border. Reciprocity (as it became known) sought to meet US demands for raw materials, while enhancing markets and reducing costs for Canadian primary producers, without sacrificing central and eastern manufacturing.[137]

Fielding presented reciprocity to the Canadian parliament on 26 January 1911 as the culmination of half a century of Canadian aspiration as well as plain common sense: 'we are sending our commercial agents to the utmost ends of the earth to seek for business; why not seek it from the 92,000,000 people who live side by side with us?'[138] W. L. Griffith, Canada's deputy high commissioner, thought the agreement to be, 'the biggest strike that Sir Wilfred Laurier's government have done, and one of the finest things for Canada that has happened in my lifetime'.[139] While Borden criticised the disruption of Canada's stable economic conditions, behind the scenes many Conservatives thought the Liberals had made another shrewd move.[140]

Despite this, a fierce debate developed in the Canadian parliament, press, and in Britain.[141] Discussion focused not just on the agreement itself but also on its implications for Canada's future economic and geopolitical orientation. It dominated the September 1911 election, except in Quebec where Laurier's naval plans attracted more attention.[142] As this chapter has suggested, the need to maintain credit was widely acknowledged and publically articulated in Canadian political life. However, as we saw in Chapter 3, the City could not agree on either the economic or imperial repercussions of reciprocity. Despite this, both sides in Canada watched and sought to manipulate the debate in the City. Soon after the agreement was announced, Fielding was warned by governor-general Earl Grey that, 'The annexation talk is beginning to create a feeling of insecurity in the British investment market and brokers have already received orders from frightened investors to sell their Canadian securities'.[143] Grey (a supporter of the agreement) thought it essential to, 'press as strongly as possible the arguments... that a prosperous people is a contented people and that the greater the material wellbeing of Canada the stronger will be her loyalty.'[144] The government considered it essential that their opponents did not make the running in London. The High Commission kept Fielding well informed about coverage in the press. The deputy high commissioner worried that critical comments by the London managers of the Bank of Montreal and the Canadian Bank of Commerce would 'prejudice' Canadian interests.[145] When Arthur Balfour described the agreement as an 'imperial disaster' in Westminster, Fielding used this controversial slight against Canadian self-government as an excuse to telegraph a long and widely reproduced justification of reciprocity.[146] Despite divisions in the City, the government took nothing for granted, watched the debate closely, and sought to ensure that its case was heard.

The possible effects on credit and investment featured in the cases made by opponents and supporters of reciprocity in Canada. Conservative speakers during the rambling debate occasionally mentioned capital inflows. On 14 February, for example, George Foster argued that reciprocity would import 'unstable conditions' from the US, jeopardising the $150 coming annually from Britain.[147] On 5 April another MP argued that, 'British and foreign capital would not trust itself in a country so unstable in its fiscal policy'.[148] Beyond Ottawa R. P. Roblin, the Conservative premier of Manitoba, listed the devaluation of 'the securities of the Britishers who have poured millions into Canada for her development' among a number of grounds for opposition. However this was not the crux of Roblins' case, nor that which the Conservatives developed through 1911. As Roblin concluded:

> [Reciprocity] will darken the sun of our prosperity; it will cloud our future with uncertainty and divert... the channels of trade to the south of us into ways which we know not and an end which may be more disastrous than financial loss, namely the loss of our independence as a Dominion of the British Empire.[149]

Broader economic and geopolitical considerations ultimately formed the core of the Conservative critique of the agreement.

A second pillar of opposition to the agreement came from Toronto's Liberal financiers and manufacturers – most of whom had links to the Canadian Bank of Commerce. B. E. Walker soon overcame reservations about alienating clients who supported reciprocity, and, on 16 February, backed a motion at the Toronto Board of Trade opposing the agreement.[150] Walker then led the defection of 18 prominent Torontonian Liberals, who two days later issued a 12 point manifesto denouncing reciprocity. The second point argued that the railways' freights would be disrupted, the eighth discussed ties to the empire, and the manifesto concluded that 'Canadian nationality is now threatened with a more serious blow than it has hereforeto met with'.[151] Surprisingly, credit was not mentioned explicitly, even though these points could all potentially be linked to the interests of investors. The Toronto Eighteen became a powerful political force. Zebulon A. Lash, (the CNR's lawyer) and W. T. White (of the National Trust Company) were effective on the stump. Lash chaired the Canadian National League, formed to rally opposition.[152] Credit failed to feature that prominently in their campaign. Thus a typical pamphlet argued that, 'the overshadowing feature of our commercial relationship with Great Britain has been the investment of capital in every field of Canadian enterprise', and noted that Canada's popularity in Britain 'has been of the greatest value in financing government and other undertakings'.[153] However it never claimed that this popularity would be undermined, focusing rather on economic dislocations and Canada's place in the empire.

It is worth pondering why credit did not feature more in the campaign. In part Canadians raising capital in London were caught in a dilemma. Few were certain that the agreement would fail, and causing alarm by arguing that it might harm British investors risked stemming the flow of capital.[154] Yet men such as Walker publically opposed other measures on such grounds, running similar risks. The Canadian managers of the Canadian Bank of Commerce and Bank of Montreal both spoke out against the agreement despite this risk. Furthermore, emphasising broader economic and imperial dislocations could also cause disquiet in London. It is, therefore, more likely that credit did not feature more prominently and explicitly in the arguments of reciprocity's opponents because a divided City made warnings of dangers to credit implausible. Indeed, supporters of reciprocity could use signals from the capital markets to counter predictions of dire consequences for the Canadian economy. In March, Griffith sent Fielding a list of 11 Canadian issues made since the agreement worth £4,531,871 of which seven had been oversubscribed to help the finance minister counter the 'foolish assertion... that the reciprocity agreement would have the effect of making investors on this side chary of putting their money into Canadian issues'.[155] In February, a letter to the *Halifax Chronicle* observed that, 'in spite of assurance that the reciprocity treaty would go through, and that if it did the company's business would be considerably curtailed east and west, the C.P.R stock has been remarkably strong under the lead of London and New York'.[156] Later in the year the same paper observed that if reciprocity was likely to result in economic disaster, 'proverbially timid capital' ought to be fleeing, but instead CPR and Canadian banking stocks rose, as did the volume of investment from Britain.[157]

Ultimately the Conservatives' victory in the September 1911 election (on a 2.8 per cent swing) sealed reciprocity's fate. Possible economic dislocations, fears of American annexation, and the ephemeral threat to Canada's membership of the empire swayed large swathes of anglophone Canada.[158] Despite divisions in the City, its views featured occasionally in the reciprocity campaign. It was not neglected by opponents or defenders of the government, and both sides competed in London as well as in Canada. This reflected the extent to which Canadian politics and London finance were linked. Yet the obvious divisions in City views, and the mixed signals from the capital markets, made it impossible to argue (or at least to argue irrefutably) that the agreement would either destroy (or enhance) credit. At this moment when Canada's entwined economic, national, and imperial projects were thought to be at stake, a divided City had little purchase, but was drawn into the political process by Canadians themselves.

Conclusion

This chapter has charted the links between Canadian politics and London finance during the great boom from 1896 to 1914. It began by showing how Montreal's and Toronto's financial elites saw credit as crucial to their own, and to national, interests. Men such as E. S. Clouston or B. E. Walker intervened frequently to oppose measures they thought likely to lead to an erosion of credit. They conducted the rules of the game (whose premises and assumptions they basically shared) into Canadian economic and political life, often finding Canadian governments receptive. Imports of capital – especially for railway construction – were widely seen as integral to Canada's economic wellbeing and emerging nationhood. Liberal and Conservative politicians paid close attention to signals from the capital market, shaping their budgets accordingly. However, maintaining credit was rarely an end in itself. Improved credit could be a badge of honour, but could also be used to reduce debt service or to pursue construction projects which delivered tangible political dividends. Laurier's railway policy was conceived in this way, and bound both Liberal and Conservative governments to London opinion. The links between Canadian political life and the City were so pervasive, so routine, that the reciprocity campaign was – in part – fought in London. In this instance neither side was able to rally City opinion to their side. A City deeply divided on the merits of protectionism, and by tariff reform, could never have reached consensus. But this did not prevent it becoming an element in the reciprocity debate.

Ultimately these links were based on the widespread belief that British capital was an integral component of Canadian development. Few in the upper echelons of Canadian political and economic life questioned the need to keep British money flowing. The long boom made this case all the more plausible, accentuating sensitivity to the City's opinions. In all these matters Canada contrasted with Australia in this period. There the economic problems of the 1890s, the difficulties in raising new British capital, the weaker integration of business and politics, and the questioning of the virtue of overseas debt by a large section of the emergent Labor party led the politics of finance to take a different form.

6

The Politics of Finance in Three Australian States: Victoria, New South Wales, and Western Australia, 1901–1914

In the northern dominion the political influence of powerful financial institutions committed to borrowing in Britain, the ubiquitous connection made between credit and national development, and transcontinental railway construction all combined to make the federal government in Canada peculiarly sensitive to signals from the City. The next two chapters examine the very different intermeshing of London finance and Edwardian Australian politics. The next chapter explores the experience of the Commonwealth from its inauguration in 1901. This chapter first examines the attitudes to borrowing prevalent in Australian politics, and then charts the ways relations with the City interacted with politics in three states: Victoria, New South Wales, and Western Australia. Both show that relations with the City featured strongly in federal and state politics. In each case the politics of finance took different forms, and produced different levels of influence. However, the outworkings of the politics of finance in these states (as well as in the Commonwealth) can only be understood against the backdrop of broader developments in Australian politics.

Australian politics, 1890–1914: Federation and Labor

The 1890s and 1900s saw two fundamental reconfigurations in Australian political life. Firstly, the project of uniting the continent finally came to fruition in 1901 when (by an act of the Westminster parliament) the Commonwealth of Australia came into being. The idea of promoting greater unity between Britain's Australian colonies was periodically proposed in the 1880s for defensive reasons and to restrain non-White immigration.[1] A convention to discuss federation was held in 1891, and the project revived with a further gathering in 1897. By then additional concerns had emerged: to revive the economy and credit through broadening markets (and hence the tax base), and to obtain a more unified voice within imperial politics.[2] The forces behind the federation project were complex and strangely fragile. Voters in New South Wales failed to pass one draft constitution in 1898 by the required majority, while Western Australia only decided to join in 1900.[3] The functions the new federal government would adopt were far from clear on its formation in 1901. Many expected it to take a relatively minimal role focusing on the policing of Australia's borders and the creation of a single market and tariff policy. However, pressures at the conventions, particularly from Victorian progressives, meant that the constitution allowed the Commonwealth government to enter a wide range of other policy areas, especially in social and industrial relations. These were soon exercised and, by its tenth anniversary, and despite the actions of the Supreme Court which disallowed many initiatives, the federal government had become a much more powerful entity.[4]

Many contemporaries attributed this to a second development, again first clearly visible in the early 1890s, and gaining pace after 1900: the rise of Labor. In the 1870s and 1880s, eastern Australia saw the emergence of an increasingly virulent trades unionism, particularly in the pastoral and maritime industries, and also amongst miners at Broken Hill in New South Wales. In the early 1890s a string of defeats in industrial disputes set the movement back. At times it is argued that, finding industrial activism ineffective, labour turned to politics.[5] Nonetheless, the dire economic fortunes of eastern Australia in the 1890s were also important. The crash of 1893, the subsequent depression deepened by state retrenchment, and the drought all had a heavy impact on large sections of the working and lower middle classes. These diverse groups came to be united by a common 'populist' rhetoric at the core of which lay the idea that the interests of the masses had been betrayed by the ruling elites under the influence of the 'money power'.[6] The federal and state Labor parties slowly tapped this groundswell of discontent, although the timing and strength of their emergence varied greatly.

These parties inserted themselves into a complex political situation. In most states, Free Traders vied for office with Protectionists, who often also had progressive leanings (meaning a greater willingness to regulate the economy on behalf of the working classes). The divisions between the non-Labor parties often also had sectarian undertones, with Protectionists tending to draw support from Catholics and Free Traders enjoying closer links to protestants, temperance movements, and Orange Lodges. Federation ended the states' responsibility for tariff policy, beginning an erosion of the old economic dividing lines. As a result, political nomenclature shifted rapidly in this period. Generally Protectionists became Progressives; Free Traders became Liberals or Anti-Socialists. Through the course of the subsequent decade, Progressive votes became squeezed and the non-Labor parties coalesced, emerging as Liberals.[7] In order to understand how these shifting political groupings interacted with the City, it is necessary first to examine the views held about overseas debt in Australia.

Australian attitudes to domestic and overseas borrowing

In Canada there was a virtual consensus that borrowing was essential to economic and political progress, powerfully articulated by Canada's financial elites and journalists. By contrast in Australia, financiers and businessmen took less of a lead in interpreting the implications of external financial connections, and lobbied less on the City's behalf.[8] As a result, politicians, civil servants, and journalists played a greater role in forming ideas about financial relationships. Financial journals and journalists came closest to performing the part played by leading financiers in Canada. The *Australasian Insurance and Banking Record*, published in Melbourne from 1877, provided a united voice to Australian finance, supplemented by the daily press in the state capitals. Australia's answer to Canada's F. W. Field was R. L. Nash, financial editor of the Sydney *Daily Telegraph* and compiler of the *Australian Joint-Stock Companies Yearbook*.[9]

Yet it is telling that the statistical basis of much Australian thinking about debt was provided by a government employee: Timothy Coghlan, New South Wales' official statistician from 1886 to 1904, and agent-general from 1905. His *Wealth and Progress of New South Wales* (1887 onwards) and his *Statistical Account of the Seven Colonies* (1902) became standard reference works in both hemispheres. Recognising his early achievements, the Royal Statistical Society made Coghlan a fellow in 1893. He was no mere number cruncher, and in the 1890s was frequently to be found at the heart of political life; he had strong links to leading lights of the radical and nationalist Sydney *Bulletin*.[10] His official writings reveal subtly stated commentary, often made more explicit in articles in the *Freeman's Journal*, the Sydney *Daily Telegraph*, and the Sydney *Bulletin*.[11] Coghlan wrote ambivalently on the value of overseas borrowing. In the *Seven Colonies*, he estimated that since 1871 debt had increased by £260,682,000 (£165,821,000 on public account, and £94,682,000 on private account). Servicing this debt required Australia to pay an annual 'tribute' (a revealing phrase) of £16,261,000 to Britain. Since £125 million had been paid on the public debt, Coghlan suggested that only £30 million of capital had permanently been transferred to Australia, while private borrowing had generated an *outflow* of £30,574,000. He criticised the excessive borrowings of the 1880s but concluded overall that, 'by far the larger portion of loans has been well expended'.[12] Such lukewarm comments, the placement of debt towards the end of the *Seven Colonies* and *Wealth and Progress*, suggests a view that capital import was ancillary to Australian development.[13]

Coghlan's ambivalence reflected widespread difference of opinion over the past, present, and future utility of overseas borrowing. Views on the left were complex. On the one hand, many supported borrowing (overseas or in Australia) in order to provide employment for working men, especially during the lean early years of the twentieth century (Noel Butlin's 'colonial socialism').[14] New South Wales Labor supported borrowing for these reasons around the turn of the century and just prior to the Great War.[15] On the other hand, as Peter Love has shown, the economic crises of the 1890s led to the emergence of a powerful critique of external borrowing and of the exploitative role played by the 'money power'.[16] Indeed the money and land monopolies competed for pride of place in populist thinking as the greatest enemies of the common man.[17] As a result, many on the left opposed further borrowing and further dependence on this money power. In 1902 the Federal Labor Party's 'Fighting Platform' (its manifesto) pledged the cessation of public borrowing.[18] Some Progressives drew similar conclusions. In 1904, Bernhard Ringrose Wise (a New South Wales Progressive) told an audience at Sydney's Protestant Hall that, 'The financial methods of the past must be abandoned because they are leading us not to prosperity but to ruin'. 'Australia', he continued, was owned by, 'the holders of her bonds in London', making Australians, 'slaves of the worst of all bondages – the bondage of the money tie'. Wise concluded, 'If we would make Australia great, if we would make Australia free, the first and essential measure is to take Australia out of pawn'.[19]

In this discourse, the City was frequently portrayed as the global centre of the money power and as un-British, ideas tinged with anti-Semitism.[20] As we saw at the start, Edward De Norbery Rogers' depicted John Bull himself as the partner of a Jewish financier, Mr Wrathchild (even though the Rothschilds had no significant dealings with Australia). The *Bulletin* went one step further, portraying John Bull as a Jewish pawnbroker.[21] In similar vein, others wrote of 'Bull Cohen', who, as one Australian correspondent to *The Times* explained, was, 'the grasping money-lender, the slave driver, the nation whose only interest in anything human or divine is centred in its money value. Avarice and treachery, cowardice and stupid meanness, all views the bushman hates, are combined in the Bull-Cohen monster'.[22] The Melbourne *Argus* worried that London might think these views to be widespread.[23] Perhaps in reply to such ideas, those who advocated borrowing emphasised the *Britishness* of the City. Thus B. Rosentaumm (of the Perth Chamber of Commerce) thought it, 'a matter for congratulation that most of our loans are floated in London, that the investors are the people of Great Britain', since, 'if the word "empire" is worthy of the expression, it must mean that in borrowing from the British people, we are borrowing from ourselves'. 'Besides', he added, 'it often happens that the British investor of yesterday is the citizen of Australia tomorrow'.[24] As in Britain so in Australia, notions of a Greater British or pan-imperial community entered discussions of financial relations, here in the context of a highly charged debate linking race and political economy.

Amongst businessmen, financiers, and non-Labor politicians, attitudes to the City were less hostile. Most of these groups thought that Australia's past borrowings had been necessary. In 1900 the *Australian Insurance and Banking Record* (*AIBR*) denied Australia's debt burden was 'particularly heavy', 'especially as without it the development of the colonies to the present extra-ordinary [sic] degree would not have been possible'.[25] In 1906 the *Sydney Morning Herald* observed that 'had Australia depended entirely on her own resources in the past and had not the advantage of the use of the accumulated savings of the old world, she would not have progressed with anything like the rapidity with which she has done'.[26] The pressing question was whether Australia should raise capital in the present and in the future. At the turn of the century, some members of the financial and commercial classes supported a cessation of borrowing on business and political grounds. In 1901 R. L. Nash told the Institute of Bankers in New South Wales that there was little room for productive investment in Australia. He acknowledged the necessity of borrowing for public works 'which earn as much, if not more, than has to be paid out on their cost' but worried that politicians were using unproductive public works to gain votes. Many agreed with Nash that, 'State despotism is held in check by the inability to borrow fast enough'.[27]

From 1902 until 1910 Australian states (especially Victoria) raised capital locally, adding a further element to the debate. The relative merits of borrowing in Australia and Britain were frequently discussed. In 1905, the *Sydney Morning Herald* argued that borrowing locally would raise interest rates, observing that 'the struggling farmer', the 'small butter factory', and the 'manufacturer… all suffer from dear money'.[28] In this way, New South Wales' treasurer justified issuing £1mil treasury bills in London in 1901 even though interest rates were lower in Sydney.[29] In 1902 the *AIBR* warned that relying solely on local capital would tighten local interest rates and ran the risk (by making Australia's resources appear exhausted) of worsening terms in London.[30]

Against such views, some supporters of local borrowing argued that it allowed Australia to retain the full benefits of investment. In 1903 the president of the Melbourne Chamber of Commerce called for government loans to be placed, 'as far as possible in the Commonwealth to avoid the drain of annual payments'.[31] In January 1906, when Victoria floated a £1.6 million 3.5 per cent loan in the state (to repay £1,513,000 maturing in Britain), the chairman of the Melbourne Stock Exchange pointed out that, 'the people of Victoria will get the interest to spend, and that is much better than it going away and our getting nothing'.[32] When in 1905 interest in Western Australian mining looked likely to revive in London, the *Coolgardie Miner* wished, 'it were possible for local people to open up the mines and secure the good things for themselves'.[33]

Others emphasised that local borrowing could complement relations with the City. In 1906, the Melbourne *Argus* predicted, 'The willingness and ability of the Australian investing public to aid in the redemption of existing loans will greatly facilitate the work of [loan] renewal, particularly by the impression it will make upon the British creditor'.[34] Many in London welcomed local borrowing, and, in 1904, the Victorian agent-general thought any opposition there was, 'chiefly confined to those who have secured large commissions on our former loans'. 'The general public', he proceeded, 'view with satisfaction and agreeable surprise, the ability of the state to reduce its liabilities on this side'.[35] Borrowing locally was not necessarily understood as a declaration of financial autarky.

Few thought Australia could really rely on its own capital indefinitely, a view that strengthened as the limits of the local capital market were tested in the half decade prior to the war. When in 1907 New South Wales' premier, Joseph Carruthers, argued that his state could soon dispense with borrowing in Britain, the *Sydney Morning Herald* pointed out that with £16,308,661 of loans maturing in London down to 1912, with domestic interest rates tightening, and with 'other states also having heavy commitments', it was, 'absurd to tell the money-lender abroad in effect "We have used you in the past, but we are done with you for the future"'.[36] In 1912, R. L. Nash told the Dominions Royal Commission that Australia 'must go very slowly if we have to depend entirely on our own capital'.[37] This reiterated Alfred Deakin's earlier (and possibly satirical) observation to readers of the *Morning Post* that, 'under the

Commonwealth we look for larger investments of British capital, for the development of our immense natural resources, for an inflow of population and an outflow of products which shall secure us fat years and "many of them"'.[38]

All of this contrasted with the Canadian consensus that it had been, and would continue to be, necessary to borrow in Britain. A number of views on the value of borrowing were current in Australian politics. On the left, many populists and monetary radicals thought the debts amassed in the past had simply resulted in the exploitation of the working man; opposition to borrowing became a Federal Labor's policy. Some progressives shared similar views. However, others in the labour movement embraced borrowing in order to allow state expenditure to soften economic downturns. Beyond labour ranks there tended to be a consensus that Australia's past borrowings had been sound but there was less agreement on the best future course. Hence, local borrowing was seen by some as a means of lessening a 'drain' to Britain, and by others as one means to restore Australia's credit in the City. As local capital reached its limits, the attractions of borrowing in Britain reasserted themselves. These competing conceptions framed interactions between Australian political life and London finance.

State politics and London Finance

The state governments had strong reasons to watch the London market. They were Australia's leading borrowers and even between 1904 and 1912, when little fresh borrowing occurred, they had to undertake a number of renewal operations. Since the interest payments on new or renewed debt depended in large part on the prices prevailing in the London Stock Exchange, state politicians had a direct incentive to guard their credit. From about 1904, as Chapter 4 showed, this led to more assertive self-promotion and defence against defamatory remarks by a new generation of agent-generals such as Coghlan, Taverner and James.[39] The remainder of this chapter examines how far the need to maintain credit affected political life and policy as well as presentation in three states: Victoria, New South Wales, and Western Australia.

As we have seen, accusations of profligacy lay at the heart of a good deal of criticism of Australia in London, much fuelled by groups in the Commonwealth. Yet calls for retrenchment, especially in loan expenditure, had to find support within the framework of colonial democracy where manhood or even universal suffrage applied. The result, as Macintyre has observed, was that, 'The successful administration was

Table 6.1 Difference between Revenue and Expenditure as a percentage of Total Revenue, New South Wales, Victoria, and Western Australia, 1900–1914 (per cent)

Year	New South Wales	Victoria	Western Australia
1900	–24.20	–10.71	–10.71
1901	–27.36	–11.23	–37.64
1902	–44.68	–18.75	–27.37
1903	–43.24	–8.05	–21.63
1904	–20.99	–6.39	–19.57
1905	–12.60	–1.99	–6.92
1906	–3.77	–1.49	–0.93
1907	3.36	–2.20	–6.82
1908	–0.72	–3.58	–7.70
1909	–15.78	–13.52	–16.27
1910	–11.99	–14.35	–6.83
1911	–28.12	–28.76	–29.01
1912	–31.66	–29.49	–49.04
1913	–52.59	–21.61	–67.48
1914	–46.62	–30.73	–42.24

Calculated from W. Vamplew, ed., *Australians: Historical Statistics* (Broadway, N.S.W, 1987), Series G46-75, G 121-135.

the one that allowed citizens to prosper and made the benefits of material progress available to a sufficiently wide clientele'.[40] State governments may have needed to restore credit in the City, but also had to win votes from a broad electorate. Figure 7.1 above charts taxation and expenditure in the three states which feature in this chapter.[41] In the east, the depression of the 1890s created large-scale unemployment and strong pressure for greater state intervention.[42] Public works enabled politicians to court the classes most affected by providing employment and an indirect means to regulate wages in the rest of the economy.[43] As a result public borrowing in Victoria and New South Wales increased around the turn of the century. This political conjunction was challenged earliest and most forcefully in Victoria.

Victoria

Although Victoria never faced as deep a deficit as New South Wales, it still spent loan money to alleviate the effects of the depression. By contemporary reckoning in 1901–1902 it had a deficit on current account of £437,611.[44] Around the turn of the century the ministries of George Turner and A. J. Peacock sought working class support – indeed their minister of public works, W. A. Trenweth, came from Victorian Labor's moderate wing.[45] In 1902 the *AIBR* argued that Victoria's deficit was largely due to the establishment of old age pensions and the uneconomical running of the railways, criticised the 'inferior men who have been tolerated as treasurers in the Victorian parliament', and thought, 'financial administration has been conditioned too much by political considerations'.[46] The journal complained that, 'a combination of various departments of a large civil service, with the help of the votes of… the railways, is able… to settle the fate of a ministry', leading to high expenditure.[47]

By then Victorian politics were being dramatically transformed by the emergence of a broadly-based movement advocating the 'reform' (meaning retrenchment) of state expenditure. This began in depressed rural Victoria in 1901 when a farmer at Kyabram in Goulburn Valley, G. H. Bishop, discussed the problems of the state with a local newspaper proprietor. A subsequent meeting on 13 November called for a reduction of the number of members of parliament, public servants' salaries, and state expenditure in general. The 'Kyabram movement', and its official body, the National Citizens Reform League (established in April 1902), obtained the backing of Melbourne's financial and industrial interests, along with the *Age* and the *Argus* (Melbourne's leading dailies). By the end of 1902, the league had 210 branches and 15,555 members concentrated in rural areas, which were disproportionately represented in the Victorian assembly.[48]

Against this backdrop, in June 1902 a conservative MLA, William Irvine, forced a no confidence vote and took over as premier. He sought to reduce the size of the legislature, the salaries of politicians and public servants, and expenditure generally. In September, his minority administration was defeated seeking to reduce public servants' salaries.[49] An election was called in which the *AIBR* hoped, 'Victory will be overwhelming, so that the public service and labour party will be taught that the general public resent their unholy alliance in favour of a course of extravagance that, if continued, will ruin the country'.[50] This wish was fulfilled and, in alliance with the National Citizens Reform League, Irvine won a majority of 23 in the election.[51] Irvine then pursued reductions in expenditure, justifying this economy drive as a means to save money for development.[52] He was also keen that these changes were duly acknowledged in London. He even telegraphed the agent-general in October 1902 hoping that details of the latest budget figures would improve the prospects of a loan then under negotiation.[53]

Irvine also sought to neutralise the supposed political influence of public employees. His government established separate electoral roles for civil servants and railway workers and, in January 1903, forbade the railway unions from affiliating with the Trades Union Council – the central body co-ordinating Victorian unions. In May 1903 the railwaymen struck in protest. Within Victoria, Irvine rallied middle class opinion. The *Age* condemned a, 'mutiny against constituted authority' and the government passed a strike suppression bill which banned the collection of donations and prohibited meetings of more than six people. The strike collapsed after a week.[54] These events gained applause in the City, leading Victoria's agent-general, A. J. Dobson, to congratulate Irvine for the 'splendid services you have rendered not merely to Victoria but to Australia'.[55] Irvine's successor, Thomas Bent, continued to enjoy the fruits of the goodwill created by this confrontation, and the improving health of Victoria's finances. In January 1907 J. W. Taverner, who replaced Dobson in 1904, informed Bent that, 'In financial circles in London I am glad to inform you satisfaction is expressed of your successful financial administration of Victoria'.[56]

These events need careful analysis. Irvine had confronted organised labour and reduced expenditure in ways which the City applauded, and he and his successors certainly had an eye on the City's opinion. Yet it would be an exaggeration to suggest that these actions were undertaken in order to restore credit in London. It was Kyabram which transformed Victorian politics *prior* to the final weakening of Australian credit in London in July 1903 (when, as we saw in Chapter 3, underwriters temporarily refused to underwrite colonial stocks); and it was the strength and range of support that this movement placed behind Irvine which enabled him to tackle the unions and expenditure in such a forthright manner. In other words, the policies approved of in the City were generated by specific conjunctions within Victorian politics. Despite the class mythology that grew around the 1903 strike, Labor's weakness in the countryside, its difficulties in securing union support, and an electoral system favouring rural areas prevented it obtaining power down to 1914.[57] Ironically, the state with the deepest capital markets, and hence the greatest degree of independence from the City was also the one whose politics most conformed to its expectations. New South Wales, the heaviest borrower in the City, was a very different case.

New South Wales

Events in Victoria were followed eagerly by conservative groups across the Murray who hoped to see similar medicine prescribed in New South Wales. Around 1900, the Progressive governments of William Lynn and John See undertook extensive public works programmes (overseen by their Minister of Public Works, Edward O'Sullivan) financed by borrowing in London to create work and alleviate unemployment.[58] This drew considerable support from the urban working classes in Sydney, but also from the New South Wales wheat belt – Labor's heartland. Unlike their Victorian counterparts, the state's wheat farmers worked periodically in the pastoral industry, and had suffered from its contraction in the late-1890s.[59] These factors explain the greater interest in borrowing in London; hardly reasons which financiers and investors found endearing but which, nonetheless, created a deep link between New South Wales' politics and the City.

The government's finances were criticised in Australian financial circles. The *AIBR* thought the state's 'public expenditure too extravagant', especially its 'unregulated loan expenditure'.[60] When in 1902 £7 million of borrowing was announced (against the advice of the treasurer, Thomas Waddell), the journal condemned what it saw as unsustainable spending, and complained that 'the popularity gained by loan expenditure is regarded as of more consequence than economic principles'.[61] The *Sydney Morning Herald* and the Sydney *Daily Telegraph* joined the attack, publishing strings of articles decrying the state of the public finances.[62] The latter warned that a 55 per cent increase in expenditure in four years would be 'gravely questioned, not only in Australia but in England', and would lead the state's resources to be 'swamped in interest charges'.[63]

Nonetheless, it proved harder to construct an alliance in favour of 'reform' in New South Wales. The Sydney manager of the Australian Mercantile Land and Finance Company thought that without 'providing the labouring man with employment at remunerative wages... it would be impossible for any ministry to hold office at the present time'.[64] As we have seen, public works cemented an alliance between the Protectionists/Progressives and Labor in the legislative assembly. Hence attempts to imitate the Kyabram movement proved less successful in New South Wales – it was much harder to engineer the combination of rural voters and coastal businesses that rallied behind Irvine. In 1902 a Taxpayers' Union was founded to imitate the National Reform League and unite the state's Liberal party and other conservatives. It soon split when the new

Liberal leader, Joseph Carruthers, proved unwilling to discuss specific economies, especially reducing the size of the assembly. Two organisations emerged from the split. Carruthers' Liberal and Reform Association achieved a following comparable to Kyabram, while a more hard-line rival, the People's Reform League, failed to gather widespread support.[65]

With a powerful Progressive-Labor alliance enjoying broad approval, Carruthers' reconstructed Liberal party needed to connect economy with the interests of urban and rural workers. Debt and its repercussions featured prominently in this case. One manifesto attacked the ministry for seeking to 'maintain an artificial state of prosperity [which] is more than the country can bear', resulting in 'less employment for the people, more money going out of the country to pay English creditors and harder times for everybody'.[66] Similarly, in 1903, Carruthers estimated that borrowing £17 million had increased interest payments by £510,000 which could have employed 5,000 men at 7s a day. 'Any spendthrift', he declared, 'could boom the times by borrowing [which might] boom labour temporarily but put the shackles on it permanently'.[67] During the 1903 Victorian railway strike, he argued (in criticism of Irvine) that economy should not, '[make] any class bear the burden for the whole community'.[68] This conciliatory approach to labour led many in business circles to wish New South Wales, 'had a man of the type of the new Victorian premier'.[69]

Carruthers successfully constructed a mass movement between 1902 and 1904. Yet, unlike in Victoria, it was not the success of this movement which began the overhaul of New South Wales' finances. In their last years the Progressives changed tack and began retrenching, a move initiated by difficulties in London. They had always been divided on their loan policy, with treasurer Thomas Waddell in particular opposed to O'Sullivan's schemes. The issue came to a head when the July 1903 underwriters' strike signalled the febrile state of the London capital market.[70] Worried that capital would soon be in short supply, the ministry began cutting expenditure. Waddell's 1904 budget promised economy and a reduction of borrowing by £600,000 to £1.5 million per annum. In July 1904, John See resigned as premier. Waddell emerged as his successor, pledging to place, 'the public accounts and the credit of the colony on the surest footing known since [its] foundation'.[71] Waddell's assurances of restraint were insufficient for one rival, Bernhard Ringrose Wise, who resigned from the government citing as one major reason the belief that 'the only sound basis for financial reform is the immediate stopping of all public loans except to meet existing liabilities and renewals'.[72]

Table 6.2   New South Wales Legislative Assembly Election Results, 1901–1913

	Progressive	Liberal	Labor	Other	Total
1901	41	37	24	22	124
1904	16	45	25	4	90
1907		45	32	13	90
1910		37	46	7	90
1913		28	49	13	90

Source: Hughes, C. A. and B. D. Graham, *A Handbook of Australian Government and Politics, 1890–1964* (Canberra, 1968), pp. 435–44,

As we saw earlier, Wise was influenced by populist and nationalist critiques of the 'money power'. Similar reasoning led the New South Wales Labor party to place a cessation of borrowing on its 'fighting platform'.[73] Thus the change of tack in government policy was precipitated by weakening credit in London (a moment that might be described as a clear 'relational' manifestation of structural power), which in turn galvanised opposition to borrowing within New South Wales, although ironically in part by strengthening socialist and nationalist critiques of money-lenders. The August 1904 election took place against the backdrop of this shift in political discourse. Carruthers campaigned for more stringent economising than Waddell, gaining reluctant support from the People's Reform League, as well as the *Sydney Morning Herald* and the Sydney *Daily Telegraph*. Bereft of the public works policy, Progressive support fell: the party secured only 16 seats, Labor gained one, and Carruthers' Liberals won a small majority (with independent support).

In the early months the new premier declared that the 'main work of the government' was the 'restoration of credit'.[74] Over the next three years, credit lay at the heart of the state's politics, driving an ongoing tussle between the premier, the *Sydney Morning Herald* along with the more conservative elements whose views it often articulated. Late in 1904 the paper condemned a proposal for £600,000 of new borrowing which it thought would 'no more satisfy our London creditors than the people of the state'. With £4,000,000 soon to be renewed, 'it was incumbent to make an instant impression on the London Money Market'.[75] In early 1905, Carruthers boasted that loan expenditure had fallen by £800,000 in the last quarter and the state's finances showed a 'betterment' of £100,000. 'If the most ardent reformer expected more than that', he jibbed, 'I never heard him utter it during the reform campaign'.[76] The *Herald* retorted that the recovery of the pastoral industry had done most to restore the finances and urged the premier to 'assure our creditors that he intends to spend very little money'.[77] In June, Carruthers announced a £300,000 surplus which he thought 'completely satisfactory to the people' and likely, 'materially to influence our public creditors'. The *Herald* snipped that his government could 'only take a negative sort of credit' that it had not 'hindered' the improvement.[78]

When a £536,000 surplus was announced in 1906, the *Herald* changed tack and argued that a reduction of taxation (the other facet of 'sound' finance) would, 'make it possible to establish the state's credit on an enduring foundation'.[79] Carruthers preferred to fund non-reproductive public works on the basis that 'a first consideration must be to live within our own means and cease borrowing'. 'It was', he claimed, 'unfair to tax the present for posterity; but equally unfair to saddle posterity with our debts without assets equivalent thereof'.[80] By 1907, though, Carruthers had reduced taxation as surpluses continued to expand rapidly.[81] This tit-for-tat reflected a deeper divide over the purpose of 'reform'. Carruthers was seeking to restore credit to perpetuate an existing pattern of political economy. His approach – economising mildly and allowing increasing revenues to restore balance to his state's finances – was ideally suited to preserve the working and middle class alliance on which his political success depended, while also maintaining goodwill in London. The *Herald* wished to see a reduction in the role of the state. Both agreed that credit was essential while arguing that their preferred ends were the best means to its restoration.

In 1907 Carruthers retired after seeking to obstruct Commonwealth tariffs on wire netting imports, a key form of imported pastoral capital.[82] By then Waddell's Progressives had become virtually indistinguishable from the Liberals, particularly on economic policy. Carruthers' successor, C. G. Wade, united the two groups, although a few Progressives (including O'Sullivan) joined Labor.[83] Waddell returned as treasurer and, in his first budget, portrayed his last years in office and Carruthers' tenure as a single continuous period of economic reform.[84] Perhaps seeking to ensure that this message was heard in London, Waddell sent a copy of his first budget to the earl of Jersey; New South Wales' long time ally sent a laudatory reply.[85]

As economic recovery set in, politics in New South Wales (and attention in the City) turned to other issues; especially industrial unrest. Wade's government confronted labour in a forceful manner reminiscent of Irvine. In early 1908, it passed a new Industrial Disputes Act which introduced Victorian-style wages boards.[86] A strike by Sydney tram workers in protest was defeated. Further unrest followed, encouraged by radicals, including the British-born syndicalist Tom Mann. From January to May 1909 Mann led workers at Broken Hill in a succession of strikes (again raising disquiet in the City), while in November a strike by coal miners in Newcastle paralysed the continent. In response, Wade's government, passed what opponents dubbed 'Coercion Acts' making unlawful strikes (and lockouts) punishable by imprisonment. Mann, along with other radicals, was jailed until the summer of 1910.[87]

Wade gained widespread anti-Labor backing in Australia, but his interventions contributed to a rise in Labor support. In October 1910 he was defeated in the state elections in which the strikes featured prominently, just as they had in the earlier federal elections of that year (which Labor also won).[88] After initially preaching economy, the government of J. S. T. McGowen embarked on an expanded programme of public works funded by borrowing, despite opposition in its own ranks based on the lingering suspicion of financiers. This conversion owed much to the desire to promote closer settlement (discussed further in the next chapter) which required denser transport connections, especially along the state's underdeveloped coasts.[89] This *volte farce* was facilitated by the renewed availability of capital in London, with the City beginning to look askance at Canada, and with memories of past imprudence fading.

Despite the City's willingness to accept New South Wales' stocks, the Liberal opposition developed a refined critique of Labor finance which continued to place overseas investment at its heart. This critique started from the premise that, (in Waddell's words), on 'the maintenance of the country's credit and revenues depends the whole fabric of government and to a large extent the industrial life of the state'. He proceeded that the government was spending too fast, that credit in London could not last, that terms were worsening, and that government borrowing had raised domestic interest rates to their highest level in 40 years.[90] At the end of 1913, Waddell claimed the state was near bankruptcy.[91] By then Waddell had added a new element to his case: that Labor was driving out *private* British capital even as it amassed debts. As the Sydney *Daily Telegraph* explained: 'Instead of the outflow of British capital, apart from the government, we need an inflow, and the ridiculous notion as Mr Waddell puts it, that "we don't mind how many millions in interest leave our state every year but no money made as profits shall go" requires to be exploded'.[92] Thus, by 1914, the Liberals argued not only that state credit would ultimately be sacrificed, but also that private investment (which had all ready contracted) as well as public borrowing was necessary for development. Relations with the London capital market and British investors were crucial components of a developing critique of 'colonial socialism' which questioned not only the level and purpose of borrowing but also the balance of public and private relations.[93]

New South Wales was a heavier borrower than Victoria. Credit and the London capital market's views were central in political discussions. Nonetheless this London connection was refracted through the structures and exigencies of local political life. The strength of labour and the importance of public works made maintaining credit important, but also created countervailing pressures toward higher expenditure and borrowing. The stronger labour movement also made industrial relations more problematic from the City's point of view, and limited the scope for direct confrontation (without sacrificing support). The close structural connections between New South Wales and the City, reflected in political discourse, also revealed the presence of political forces which paradoxically limited the City's influence. Western Australia (the second largest Australian government borrower between 1896 and 1914, as Table 2.1 shows) was different again. The state was a late developer economically, and, in contrast to the eastern states, private investment (especially in mining) loomed much larger in political calculations. Examining Western Australia shows again how local circumstances and the specific nature of connections with London shaped the politics of finance.

Western Australia

In the 1890s, and while eastern Australia's economy struggled, the discovery of gold at Coolgardie and Kalgoorlie brought boom conditions to the continent's western third. After the concession of responsible government in 1890, development was also facilitated by a dramatic programme of public works under premier John Forrest, funded through fresh borrowing in London.[94] However, the turn of the century saw a number of dislocations in Western Australian political and economic life. Forrest departed for federal politics, leaving an unstable political vacuum which saw the state led by eight premiers in the 12 years following federation. At the same time, Labor emerged as a political force, and two of its leaders became premiers: Henry

Daglish (1904–1905) and Jack Scaddan (1911–1916).[95] Economic circumstances were equally febrile. The collapse of the gold mining boom in 1900–1901 curtailed the inflow of private capital. Subsequently the industry contracted, reducing employment, and, through slackening imports, weakening the state's finances which relied on tariffs revenues. The finances were further complicated by federation. The state had been particularly dependent on intercolonial tariffs, and while special financial provisions had been made to smooth the transition to internal free trade, uncertainty surrounded the state's finances once this supported ended.[96] In 1906 the land and income taxes were introduced to plug this gap, while successive governments sought to revive the goldfields and expand wheat production.

In this context, loans continued to be an important element in Western Australian politics and development. It has been claimed that political instability in the post-Forrest era lessened borrowing; however net borrowing in London continued to match levels seen in the 1890s until 1903. A reduction came in 1903 (coinciding with the London underwriter's strike) and 1904. After a return to the market in 1905, the slowing continued in 1906.[97] Attitudes to borrowing in the state were highlighted during this slow down, especially during the minority Labor administration of Henry Daglish, which restrained loan expenditure. In November 1904 the state faced a deficit on current expenditure. The *West Australian* (Perth's leading daily newspaper) criticised the government for the 'inevitable result of a suddenly and violently curtailed loan expenditure', since 'there can be no "marking time" in the case of a young country'.[98] The *Coolgardie Miner* agreed, 'Anyone can improve the finances by cheese-paring and curtailing the expenditure while compelling the people to provide the revenue. That simply means that the individual is made to suffer till the treasurer's books are showing a balance on the right side'. The paper continued, 'What the people want is progress as well as good financing, and they see no reason why we cannot have it while we have abundant resources'.[99] In May 1905 the *West Australian* compared the state to 'a large estate only partially developed' which it was the government's duty to make, 'fit not only for the occupation of our own people, but for the purposes of those whom we hope to attract to our shores'. Hence, borrowing needed to resume and 'the people of Western Australia ask for bread in the shape of a sound development policy'.[100] Thus, in contrast to the norm in the east, Labor was criticised for reckless prudence. After Daglish's administration fell in August 1905 (on which more below), the ministries of Cornthwaite Hector

Rason, and his successors N. J. Moore, F. Wilson and Labor's Jack Scaddan resumed borrowing.[101]

Unlike in Victoria and New South Wales, British investment in the private sector also attracted attention from Western Australian politicians. For much of the 1900s, it was hoped that a revival of the gold mines would attract fresh capital, and generate revenues. As a result, successive governments devoted attention to the industry's speculative excesses once these began to deter investment. The collapse of Whittaker Wright's empire in 1901 led the state to establish a royal commission, and in 1904 a further commission investigated fraud at the Great Boulder Proprietary Mine, controlled by the London-based American financier, Frank Gardener.[102] The second commission's 1905 report offered a prime opportunity to re-establish confidence in the industry. As agent-general Walter James explained to *The Times*, 'until the real evil [of speculation in London] was recognised at this end and shareholders became less inclined to accept every failure as due to state laws or local management, it appeared impossible to intervene [to restore confidence] with success'.[103] James was pleased that widespread coverage of the report in the press, led to 'wide approval' of the state's 'honesty' in 'expos[ing] the scandals and endeavouring to check them'.[104] He also promised to consult widely about any proposed legislation to avoid the risks of 'a hasty attempt to remove the admitted evils'.[105] On 3 June 1905 Daglish introduced legislation based on the commission's report, seen into law by Daglish's successor, C. H. Rason (not before James urged further delays to ensure that London interests were contacted as an 'act of courtesy').[106]

James and Daglish devoted particular attention to the stockbroker Francis Govett, who (as we saw in Chapter 2) was emerging as a major player in the reconstruction of the industry in close co-operation with Berwick, Moreing and Co and their star engineer, Herbert Hoover. James informed Daglish that Govett was 'in sympathy with us and quite prepared to work fairly with the state authorities'.[107] He explained that 'a London friend' would be 'most useful' if the 'the old excuses for failure, state legislation and labour troubles' again led Western Australia to be blamed for failures of the industry.[108] That year Govett met the premier during a visit to the state and was impressed, assuring the Ivanhoe Gold Mining Company AGM that the state government was, 'uniformly anxious to do whatever might be shown to be in the true interests of the mining industry'.[109] After Daglish's resignation, the new premier, Cornthwaite Hector Rason, failed to reply to one of Govett's letters. James urged Rason to be less tardy as Govett had, 'always shewn

[sic] a decided inclination to help the government when attacked by other mine owners'.[110]

This close attention both to re-establishing confidence in the industry, and to ensuring that mining interests in the City approved of the methods used to this end, highlight the continued importance of British investment in mining to the state. James was convinced that 'our great drawback now is the absence of new mines', and expected, 'two or three big shows would send millions into Western Australia and lead to a much more thorough prospecting'.[111] On one occasion Hoover informed the agent-general that many mines had large financial reserves seeking suitable outlets for investment.[112] Probably with this in mind, Daglish forwarded information regarding the latest mining prospects, for example informing the agent-general in June 1905 that Kalgoorlie was reviving and of promising new discoveries at Southern Cross.[113] In the end a small boom came in 1910 associated with discoveries surrounding the Bullfinch Proprietary Mine.[114] Especially in the straightened circumstances of 1903–1905, Western Australia courted a very different section of the capital market from its eastern counterparts.

In the end, wheat not gold saved the state's economy and finances. Between 1905 and 1911 the area of the state under the plough expanded from 138,000 acres to 1.4 million, and the size of the harvest trebled. Developing agriculture lay at the heart of both public works spending and much other developmental policy.[115] It also laid the foundations of the bitter confrontation between the state and another City interest: the Midland Railway Company of Western Australia already encountered in Chapters 3 and 4. The Midland was an anomaly, one of just two expatriate-owned private railways in the continent.[116] In the second half of the 1880s, a London-based syndicate led by an engineer, John Waddington, had negotiated a concession to construct a line from Perth to Geraldton. Investors were to be attracted by land grants on the model of the CPR and many other North American Railways; the line was granted 3,540,000 acres on condition that it attracted 5,000 European migrants within seven years.[117] When finally floated in 1890, the railway had a total capitalisation of £2,240,000 equities (of which £1 million were to be held in reserve) and £1,000,000 debentures guaranteed by the state. By then the emerging financial problems of eastern Australia and Argentina had soured investors' confidence, and only £500,000 was subscribed – £200,000 from the investing public. Despite continued state aid, in 1895 it went into receivership with its lands largely mortgaged to the government and its creditors.[118] In that year the Western Australian government looked to purchase the line but the company asked too high a price.[119] Thereafter the Midland limped on into the new century. As agricultural development became an increasing priority, the Midland's land grant attracted criticism. The line was accused of holding its acquisitions in anticipation of rising prices and speculative gains rather than releasing them to settlers.[120] In 1903 Walter James' government attempted a second purchase but again found the price too high. Thereafter it introduced a number of regulatory measures: a rail traffic bill controlling freights and other aspects of its operation; a mining bill which affected its rights to mineral finds on its lands; and a subsidised steamer from Perth to Geraldton competing with the line.[121] The company's directors saw these measures as attempts to undermine its revenues, obstruct its attempts at settlement (a counter allegation frequently levelled at the government); and drive down its value.[122] As we saw in Chapters 3 and 4, the company first petitioned the colonial office and then conducted a campaign in the London financial press, accusing the state of violating property rights. The rail traffic bill was dropped in early 1904, possibly a temporary victory against a state looking to borrow in the London capital market.[123] The Midland's secretary later boasted that it had, 'sufficient friends who are powerful enough, and who hold prominent positions in the financial world, to frustrate any attempt to carry a loan through here'.[124]

When James gave way to Daglish in 1904, the new Labor premier revived attempts to purchase the line. After negotiations between a reluctant James (now agent-general) and Mr Mendie of the Midland (described by James as 'a financial Jew as keen as mustard'), a sale was agreed at £1.5 million, which James thought too high.[125] Daglish's commitment to the purchase seems to have originated in a determination to accelerate settlement.[126] He was under considerable pressure from the state's press. The Perth *Morning Herald* thought failure to buy the railway would be 'unpardonable folly'.[127] Moreover demands to revive public works, along with a deficit of £40,000 on current expenditure, had led Daglish back to the capital market.[128] In June 1905 the state floated a £1,400,000 $3\frac{1}{2}$ per cent loan at £96 10s, compared to £102 10s in 1902.[129] The Perth *Sunday Times* thought the loan 'the biggest failure in the history of Australian borrowing'.[130] Having decided to resume borrowing, and given these difficulties, purchasing the Midland would also have silenced a group of vocal critics in London, and (hopefully) have improved the prospects for future loans. In the end a majority of the Western Australian legislative assembly (including Labor's rank and file) agreed with Walter James that the price was too high.[131] On

25 August Daglish resigned after a motion to authorise the purchase was defeated. The Labor proselytiser, W. G. Spence, thought it 'creditable to the Labor Party that they preferred to see a Labor ministry out of office rather than help to benefit a rotten private enterprise, at the expense of taxpayers'.[132] The fall of Western Australia's first Labor government was clearly linked to London finance, and the suspicions of a particular branch of London finance in the state.

Subsequently Daglish's successor, C. H. Rason, dropped proposals to purchase the line. Although James concluded that the Midland's opposition 'did not count for a cent', Rason and his successors sought to maintain a good relationship, for example lifting restrictions on the company's land sales.[133] With a new programme of borrowing underway there was little to be gained by further confrontation. For its part the company began promoting settlement and even described itself as 'Fairy Prince to the Cinderella State of Australia'. Unfortunately, its practice of offering model farms at high prices failed to attract many settlers when land was available at lower cost elsewhere.[134] The Federal Land Tax of 1910 and the construction of a competing line by Scaddan's administration meant that by the eve of the Great War the company's directors and shareholders were again complaining of unfair and (as we saw in Chapter 4) un-British treatment.[135]

The late development of Western Australia relative to its eastern counterparts produced intimate but contrasting connections with the London capital market which were deeply implicated in issues at the heart of political life. The importance of mining capital meant that as well as courting potential bondholders and Robert Nivison, the leaders of successive governments also had their eyes on the mining interests largely ignored by their eastern counterparts. Equally the case of the anomalous Midland Railway Company (politically unpopular but whose power in the City the state seemed reluctant to test) was deeply entwined with the desire to develop the state's agriculture. Close and complex connections existed between Western Australian political life and the City, and their pattern took a very different form to those seen in New South Wales and Victoria. Only in Western Australia was Labor criticised for *opposing* public works!

Conclusion

This chapter has examined the continuing impact of the City on political life in three Australian states in the early years of federation. Unlike in Canada, this took place in the context of a dense and shifting range of views on the necessity of borrowing (and therefore maintaining credit) for development. Yet even in the absence of consensus, the legacy of past borrowing, the pressures of renewals, continued commitments to development, and the political dividends public works could deliver, all kept state politicians' eyes on London. Yet the impact of the City was tempered by and refracted through local political circumstances. Ironically the state most favourably viewed in the City – Victoria – was least dependent due to Melbourne's capital market. In the early 1900s the City approved of the unusual alliance between urban capital and rural interests embodied in Kyabram. However, while the eventual beneficiary, the Victorian premier W. H. Irvine, showed concern for the City's favour, Victoria's popularity in London was an unintended repercussion of political gyrations over which the City had limited purchase. Indeed, this seeming independent guarantor of probity was precisely what a City often acutely aware of its limited political purchase welcomed. Its influence in New South Wales was greater in part because political circumstances there were less benign. There retrenchment was precipitated by declining credit in London and London's views featured heavily in political discourse. Yet the strength of Labor, and the possibility of public works generating support, tempted administrations both to deviate from London's notions of sound finance and labour policy, and to borrow more in the process. Western Australia's different stage and pattern of economic development made the City much more central in political life and also highlighted how particular patterns of investment could produce a very different politics of finance in which gold mining and even, at times, the anomalous Midland Railway played an important part. Ultimately political life in all these states reflected the structural linkages between their economies and the City, forged by British overseas investment. Certainly the degree and extent to which this translated into influence depended on local economic and political circumstances. Nonetheless, the legacy and continued reality of state borrowing in Australia maintained close if differing connections. By contrast, the new federal government had no such legacy, and did not borrow overseas before the War.

7
Influence Stumped? The Commonwealth and the City, 1901–1914

In 1908, New South Wales' ex-premier, Joseph Carruthers gave an interview to *The Financier* while visiting London. In it he stated that 'all the unpopularity accruing to Australia in the eyes of the British investor has arisen from federal acts not state legislation'. The 'commercial and trading classes of England' were harassed by restrictions on trade and shipping. Since these were the classes 'that the Commonwealth would have to appeal to for money', they would respond to 'unpopular legislation in Australia by buttoning up their pockets when asked to subscribe to loans'.[1] Carruthers spoke in the context of an ongoing debate about the Commonwealth taking over the states' debts, something his comments were probably intended to obstruct as part of a broader defence of states' rights.[2] It is unclear that connections between commercial and financial interests were as close as Carruthers implied, and the City often found much to criticise in state politics. However, in the wake of 'reform' in New South Wales and Victoria, criticism in the City did indeed focus on the Commonwealth government. Its expanding budgets caused disquiet, as did the leftward and progressive drift of its social policy, and the growth of the Federal Labour Party (FLP).

In some ways, one might expect that the Commonwealth would prove unresponsive to the City. After all it had no debt in London and did not borrow there before 1914. Yet there were still links to the City. Firstly, although the Commonwealth did not borrow in London prior to 1914, this could not have been anticipated in 1901. At several junctures loans were proposed. Secondly, three-quarters of Commonwealth revenue returned to the states in its early years and their ability to service their debts depended on this revenue. The control of borrowing and the states' debts was itself a central aspect of financial relations between the two tiers of Australian government. Finally, given the positive or negative linkages many continued to make between capital imports and development, borrowing overseas featured in broader debates about the Commonwealth's custodianship of the economy. Some on the right argued it was necessary to pursue policies likely to attract fresh capital; others, especially on the populist left, saw the new tier of government as a vehicle to escape the thraldom of the money power.

This chapter explores the most prominent outworkings of these connections. First it focuses on budgetary policy and the emergence of 'anti-socialism' between 1901 and 1910. It then examines actions of the 1910–1913 Labor government (the first to enjoy a majority in both the Senate and the House of Representatives), particularly on that government's policy of progressive land taxation. It highlights the frequent connections made between Commonwealth politics and London finance. Yet it also shows that these connections were – ultimately – tempered by the complex politics of the early Commonwealth, and by the scepticism widespread on the left as to the value of borrowing in the City. These local political factors curtailed the influence of the City despite the structural connections between federal politics and the City forged by debt and the desire of the states and many businesses to borrow. It is to the politics of the 'emergent Commonwealth' that we now turn.

Three elevens: Federal politics, 1901–1910

In 1901, the new Commonwealth of Australia came into being, with its parliament sitting in Melbourne prior to the construction of a new capital. The new legislature had two houses, the House of Representatives and the Senate. Although these were named after their American counterparts, Australian politics remained closely tied to the Westminster model. Members of the Representatives represented approximately equal populations, leading to a preponderance of members from populous New South Wales and Victoria. Elections were held triennially, initially on the franchises of the individual states. From 1903 the vote was extended to all British subjects over 21 (including women but excluding aborigines).[3] The Senate comprised six senators from every state, with the further franchise requirement that the voter be a state elector. Senate terms ran for six years with half the seats contested at each triennial federal election.[4] Its composition approximately generally reflected that of the parties in the lower house.

Until 1907 tariff policy remained a defining issue in federal political life (as it had been prior to federation in most states).[5] The two largest parties in the new parliament in 1901 were the Protectionists, led by

Table 7.1 House of Representatives Election Results, 1901–1913

	Protectionist/Progressive*			Free Trade/Anti-socialist*		Liberal	Labour			Other	
	Votes	%	Seats	Votes	%	Seats	Votes	%	Seats	Seats	Seats
1901	185,943	43.7	31	151,960	35.7	28	79,736	18.7	14	2	
1903	214,091	29.7	26	223,163	31.0	25	247,774	34.4	23	1	
1906	156,425	16.4	16	363,257	38.2	27	348,711	36.6	26	2	
1910				596,350	45.1	31	660,864	50.0	43		
1913				930,076	49.4	38	840,420	48.7	37	1	

*These parties united in 1909 to form the Liberal Party.
Source: Hughes and Graham, *Handbook of Australian Government and Politics,* pp. 286–310.

Edmund Barton, and the Free Traders, led by George Reid. The chief bone of contention between these groups revolved around whether tariffs should provide protection to Australian industries or act as purely revenue raising devices – an issue only finally resolved in favour of protection with William Lyne's revision of the tariff in 1908.[6] The word party requires careful qualification. The Free Traders (later Anti-Socialists) and the Protectionists (later Progressives) were not tight units. The Protectionists under Barton, and his successor Alfred Deakin (the dominant political figure of the early Commonwealth) encompassed a range of views on social matters from conservatives such as William McLean or John Forrest through to radicals such as H. B. Higgins, Isaac Isaacs, and William Lyne. The Free Traders, while generally more conservative, also possessed a range of views; even their leader George Reid was far from a reactionary on many social issues.[7]

The emergence of the Federal Labor Party in the first decade of the Australian Commonwealth further complicated the political situation. Its performance in the first federal election prevented either of the other two parties from achieving an overall majority. Thereafter it gained in strength and in 1910 Andrew Fisher became the first Australian prime minister to enjoy the support of a majority of representatives and senators. This reflected the continued vigour of Australian populism and rapid unionisation in the first decade of the new century, both of which drew increasing numbers of Australians into the Labor fold.[8] The party was marked off from its political rivals by the rapidity and novelty of its emergence, and to some extent by its social composition. Its opponents also identified and condemned differing political methods. The FLP offered candidates for election on the basis of statements of general principle, agreed at party conferences, along with an elaborate programme (or 'fighting platform') broken down into numerous 'planks'. Labor candidates in theory pledged to support this programme in parliament, and to vote as directed by a caucus of Labor M.P.s.[9] This violation of Burkean conceptions of representation attracted criticism from non-Labor commentators, and was one important dividing line between Labor and socially advanced Protectionists.[10] Yet it is possible to overstate the cohesion of Labor in the early years of federation. Initially the party was divided on the fiscal question (with New South Wales' representatives tending to favour free trade, and Victorians tending to support protection). This division only closed in the mid-1900s when Labor subscribed to 'new protection' (legal measures to ensure that protected industries shared the fruits of tariffs with their workers).[11]

A Labor ministry (led by J. C. Watson) held office in early-1904, and an alliance of Free Traders and conservative Protectionists (the Reid-McLean ministry) between the end of 1904 and early-1905. Excepting these interludes, the government of the early Commonwealth was dominated by the Protectionists led first by Edmund Barton and then by Alfred Deakin, despite a declining vote. Many early commentators ascribed the leftward drift of Commonwealth politics to Labor propping up the Protectionists in exchange for various measures: federal conciliation and arbitration, restrictions on immigration (including from Europe), new protection, and federal old age pensions. Yet this 'support for concessions' model oversimplifies the political forces at work. Labor's bargaining position was weaker than it first appears. While Labor was divided on the tariffs it could not prop up a Protectionist government on this critical issue, and voting in parliament was not always conducted on party lines, making the Protectionist position less vulnerable than might be expected. Labor could only exert a strong influence if a plausible alternative alliance were possible; however, Labor support for the Free Traders was not likely, especially once the latter re-branded themselves 'Anti-socialists' in 1906.[12] While Labor was an important advocate of socially advanced legislation, many Progressives, including Deakin, also genuinely supported such measures, indeed often the initiative lay with them.[13]

Thus, the leftward drift of the early Commonwealth did not, then, result from the capture of the Protectionists by Labor. Rather, while the tariff remained a live issue, it was the product of a situation in which the Protectionist-Labor rapprochement constituted the only viable alliance within federal politics. It functioned because centre and left-leaning Protectionists and Labor's moderate majority shared a vision of the Commonwealth's future. Often this vision involved expanding federal expenditure. The next section examines aspects of the Commonwealth's finances and their links to the City.

Budgets, borrowing, and the states' debts

Few aspects of government policy attracted closer attention in the City than budgetary policy. While confidence in Canada was underpinned by her buoyant revenues, the Commonwealth presented a less edifying picture. Since the constitution required surplus revenues to be returned to the states, the federal government could not run a surplus (something not necessarily appreciated in London).[14] Moreover, the Commonwealth's own expanding expenditure – which outpaced revenues – caused

Table 7.2 Commonwealth Government Finances, 1901–1914 (£000s and per cent)

Year*	Debts	Revenue Total £000s	% Change previous year	Expenditure Total £000s	% Change previous year	Expenditure after payments to states Total £000s	% Change previous year	Commonwealth Capital Formation as a % of expenditure after payments to the states
1901		4,895		4,890		1,296		0.00
1902 $		11,297	15.39	11,301	15.55	3,933	51.74	20.34
1903		12,075	6.89	12,101	7.08	3,901	-0.81	8.20
1904		11,631	-3.68	11,635	-3.85	4,253	9.02	6.11
1905		11,465	-1.43	11,465	-1.46	4,323	1.65	4.63
1906		11,882	3.64	11,884	3.65	4,498	4.05	3.56
1907		12,832	8.00	12,822	7.89	4,977	10.65	6.43
1908		15,018	17.04	14,829	15.65	5,969	19.93	7.71
1909		14,350	-4.45	13,884	-6.37	5,957	-0.20	10.24
1910		15,540	8.29	16,587	19.47	8,091	35.82	7.79
1911	5,897	18,807	21.02	18,270	10.15	12,667	56.56	7.11
1912	6,372	20,547	9.25	21,063	15.29	15,239	20.30	15.09
1913	7,431	21,906	6.61	21,997	4.43	15,877	4.19	17.57
1914	9,395	21,743	-0.74	24,431	11.07	18,148	14.30	22.04

* – The Commonwealth financial year ended on 30 June. The figures 1901 are for six months only.
$ – As the 1901 figures are for six months only, the 1901 figure has been doubled in the first calculation.
Source: Vamplew, Australians: Historical Statistics, G8-14.

greater concern. These are represented in Table 7.2. Until 1908 expenditure and revenue balanced, but overall Commonwealth expenditure was clearly accelerating. In 1901 E. T. Doxat wrote in London that, 'it looks as if the immediate advantages [of federation] are rather doubtful and that instead of a saving in expenses the boot will be on the other foot'.[15] These rising outgoings were not in large part expended on the reproductive works favoured in the City. Only 13 per cent of expenditure after payments to the states was devoted to capital formation between 1901 and 1914, accounting for just 9 per cent of total public capital formation. This may have been a function of the distribution of responsibilities between the federal government and the states, but it still helps explain why questions were asked in the City.[16]

Some contemporaries ascribed these rising costs to an absence of direct pressure from the City. In October 1904, the federal treasurer, George Turner estimated that in the next financial year (1904–1905), federal expenditure would rise by £600,015, or 13 per cent. Contrasting the federal government with the economising administrations in New South Wales and Victoria, the *Sydney Morning Herald* complained that calls for economy there fell on deaf ears since 'the federal departments have born no share of the pressure put upon the states by adverse financial conditions'.[17] However, Commonwealth borrowing in London was not out of the question. Prime Minister Edmund Barton sounded out the City at the 1902 Colonial Conference. According to W. G. Spence, Labor's opposition derailed this 'attempt to perpetuate the mad borrowing craze'.[18] More importantly, Alfred Deakin threatened to resign in protest against this and against proposals to raise MPs' salaries. Deakin thought both moves unjustified in the context of the drought and criticisms of Australian extravagance.[19]

Despite this early aversion to borrowing, Deakin and his fellow Protectionists remained interested in the City. The first Commonwealth treasurer, George Turner, does not seem to have had close links there (although he represented Victoria as premier at the 1897 Jubilee).[20] However, his successor, the former Western Australian premier John Forrest, certainly paid close attention to the Square Mile. As treasurer, Forrest courted the opinions of London financiers and British politicians, probably using contacts made while premier of Western Australia. He sent a copy of his first budget to the former colonial secretary Lord Knutsford, receiving cautious praise.[21] Another London acquaintance applauded his 'endeavours to place the finances of the Commonwealth on a basis which... may... meet the approval of the whole financial community'.[22]

Forrest consulted a wide range of City and Treasury authorities before proposing new federal banking regulations in 1907, and on proposals for a Commonwealth note issue and central bank.[23] Forrest's attention to the City was not unique, nor was his management of the Treasury a great departure from Turner's. As Deakin told readers of the *Morning Post*, 'nothing is changed except the man'.[24]

While no departure occurred in budgetary policy, the second Deakin administration began exploring another proposal that closely bound Australian politics to the City. The states' debts were a central element in financial relations between the two tiers of government. The states were responsible for debt service and held the assets (especially railways) constructed through borrowing. Thus although in 1902 Deakin observed that the constitution left the states 'legally free but financially bound to the chariot wheels of the central government', the debts created a powerful moral claim on federal tariff revenues; a claim only guaranteed by the constitution until 1911.[25] Thus control of the debts affected the balance of power between the two tiers of government. The constitution gave the Commonwealth the right to assume responsibility for debts amassed until 1901. This would, potentially, strengthen the central government. It was also widely believed that combining the states debts would bring economic benefits. According to one prediction in 1905, since the Commonwealth would borrow at 3 per cent while the states borrowed at 3.5 per cent, resulting in an annual saving of £1,350,000 (or 12 per cent of the £11.5 million was transferred from the Commonwealth to the states in 1904–1905).[26]

With these political and economic advantages in mind, Forrest visited London at the end of 1905, consulting widely on the practicalities of debt consolidation.[27] During these discussions it became clear that the anticipated savings – and hence the main politically-neutral attraction of the scheme – depended on the ability of the Commonwealth to borrow more cheaply than the states. Doubt was thrown on this assumption by the weak prices of Australian stocks. Timothy Coghlan seized on this point in a wide ranging report. This emphasised the depressing effect of the 'political predispositions and prejudices' of 'the investing public and their brokers' who distrusted Australia due to the, 'ludicrous but oft repeated assertion that there is a considerable section of the Australian people who favour legislative proposals tending to diminish private property'. He warned that 'so long as Australia seeks further money from the London market, either for her undertakings or for renewing old loans, attention will have to be paid to the opinions of British investors on certain political matters', and concluded that this ought:

> to teach our people the necessity of self-dependence and though Australia is not yet in a position to supply the capital to take up loans... it may direct its energies in that direction, as no country can call itself entirely free that depends upon the population of a far off city.

As a result of the City's 'prejudices', Coghlan doubted the Commonwealth could borrow more cheaply that the states (at least for the time being).[28] Coghlan's report was intended to be submitted jointly with his fellow agents-general. When it was circulated, his Victorian counterpart, J. W. Taverner of Victoria, opposed the inclusion of this political commentary since, 'to admit the right of British investors to question the particular party that may be in power... would be a challenge to self-government under the British flag'.[29] Forrest and Deakin too preferred to ignore Coghlan's warnings (and Coghlan, a closet Deakinite, was further embarrassed when his views were used by the *Sydney Morning Herald* to praise Deakin's Free Trade opponent George Reid's newly launched anti-socialist campaign).[30]

A politically practical scheme proved elusive in the context of uncertainty over the final financial settlement between the states and the Commonwealth.[31] The temporary arrangements transferring customs revenue from the Commonwealth to the states were due to terminate in 1911. Forrest's successor at the Treasury, William Lyne, proposed to offset the loss of revenue to the states by the federal government assuming responsibility for their debts, with an independent body to authorise further borrowing.[32] Such moves were resisted by advocates of states rights. The argument that the City's dislike of the Commonwealth would prevent consolidation achieving savings offered a powerful obstructive argument (precisely because it was external to the struggle between the two tiers of government). It was in this context that Carruthers comments at the start of this chapter were made in 1908.

The debate was further complicated when the Commonwealth again considered borrowing in London. On entering office in May 1909, the newly 'fused' Liberal party (on which more below) resolved to offer Britain funds to construct a dreadnought and to found an Australian navy, both financed by borrowing, and in November 1909 parliament authorised the issue of a £3.5 million loan at 3.5 per cent.[33] Forrest and Deakin opened negotiations with the Bank of England.[34] Attempts to pique investors' interest began in early 1910 when the new high commissioner, George Reid, told the *Financial News* that the navy loan was, 'a noble beginning on the part of Australia [which, by] recognising her obligations to the mother country, must surely recommend it strongly if financial houses can be influenced by such sentiments'.[35] In the event, the patriotism of financiers and investors was never tested. In April 1910 the new majority Labor decided to fund the new fleet through direct taxation.[36]

Before then the spectre of Commonwealth competition, along with the looming termination of the Braddon clause, finally led the federal and state governments to reach a new financial deal. On 18 August 1909, the states accepted 25s per capita from the Commonwealth in perpetuity, with special accommodation for Western Australia. A commission would examine the consolidation of the debts.[37] The Commonwealth only had the right to take over liabilities in existence in January 1901, while more had been amassed or renewed subsequently. Thus the debt consolidation, amongst other aspects of the arrangement, required a change in the constitution. Introducing the necessary legislation, Deakin argued, 'control of the debts of Australia is the axis on which all our financial proposals revolve'.[38] However, the necessary amendment to the constitution was rejected by a referendum coinciding with the 1910 election. Andrew Fisher's Labor government reinstated the terms of the 1909 agreement on a temporary basis, leaving the debts untouched. These arrangements persisted into the late-1920s.[39]

Although the Commonwealth did not borrow in London before 1914, its financial affairs were intricately connected with the City. The possibility of borrowing was explored several times, and non-Labor politicians including Deakin and Forrest paid attention to the City's views (whatever their conservative opponents claimed). The financial relations between the Commonwealth and the states were inseparable from the state debts, again binding the balance of power in the Commonwealth to London. Yet it would be wrong to suggest that the City exerted a strong influence in the struggle between the different tiers of Australian government. Its perceptions mattered because they affected the alleged savings from consolidation, one point of agreement between all concerned. Often these perceptions turned on the fears of the power of Labor, and the Commonwealth's progressive drift. Yet when Deakin introduced the 1909 Constitutional Amendment, it was at the head of a 'fused' Liberal party opposing Labor. The next section explores the City's role in this political reconfiguration.

Anti-socialism and fusion, 1905–1909

As we saw in Chapter 3, the City feared the leftward drift of early Commonwealth politics, which was widely – if wrongly – ascribed to Labor. The Square Mile's views were extensively reported in Australia. We have already seen how, in 1904 the Melbourne *Age's* London correspondent relayed British reactions to Watson's minority Labor government to the paper's readers.[40] Earlier that year an English correspondent conveyed to Forrest his 'alarm' at the federal election result which, seemingly, left Labor holding the balance of power: 'Your Labor men are well meaning, hard working and earnest people, but you will have to teach them economics. The fear is that while they are learning their lessons the vital interests of Australia will suffer severely'.[41]

Opposing the rising tide of 'socialism' became central to the Free Traders as the tariff issue receded; indeed in 1906 George Reid's party were re-named 'Anti-Socialists'. Reid articulated a stark vision of Labor's aims and their possible impact. In March 1905, he warned a Sydney audience:

> There is a vast organization, full of enthusiasm, whose members do not even fight over the fiscal question, which is bent on overturning... the foundations upon which our industrial system and... our national prosperity are based. My grave duty at the present time is to prevent Australia going into socialistic chaos.[42]

While Deakin dismissed such heated rhetoric as an electoral ploy, Reid repeated these fears in equally stark terms in private.[43] In a memorandum during his short term as prime minister, he cautioned the governor-general against 'socialistic movement whose objective is the destruction of all private enterprise'.[44] By 1906, Reid's anti-socialist campaign had resulted in the formation of leagues across the Commonwealth to, 'fight the socialist system which aims at the destruction of rights of private enterprise and property'.[45]

Occasionally Labor's opponents did allude to the need to restore confidence in the City. For example Reid warned that the 'blight of socialism... is destroying public confidence both at home and abroad'.[46] In support of Reid's campaign, the *Sydney Morning Herald* argued that 'if confidence [amongst British investors] is to be restored, it is the caucus itself that must be attacked, and that is the objective of the liberal organizations throughout the Commonwealth in preparation for the general election'.[47] Indeed, the campaign probably fuelled fears in London. As B. R. Wise complained that 'speeches were made by loyal Australians, which did infinite mischief to Australian credit by the lurid colours in which they painted the conditions of the country'.[48] Yet, given the level of criticism in London, it is striking that Reid himself did not lay more and more explicit emphasis on Australia's status as a 'borrowing country' (the contrast with Canadian politics is striking). This may reflect the widespread unpopularity of the 'money power'. The Labor proselytiser, W. G. Spence, described the anti-socialist as 'the most unpatriotic person around', a member of the '"stinking fish" party' that 'denounces the country' and 'barracks for anything the capitalist crowd asks for'.[49] Clearly, basing anti-socialism on London financiers' views risked appearing un-Australian.

Many other Australians wished to see Reid and Deakin to bury their differences and present a united front against Labor. In 1904, Forrest urged Deakin to break his ties with Labor, and in 1907 dissatisfaction with the continuing alliance with Labor led Forrest and four other conservative Protectionists (collectively known as the 'corner') to part ways with Deakin.[50] By then voices beyond the political classes had begun to call for a broad anti-Labor alliance. In 1907 the Melbourne Chamber of Commerce argued that with the tariff question 'settled on, an anti-Labor alliance should be possible'.[51] Some referred to the City while making the case. The *Sydney Morning Herald* urged Australians to take to heart Lord Rothschild's views that tight money across the globe was caused by fears of socialism.[52] Most explicitly, Joseph Carruthers wrote to Deakin urging him to ally with Reid, complaining:

> You federal people don't understand the position because you have no financial troubles but we in the State Govt know that in our financing we discover the real opinion of Australia and the causes which continue to hold her back. The Labour party is a 'bête noir' to the forces that control our affairs...[53]

Thus in part the pressure for fusion was predicated on London's views, views which echoed and bolstered fears on the Australian right.

Alfred Deakin however long resisted such pressures. Partly as a result, Deakin and his allies sought to confront London's fears of Labor. In his *Morning Post* column Deakin attacked 'anti-socialism' for its lack of 'coherent or definable principle' and pointed out that Reid defended public ownership of railways, telegraph lines, and waterworks. Deakin also asserted that Labor's emergence caused 'no profound modifications of the real spirit or substance of our political development'.[54] While attending the 1907 Imperial Conference, the prime minister received a delegation representing British electrical companies operating in Australia to discuss their fears of Labor. He pointed out that Labor's internal divisions and the difficulties it would have in securing a working majority meant that the party was neither as radical nor as strong as the delegation believed.[55] In a way, the City could not be ignored by Deakin and his sympathisers both because of the implications for Australian credit, and because the City's endorsement of anti-socialism might prove politically inconvenient.

In the end, the unification of the Free Traders and Protectionists emerged from shifts within Australian politics. Through the first decade of the Commonwealth support for Deakin's party had been declining. They polled 43.65 per cent of the vote in 1901 but only 16.44 per cent in 1906; at the same time Labor's share rose from 18.72 per cent to 36.64 per cent. This shift had numerous causes. In particular increased unionisation widened Labor's catchment area, and Reid's strident anti-socialism created a polarised politics pitting social reform against property.[56] In this context, the Deakinite 'middle way' became difficult to sustain. the final settlement of the tariff in 1908 removed the main dividing line between the two non-Labor parties.

With its electoral star rising, in November 1908 Labor withdrew support from Deakin and formed a minority government. In May 1909, after protracted negotiations and George Reid's withdrawal from active politics, a 'fused' Liberal party emerged with Deakin at its head, and Reid's successor, the former miner Joseph Cook as deputy (some Progressives, including William Lyne, joined Labor). The new party enjoyed a majority and was restored to office at the end of the month.[57] The 'fusion' enjoyed a brief but active period in office. It arranged the formation of an Australian navy; sought a resolution to the financial relations between the Commonwealth and the states; and established a high commission. Reid was (conveniently) dispatched to the new post to 'refute' Australia's 'slanderers' in Britain.[58]

Soon after his arrival in London, this task became harder. In April 1910 Labor triumphed in the federal elections, securing a majority in both houses of the Australian parliament. Labor's support was bolstered by a number of factors. There was a widespread perception that fusion was unprincipled. Its association with Orange Lodges shifted votes to Labor in New South Wales where the Progressives had often attracted Catholic voters. Labor support also rose in the wake of the industrial disputes at Broken Hill and Newcastle, and the New South Wales premier Wade's unpopular 'coercion acts'.[59] Thus, what reassurance the City gained from a solid anti-socialist bloc was short-lived. Labor controlled Australia.

Labor, land taxation, and the City, 1910–1914

In practice, Fisher's Labor government was far less of a break with the immediate past (although that past had hardly inspired much confidence in London). Fisher espoused a pragmatic and gradualist approach, arguing that, 'No [Labour] party worthy of its name can deny that its objective is socialism, but no socialist with any parliamentary experience can hope to get anything for many years to come – other than practical legislation of a socialist nature'.[60] Labor continued many policies begun under Deakin. It sought to amend the constitution to secure federal conciliation and arbitration and new protection, supported proposals for an Australian navy, and adopted Deakin's financial scheme albeit on a temporary basis.[61] However, it also introduced several new elements which sought to tackle (or to appear to tackle) the monopolies seen by populists as the root cause of the common man's woes including the land monopoly and the money power.

Attention has focused on Fisher's monetary policies. Acts establishing a federal note issue and a central bank were passed in 1910 and 1911. Many of the 'monetary radicals' within the Labor movement (such as Frank Anstey and King O'Malley) had long seen such legislation as a means to combat the money power and escape the economic shackles of the gold standard.[62] The 1910 Labor manifesto declared that, 'Banking is one of the frauds by which capitalism bleeds the people'.[63] In 1908, O'Malley had produced a comprehensive scheme for a currency issuing central bank. In 1911 a Labor-supporting journalist wrote that a such national bank would be 'a weapon with which the people would destroy the tyranny of the money power'.[64] Such ideas aroused fears as Labor moved to introduce the federal notes. Australian banks were to be required to hold a portion of their reserves in the new currency, leading conservative commentators to condemn a raid on 'the people's savings'.[65] Yet in practice the proposals were far from radical. The gold standard was left untouched, and the banks lobbied successfully to modify certain clauses, and thereafter were happy to sacrifice a relatively unprofitable responsibility.[66] There was short-lived disquiet on the London Stock Exchange after an article in the *Sunday Times* alleged that Australian currency would depreciate, an idea quickly dispelled by a quick reply from Coghlan.[67]

The separation of the note issue and the proposal for a federal bank proved the first of a number of dilutions of radical proposals. The proposed Commonwealth Bank soon departed further from O'Malley's vision of an interventionist champion of the people. Instead, in 1911 Fisher's government outlined legislation establishing a conventional bank conducting the Commonwealth's business without broader macroeconomic powers.[68] Even such a bank might have challenged existing interests if, as one Labor activist put it, it were 'worked along socialist lines'.[69] The appointment of Denison Miller, a 52-year-old former assistant general manager of the Bank of New South Wales, made it unlikely that this would happen. The English, Scottish, and Australian Bank's Australian general manager reassured his London board that they had nothing to fear from 'a banker of such wide and varied experience, and free from political control'.[70] Miller lived up to expectations, running the new bank on conventional lines.[71]

In the end, Fisher's approach to the 'banking monopoly' did not violate either the rules of the game or British banking interests. They were largely overlooked in London. This was not the case with another of Labor's measures, the establishment in 1910 of a progressive federal land tax. This generated widespread criticism in the City co-ordinated by the London pastoral lobby – a lobby which, in the 1920s was able to bring the Queensland government to its knees.[72] It led to a revealing confrontation between Labor and the City, between 'Dr Commonwealth', and 'Mr Wrathchild' and John Bull.

Criticisms of the 'land monopoly' had deep roots in Australia. From the early days of settlement, large areas of land had been occupied by a pastoral 'squattocracy'. Their extensive holdings had long been criticised as a transplantation of aristocracy from the old world, obstructing the establishment of an independent yeomanry who would underpin colonial democracy. Radical criticisms of the land monopoly gained traction during the depression of the 1890s, when that monopoly was thought to deprive the lower and lower middle classes of an independent means of support, heightening their economic vulnerability. Radicals and populists drew on and articulated on these frustrations, drawing on British radical traditions, and on the ideas of the American Henry George, who visited Australia in 1890.[73] For example, Frank Anstey's *Monopoly and Democracy* called for a 'perpetual war' against the land monopoly in Victoria.[74] Anstey subsequently turned his fire on the 'money power' and later condemned the undue emphasis placed on land in Labor circles.[75] Concerns about land were not confined to the radical left. B. R. Wise (a Deakinite) called Australia's public lands a 'wasted heritage'.[76] Many others advocated 'closer settlement' on economic grounds, of for strategic reasons.[77]

Two main strategies emerged to 'bust up' or 'burst up' (common phrases) large estates. The first, seen in most states, was to purchase individual properties which were subsequently thrown open to settlement. This strategy generated frustration since its effects were highly localised and land values tended to rise under its influence, leading to accusations that monopolists received ill-gotten gains.[78] The second involved placing progressive taxation on land to reduce the profitability and value of large estates, and possibly to force their sale. In 1891, both the New South Wales Labor Party and the Progressive Political League of Victoria included land taxation on their 'platforms', and by 1909 most state Labor parties advocated progressive land taxation.[79] In 1902 the federal Labor conference passed a motion for federal progressive land taxation, and in 1905 this became a central plank of Labor's 'fighting platform'.[80] Labor's 1906 manifesto declared that 'the most serious obstacle to the expansion and progress of Australia is land monopoly', and again prescribed progressive land taxation, pointing to its success in New Zealand.[81]

As a result, Fisher's minority government (November 1908 to May 1909) placed land taxation at the heart of its programme. In a speech at Gympie in March 1909, Fisher declared that 'land should not be a monopoly in this country', and added that 'absentees' should 'pay more than those actually living in the Commonwealth and helping to develop it by their own brains and muscles'.[82] On 26 May, the governor-general's speech proposed a levy on the unimproved value of all estates over £5,000 rising on a sliding scales from 1d per acre to 4d per acre on estates worth over £50,000 with an additional penny paid by absentee owners.[83] Spence praised this 'first step towards striking a blow at the land monopoly'.[84] Deakin, along with his new ally, Cook, criticised the measure chiefly on the grounds that it would interfere with the finances of the states (most of which already had their own land taxes) and that land policy generally was a matter for the states.[85] The measure was lost when Fisher was ejected from office by Deakin's Liberals.

Land taxation was central to Labor's 1910 election campaign; W. M. Hughes told a Sydney audience that, 'The Labor party's chief plank at this election is to penalize the owners of large estates'.[86] The measure was prominent in the conclusion of Labor's manifesto, which asked Australian voters for 'a majority to break down the land monopoly, develop Australia, give effect to our platform, and administer our laws'.[87] Once in office, Fisher's new government found additional reasons to tax land. Fisher intended to continue Deakin's naval programme, but planned to do so without borrowing – adhering to another Labor pledge. The land tax would supply the necessary revenue. The governor-general's speech justified the measure, 'in view of the urgent necessity of encouraging an influx of suitable migrants... in order to more effectively develop [Australia's] great resources, and defend it against possible invasion'.[88] Fisher introduced the legislation personally. When it finally passed in 1910, it proposed a moderated scale (compared to 1909) of 1d per £1 for a £5,000 estate rising to 3½d for estates with unimproved values of over £75,000, and a flat rate of 1d per £1 in addition for absentees.[89] This meant an estate worth £75,000 would pay £1093.75 per annum, or £1406.25 if owned by absentees (1.5 or 1.8 per cent of its value per year). All property owned by an individual was to be aggregated to prevent paper subdivisions. Urban properties were included to avoid constitutional complications.[90]

The measure had a high potential incidence on large pastoral estates which often yielded low incomes per acre, and singled out absentee investors for particular penalisation. Opposition in Australia initially focused on the violation of the states' rights and hence the constitutionality of the measure (a challenge in the High Court on these grounds was later rejected).[91] However from August opponents began arguing that the tax would deter British investment. One Melbourne estate agent cautioned Fisher that 'national credit, nay national honour, was at stake'. 'If you make the name of Australia synonymous with confiscation', he continued, 'Australia will not be trusted [and] how is this massive continent to be developed and peopled without fresh capital'.[92] Forrest, lobbying on behalf of the Midland Railway Company, also denounced the tax as 'practically a confiscation of its capital'.[93] The Melbourne *Argus* warned 'British capitalists will be less free in lending when the states want money for public requirements. Think of the check to enterprise if the inflow of capital is retarded'.[94] Hughes countered that 'little had been heard from London on the matter'.[95]

This was soon to change. On 18 August, the *Morning Post* published a letter (widely reproduced in Australia) from 'Imperialist' reporting unease at the prospects for British companies holding land in Australia as a result of the tax.[96] In early September, the London Chamber of Commerce protested to George Reid on behalf of trustees who had invested in pastoral property and warned that capital would be directed away from Australia.[97] On 29 September leading members of the pastoral finance companies convened a meeting of the British Australasian Society (which represented investors in companies operating in the antipodes).[98] The society concluded a detailed protest against the tax by claiming that it undermined 'confidence in the good faith of Australian government'.

This would result in a 'distrust' of Australian government stocks, the withdrawal of capital, and would prevent new public and private investment, all of which was 'inimical to the best interests of the Commonwealth'.[99]

Criticism was also heard at some anglo-Australian bank meetings, since the taxation of urban properties and the aggregation of scattered properties for the purposes of valuation meant they faced potentially large payments.[100] However, many banks displayed ambivalence. The general manager of the Union Bank of Australia estimated the bank would have to pay £11,500 per year but predicted, '[as] in New Zealand so in the Commonwealth the growth of business [due to a denser rural population] will leave us a profit sufficient to cover the extra outlay'.[101] As a result of lobbying, the banks obtained the concessions reducing their potential liabilities.[102] The Union Bank's London management were not fully satisfied, however the banks subsequently played a rather half-hearted role in opposing the tax, which the Sydney manager of the Australian Merchantile Land and Finance Company attributed to 'fear of a government National Bank being started'.[103]

While the banks achieved a degree of amelioration, the more fundamental complaints of the pastoralists could not derail a measure central to the Labor programme. Hughes (then acting-prime minister while Fisher sailed to London for the Imperial Conference) met London protests squarely, arguing that New Zealand's land tax had not thwarted development. He dismissed critics '12,000 miles away' and 'apparently blind to the true position' that 'there has never been a period in the history of Australia in which new enterprises have been entered into by greater numbers or involving larger investments of capital'.[104] The bill passed with only minor modifications on 9 November 1910.[105]

The pastoral interests did not consider themselves defeated. The London Chamber of Commerce's Australasian section formed a committee (combining pastoral interests and leading figures in the chamber). In February 1911 it considered 'that some pressure might be brought... by advising British investors not to subscribe to Australian loans', but rejected this course because, 'some members held the view that the Australian government could get their loans taken up locally' (not because such an alliance was considered inherently implausible).[106] Rather than seeking a direct alliance with bondholders, the pastoral interests resolved to lobby Fisher at the 1911 Imperial Conference.[107]

On 13 June the confrontation between London capital and Labor took place.[108] The chamber's deputation placed a carefully choreographed set of concerns before Fisher. They were introduced by Stanley Machin, chairman of the chamber's council, as a representative group of members who wished Fisher to know that, 'The Australian land tax… was viewed with the gravest doubt and misgiving by those interested in Australian land and in Australian investments generally'. He suggested that given Fisher's 'imperial views' he would not wish to, 'interfere with the development of those cordial relations which they all wished to see increased between the mother country and the Commonwealth'. He was followed by Ferdinand Faithfull Begg, who explained that, 'the investor in London was in a position at any moment to divert his investments from any one part of the world practically to any other part'. This meant that, 'Any act on the part of any government in any part of the world in which investors were interested would affect the attitude of those investors, and, consequently, the flow of capital'. Andrew Williamson of the Australian Estates and Mortgage Company, added that undermining confidence in, 'the quarter to which Australia must ultimately look for any further outflow of capital for the development of its resources', would, 'put back the hands of the clock of Australian development, and ultimately tend to produce a feeling of resentment which would be most injurious from the wider and imperial point of view'. W. Capel Slaughter of the Midland Railway Company delivered perhaps the lowest blow: 'if investors in Australian enterprises were to be exposed to that class of legislation they had much better invest their money in Canada, or even a foreign country, where there was greater respect for the rights of capital'. In short, the delegation argued that the tax, by deterring investment and causing capital to flee, would hinder Australian development and sour relations with the mother country.

Fisher replied frostily that the tax was the will of the Australia people, having been 'submitted to [them] at three different elections'. Production, he told them, was increasing greatly, implicitly denying that his actions had retarded growth. The credit of the Commonwealth 'was higher than it had ever been before'. Labor, he continued, did not wish to strike at investors but, 'where those investments came into contact with the public interest the government was in duty bound to give first consideration to the public interest'. As to the British connection, he told the delegation that this was 'not involved at all'. Tempers frayed, and after a brief argument with Williamson as to whether the number of strikes had increased or declined, Fisher accused his adversary of ignorantly attacking Australia.[109]

News of the delegation's frosty reception soon reached the Commonwealth. The *Sydney Morning Herald* criticised Fisher for having 'the temerity to suggest that Australia did not care how much British capital was withdrawn'. 'Few Australians', it claimed, would subscribe to 'such a wild and stupid assertion'.[110] Of course such criticisms can have done Fisher no harm in Labor ranks, especially as the note issue and Commonwealth Bank departed from radical aspirations. The confrontation demonstrated his willingness to confront both the 'money power' and the 'land monopoly' in its headquarters. Opposition continued and after a challenge to the tax in the High Court had failed, a legal rearguard action continued over points of detail, while the pastoralists continued to lobby politicians.[111] However the tax was difficult to overturn. When the Liberals regained office in 1913, Joseph Cook's government did not seek to revoke the measure, perhaps due to the need for revenue and the difficulties of passing a repeal through the Labor-held Senate.[112] Then the need for revenue became more acute with the coming of war in 1914.

The failure of the lobbying depended on two factors. The Commonwealth was not looking to borrow (although the states were) and a close alliance was not forged with those representing British investors in government stocks. Although private investment may have been deterred, it was never clear that credit had slipped, despite E. T. Doxat's claims that no state loan could be floated for less than a nominal value of 4 per cent in the wake of the tax.[113] Moreover, the land tax was a central part of the Labor government's programme, something long advocated by a broad spectrum of Australian opinion, and the revenues were needed for defence spending. Given the benign economic circumstances of 1910, it is hard to see how these political obstacles could have been overcome.

In many respects the Labor administration proved no worse for the City than Deakin's progressives. Yet this moderation emerged more from the internal dynamics of the labour movement than from any direct pressure from (or consideration of) the views of the City – other than lobbying from banks on the details of banking and currency legislation. The land tax however generated one of the most sustained spells of pressure directed at the new federal government from the City. Debates about the tax in Australia revealed that many beyond Labor circles considered British capital to be essential for Australian development. Fisher and Hughes tended to argue that credit had not slipped, not that the views of the City were irrelevant. Even in these inauspicious circumstances strong connections remained between the City and Australian political life.

Conclusion

This chapter has analysed the way in which the City featured in the politics of the emergent Commonwealth. A number of links emerge. There was frequent contact and correspondence between many federal politicians and groups in London. Although the Commonwealth did not actually borrow, the states' debts and proposals to transfer these to the Commonwealth connected the City to the evolution of relations between the two tiers of government. The City also featured more broadly in political discourse, whether as the headquarters of the money power or as a source of capital essential for development. Thus, Australia's past burden of debt and widespread aspirations for a further influx of capital meant that the City was not ignored in debates about Australian budgets, the consolidation of the debts, Reid's anti-socialism and moves to fusions, or Labor's flagship policy of land taxation.

Nonetheless it is hard to see evidence of the City exerting decisive influence. Firstly, while the Commonwealth avoided borrowing directly, its governments were inevitably less immediately dependent on the City's goodwill. As the economy recovered in the 1900s, there were fewer economic strains exerting pressure on federal governments. Moreover, political developments within the Commonwealth constrained influence in a number of ways. The complex three way politics prior to 1909 placed a premium on alliance building. This need not have affected the City, however the scepticism of many in Labor (and some Deakinites) about borrowing meant that there was no consensus in federal politics that maintaining credit was a priority. Reid's Anti-socialists did at times articulate this need, but given the widespread ambivalence towards financiers, even Reid avoided placing this too prominently in his arguments. After fusion in 1909 the same constraints applied to the Liberals and the Labor party. Political complexity and a powerful anti-City groundswell originating in the 1890s limited London's influence. In the absence of serious economic and budgetary pressures, these political constraints proved decisive. Ultimately the City could only watch the leftward drift of Australian politics, hoping internal political dynamics would preserve its interests. The structural links generated by finance permeated but did not determine political life in the early Commonwealth.

Conclusion

This book has reconstructed the ways in which finance inflected politics in Australia and Canada in the decade and a half preceding the Great War. This politics of finance was, ultimately, generated by the processes of economic development prevalent in settler capitalist economies. As these societies absorbed large numbers of migrants they also needed capital. Railways, urban utilities, ports, farms, factories and mines, all had to be constructed to put these new hands to work. This need for capital, as Chapter 1 showed, frequently ran beyond the capacity of local capital markets, especially during booms and when large infrastructure projects were undertaken. Notwithstanding increasing American investment in Canada from 1900 and Edwardian Australia's temporary reliance on local resources, Britain was the lender *par excellence* prior to 1914. This dependence on British financiers drew borrowing groups in settler societies to the Square Mile; the need to manage past debts maintained the resultant bonds.

Nonetheless, no two settler societies were the same and differences in timing and in patterns of political economy shaped connections with London and hence the politics of finance. Chapter 1 highlighted several important contrasts between Australia and Canada, which generated different sets of relationships with the City. Firstly, the Australian state played a central role in the provision of infrastructure, while in Canada private companies (often enjoying state support) undertook this function. One result was that Canada possessed many more businessmen – particularly railway entrepreneurs – who relied on British capital. They were concentrated in the twin peaks of Canadian financial life, the clusters of businesses surrounding the Bank of Montreal and the Toronto-based Canadian Bank of Commerce. Secondly, Australia and Canada (or more accurately eastern Australia, and central and western Canada) were at different stages on their economic cycle. Canada boomed from 1896 to 1913 as population, industry, and agriculture expanded, consuming ever more British capital in the process. Eastern Australia had enjoyed dramatic growth in the 1880s, and, after a deep depression in the 1890s, only slowly underwent 'export rescue' (to use Belich's phrase). Western Australia was a partial exception to the rule – having enjoyed a boom driven by gold mining while the east suffered in the 1890s. From that boom's collapse in 1901, it too sought rescue through mining and wheat exports.[1]

Patterns of borrowing in Britain were shaped by these differences, as Chapters 1 and 2 showed. Australia raised far less capital than Canada between 1896 and 1914; its public sector dominated its borrowings; and only mines attracted significant new British capital. Managing the legacies of past debt loomed larger in relations with the City. At the same time, Canada became the darling of the London capital market and British investment flowed to rapidly expanding sectors: especially transport and the public sector (also investing in infrastructure); but also utilities, land, mines, and industry. Contrasting economic patterns also shaped the networks connecting the City and these two dominions. Booms overseas tended to see new links forged. Many Canadian financiers established connections, or even relocated to London, during this period to tap the capital market. A wide range of banks, stockbrokers, and others vied to handle profitable Canadian issues, with the Bank of Montreal and Canadian Bank of Commerce and their associated institutions together playing a dominant role. Australia by contrast saw relatively stable relations with the City, excepting the mining sector, and in particular the relationship between the states (the leading borrowers past and present) and their financial agents – especially Robert Nivison – were fundamental. The City also housed a number of banks and pastoral finance companies which operated in Australia and had been founded and capitalised prior to the period.

Economic and business patterns established the context in which the politics of finance operated, but the aspects of political economy that concerned financiers and investors in the dominions ('the rules of the game' to use Cain and Hopkins' phrase) shaped the areas of political life which this politics of finance touched. Chapter 3 argued that these rules are best thought of as partly formulated assumptions arising from an underlying concern that risks (other than those inherent in particular categories of business activity) be minimised. In this they were more like the rules observed by social anthropologists than either economists' theorems or simplistic sporting analogies. The Edwardian City broadly wished a host state to maintain: property rights and rights of contract; geopolitical security; monetary stability encompassing the gold standard (currency stability), sound banking and an absence of speculative exuberance; budgetary prudence with a preference for borrowing to fund 'reproductive works' (although tariffs and protection divided the City); high immigration (tied to the idea that young countries had a distinctive pattern of political economy, one which could absolve many economic sins); and the absence or containment of organised, radicalised, and politicised labour. The application and reproduction of these principles took place in public and private discussions of events overseas across the City – discussions fed, facilitated, and broadcast through the press. While broad agreements in principle could emerge, the City was frequently divided over how to apply them and over their relative weight. Arguably only when the City, or those in the City who handled the business of a particular region or sector, could agree would credit be restrained and a sharp signal transmitted overseas. Even so, short of this, the ebbs and flows of stock prices in part recorded the balance of opinion, and if prices declined or threatened to decline there might still be good reasons for borrowers to heed the City's signals.

Often criticism in London originated from the dominions or from interested parties attempting to apply pressure on the dominions. Australian politics in particular was fought out in part in the City. The resultant dangers of weakening credit gave colonial governments good reasons to defend themselves, especially in the London press. As Chapter 4 showed, the Australian agents-general, the Canadian, and from 1910, Australian High Commission, and, leading Canadian bankers, all sought to defend their countries before City audiences. They tended to do so not by challenging the 'rules' themselves but by seeking to alter their application in particular instances. Australia's defenders argued that Australia's Labor party was not extreme and that Australia's economic fundamentals were such that it posed little risk. Thus, as Chapters 3 and 4 argued, these colonial contributions and campaigns by interested parties in London did not write the rules. They attempted to shape the ways in which the City's assumptions, drawn from reflection on and reaction to events across the world, were applied to their particular cases. Indeed, by accepting and re-articulating much of the City's wisdom, these contests perpetuated its rules.

Frequently such contests blended ideas about empire and Britishness with economic fundamentals. This was because, as Chapter 4 showed, various aspects of empire served at times to reassure some in the City of the dominions' financial probity. Unlike Niall Ferguson, few expected much additional security to be derived from the last vestiges of executive and legislative power vested in the British government. However, the empire's strategic umbrella and its legal unification through the Judicial Committee of the Privy Council reassured many investors. Ideas of imperial loyalty also lay behind the British government's one intervention in the capital market on the dominion's behalf in the period covered by this book: the Colonial Stock Act of 1900. These institutions were, however, understood to rest on colonial consent. Hence the confidence they engendered increasingly rested on softer social and cultural factors which were also forces in their own right. The institutions and politics of empire, and its associated culture, promoted the formation of additional linkages between Britain and the dominions intensifying the cultural economy described by Magee and Thompson: as Potter has shown, an imperial press system promoted coverage of the dominions, the politics of empire promoted connections; ex-governors and governors-general could help woo British investors and manage relations with the City; colonial conferences and other imperial business brought politicians to London; while the Congress of Chambers of Commerce of the Empire drew together leading businessmen. The latter showed how business could be imagined in an imperial mould, and the culture of empire and ideas of Britishness also shaped the way some investors thought about investment. Imperialism provided a powerful shared rhetoric of loyalty, (and some investors may have sought to serve the imperial ideal) while ideas of Britishness led favourable presumptions to be made about the trustworthiness of colonial borrowers – as often as not revealed in the bitter comments made when such expectations were not met. None of this led many in the City to disregard a pre-occupation with risk. Rather risk was in part judged through the lens of empire.

The final section of this book explored how London finance affected political life in Edwardian Canada and Australia. Again the contrasting economic patterns outlined in Chapter 1, and the differing connections each dominion possessed in the City, shaped this impact. So too did the different ideas about the desirability of borrowing held by different groups within colonial politics. Chapters 1 and 3 showed that, at least until the eve of the Great War, Canada outshone Australia in the City – raising capital with greater ease and attracting far less criticism. In these relatively benign circumstances, Canada's financial elite played a prominent role in arguing (in public and private) that Canadian national development (especially the construction of transcontinental railways to bind Canada together) depended on borrowing from Britain and that as a result maintaining credit was crucial; most prominent federal politicians and a large number of journalists agreed. Successive Liberal and Conservative governments followed London's opinions and reactions to their actions eagerly. Federal budgets (a key policy area watched closely in the Square Mile) were constructed with the state of the London markets in mind. For the Liberals, improved credit paid political dividends and was used first to reduce expenditure by refloating debt, and then to construct popular new transcontinental railways. Borden's government (which had projects of its own in mind) could not escape the legacies of Laurier's railway policy. Maintaining credit was such a pronounced feature of Canadian political life that attempts were made to draw a divided City into the 1911 reciprocity debate. Similarly, the need to maintain credit was the strongest basis for the bitter criticism of Ontario's publicly-owned hydroelectric policy. In this instance, the policy was too closely tied to provincial development, and (for the federal government) the risks of upsetting Ontarians along with Quebecois commitments to provincial autonomy were too great. Clearly the City did not influence every aspect of Canadian political life, however the fact its views were considered so frequently and thoroughly reveals the pervasive bonds between Canadian politics and London.

Patterns in Australia were very different. One important reason lay in the legacy of the early 1890s. Eastern Australia's long boom turned to bust in 1890, worsened first by the 1893 banking crisis, and the drought around the turn of the century. This economic dislocation – and accompanying retrenchment in the earlier part of the 1890s – meant that a wider range of views on the utility of debt existed across Australian politics. From the 1890s many on the left opposed all borrowing, others wished to embark on public works programmes to alleviate unemployment. Across the rest of the spectrum, a range of views competed in the late 1890s and 1900s – some advocating an end to borrowing overseas, others a temporary halt for political or economic reasons. Only after 1910, and as a now booming economy reached the limits of the local capital market, did the need for imported capital re-assert itself in discourses on political economy. These divisions on the utility of borrowing played out in a political context complicated further by the rise of Labor and federation.

After federation as before, the Australian states remained the main borrowers and it was at state level that the politics of finance was most pronounced. In each though it was different, as our comparison of Victoria, New South Wales, and Western Australia in Chapter 6 showed. At the turn of the century the New South Wales and Victorian governments both borrowed in Britain to alleviate unemployment through public works – a policy criticised in London. Yet, for budgets to be balanced a political alliance had to emerge advocating change. Victoria 'reformed' first and furthest, and prior to the temporary closure of the capital markets by London underwriters in 1903, under the influence of the Kyabram movement (which connected wheat farmers and Melbourne big business) and during the premierships of William Irvine and Thomas Bent. New South Wales took longer and only begun retrenching when the temporary withdrawal of credit forced change. In part the differences between the two lay in specific local political conjunctions: the greater power of Labor in the New South Wales countryside made the urban-rural conjunction seen in Victoria less likely. Western Australia enjoyed very different connections with the capital market, a result of a very different economic trajectory through the nineteenth century. As a result the politics of finance took a rather different form. Public expenditure again was a critical aspect of the debate, but in contrast to the situation further east, pressure was much greater on governments to borrow for public works. Private capital was also sought and the state paid a good deal of attention to the mining section of the capital market, hoping to revive something of the glory days of the 1890s. The states' sensitivity to London opinion, and the power of the (at times countervailing) drive for settlement and development, was seen in the states' periodic clashes with the anomalous Midland Railway Company of Western Australia.

Despite these differences, from 1901 these states all became components of the Australian Commonwealth. The Commonwealth had no debts of its own, and it did not borrow in London prior to 1914. Labor became increasingly powerful in federal politics (to the City's dismay), first in the context of three party politics and then, after 1910, as one of Australia's two major parties. There were connections between Commonwealth politics and the City. It was never certain that the federal government would continue to eschew the capital market (borrowing was proposed in 1902 and 1909). Federal politicians were drawn from the indebted states – at times bringing with them links with, and a concern for opinions in, the City. Financial relations between the states and the federal government, and the connected proposal to transfer the states' debts to the Commonwealth, meant that London finance was deeply entwined with a crucial issue following federation: the balance of power between the two tiers of Australian government. Nonetheless, London's views did not exert a great deal of influence in a complex political context. From 1901 to 1909 the presence of three parties in the federal parliament, none enjoying an overall majority, made coalition building a higher priority than nurturing credit, especially with the Labor party officially opposed to further borrowing. Credit featured less strongly than might be expected in arguments for the fusion of the non-Labor parties in 1909. In part, scepticism about borrowing from the 'money power' made basing the case too explicitly on the need to maintain credit politically risky. In the aftermath of fusion, the Labor government's reforms of banking proved moderate, however its land tax was bitterly criticised in the City. The divisions about the utility of borrowing, and the rise of Labor and the complex political situation that emerged as a result, limited the City's impact in Commonwealth politics in this period. Yet even in these inauspicious circumstances it is possible to see interconnected groups in Australia and London transmitting London opinion into federal politics. In the early Commonwealth the politics of finance was down but not out, its presence and structure discernible even if its influence was curtailed.

The analysis presented here draws on, and refines, both the bodies of literature highlighted at the start. To a certain degree it supports the literature on the British World and networks. The networks spawned by finance should be added to the others which forged dense social and cultural connections between Britain and the dominions. Both in Britain and in Canada and Australia, ideas about finance were intermeshed with ideas about Britishness and empire. More broadly, only through a close attention to the networks linking the City and particular dominions can the points of contact between the City and political life be established. Australia and Canada were both borrowing nations receiving migrants, but only when the patterns of connection are examined do crucial differences – the products of the greater role of the state in Australia, and unparalleled role played by Canada's powerful financial elite – become apparent. Yet as useful (and in recent years as pervasive) as network theory may be, it can only explain so much. The financial networks charted in this book did not leap into existence *sui generis*. They were shaped by the need for additional capital, and by deeper patterns of colonial political economy (its cycles and internal economic structures). Who exactly was connected to whom depended to a great extent on the way these patterns produced particular conjunctions between the City and dominion borrowers. Secondly, and *contra* the emphasis on intercolonial connections in much work on 'imperial networks', the presentation here has been of essentially binary relations between Australia and Canada, and the City. This form was determined by the fact that ultimately the City was the gateway to British (and continental) capital, and as often as not Australians and Canadians were rivals for this largesse. There was not a significant intercolonial politics of finance for the simple reason that the key relationship was between creditor (or rather financier) and debtor, not between debtors. Thirdly, Britishness, and ideas about empire, did occasionally become entwined with ideas about dependence and their political outworkings. Nonetheless this should not be over-emphasised. Whatever impact culture had on the practices of finance, both creditors and debtors were ultimately bound by economic fundamentals and by their conceptualisation in the 'rules of the game'. Cultural economy was ultimately subsumed within political economy. Finally, the networks described in this book did not always promote harmony. Connections with the City could prove controversial. In much writing on the British World there is a danger that the tensions between its various elements have been underplayed.[2] Finance was fundamental to the emergence of the British World but – especially in the Australian case – it proved a disruptive element. Moreover, at their base, financial relations were unequal. A shared Britishness could not imagine away the fact that this was a relationship between creditor and debtor, between a have and have nots.

This is then, in part, a restatement the earlier work of Cain and Hopkins.[3] This book draws on their model of 'informal imperialism', but refines it. In particular it has been suggested that, in order to analyse the repercussions of financial relationships, we need to firmly distinguish two distinct structures within which the politics of finance operated: an economic dependence on British capital; and the City's understandings of political economy – the rules of the game. Equally, it is suggested that, in order to explore the repercussions of financial relationships in colonial politics, we need to explore the understandings of the role of debt in economic development held by different groups in the colonies, and their relative strengths. In some ways this means that the influence of the City could at times have been *more pervasive* than Cain and Hopkins' emphasis on moments of crisis and reconstruction allows. Booming Canada was more sensitive to the City than Australia during recession and 'export rescue' because Canadians virtually all agreed that British capital, and credit in London was fundamental to their economic and national development. Following these refinements, it is clear that finance did create a structural and occasionally influential connection between dominion political life and the City. It is, however, necessary to qualify the misleading equation of that with 'imperialism' or structural 'power'. For Susan Strange the latter implied 'the power to *decide* how things shall be done' (my italics).[4] While the City's views on political economy collectively shaped financial relationships, it was certainly not possible for any group in the City to alter overnight assumptions about political economy that had accumulated over generations. Thus it did not possess a conscious 'power to decide' to be exercised *at will* by any group within its boundaries. It was trapped within its discourses of political economy and reacted reflexively to events overseas, which is not to deny that these reflexes could have profound repercussions for borrowers. The views and assumptions of groups in the City could affect access to capital on good terms, and in rare instances deny it. Such views could not be disregarded as long as borrowing was considered desirable. Thus, little about the politics of finance would make sense if this basic fact of dependence were denied.

In the end then, the politics of finance was underpinned by a structural economic imbalance between British investors and debtor nations whose economic development required (and was widely thought to require) frequent lashings of British capital. The legacy of past borrowing created an ongoing bond as long as the consequences of repudiation, or even weakened credit, were too dire to contemplate. The impact of this dependence, though, depended on creditors' and debtors' conceptions of political economy, and on evolving political dynamics. Financial dependence only touched those matters creditors thought relevant to their interests, and only mattered if debtors thought it in their interest to maintain their creditors' goodwill. Equating structure with power (or thinking too crudely in terms of static 'frameworks') is misleading, but it would be equally misleading to disregard more nuanced notions of structure. By focusing on economic structures and ideas about political economy, and then tracing their political outworkings, this book has shown that financial relations with the Square Mile pervaded many aspects of political life in Edwardian Australia and Canada. It constituted a crucial component of their relations with Britain, one which influenced decision-making at times in decisive ways. Recent analyses have too often been blinded by a search for moments of decisive control, or shied away from an area too closely associated with older debates on imperialism. This has obscured the ways in which the politics of finance pervaded, underpinned, and yet disrupted Britain's relations with the old dominions.

Notes

Introduction

1 E. de Norbury Rogers, *The Australian Case against John Bull & Co* (Sydney, 1905), quotes at pp.12, 14–19, 78, 102–3.
2 Ibid., pp.131–2.
3 For the final parting of ways, see S. Ward, *Australia and the British Embrace: The Demise of the Imperial Ideal* (Carlton South, Vic., 2001).
4 J. Darwin, *The Empire Project: The Rise and Fall of the British World-System, 1830–1970* (Cambridge, 2009), p.177.
5 J. Eddy and D. Schreuder, 'The Context: The Edwardian Empire in Transformation and Decline, 1902–1914', in J. Eddy and D. Schreuder (eds) *The Rise of Colonial Nationalism: Australia, New Zealand, Canada and South Africa First Assert Their Nationalities, 1880–1914* (Sydney, 1988), p.20.
6 P. P. Burroughs, 'Colonial Self-Government', in C. C. Eldridge (ed.) *British Imperialism in the Nineteenth Century* (London, 1984); A. F. Madden, 'Changing Attitudes, Widening Responsibilities, 1895–1914', in E. A. Benians, J. Butler and C. E. Carrington (eds) *Cambridge History of the British Empire* (Cambridge, 1959), iii.398.
7 Dilke included the US in Greater Britain in his earlier writings. See C. W. Dilke, *Greater Britain: A Record of Travel in English-Speaking Countries During 1866 and 1867* (London, 1868); C. W. Dilke, *Problems of Greater Britain* (London, 1890); J. R. Seeley, *The Expansion of England* (London, 1883). For a recent overview, see D. Bell, *The Idea of Greater Britain: Empire and the Future of World Order, 1860–1900* (Princeton, N.J., 2007).
8 G. N. Curzon, *Speeches on India, Delivered by Lord Curzon ... While in England in July–August, 1904* (London, 1904), pp.3–4. Andrew Thompson and Simon Potter have rightly emphasised the importance of the settlement empire. See A. S. Thompson, *Imperial Britain: The Empire in British Politics, c.1880–1932* (London, 2000); S. J. Potter, *News and the British World: The Emergence of an Imperial Press System, 1876–1922* (Oxford, 2003). For a survey of the vast literature on Empire and British culture, see idem, 'Empire, Cultures and Identities in Nineteenth- and Twentieth-Century Britain', *History Compass*, 5, no. 1 (2007).
9 J. D. Startt, *Journalists for Empire: The Imperial Debate in the Edwardian Stately Press, 1903–1913* (New York, 1991), pp.4–5; Eddy and Schreuder, 'The Edwardian Empire', pp.39–50; A. S. Thompson, 'The Language of Imperialism and the Meanings of Empire: Imperial Discourse in British Politics, 1895–1914', *Journal of British Studies*, 36, no. 2 (1997); S. J. Potter, 'Richard Jebb, John S. Ewart and the Round Table, 1898–1926', *English Historical Review*, CXXII, no. 495 (2007).
10 Eddy and Schreuder, 'The Edwardian Empire', 31–2; Thompson, *Imperial Britain*, pp.110–32.
11 F. Crouzet, 'Trade and Empire: The British Experience from the Establishment of Free Trade until the First World War', in B. M. Ratcliffe (ed.) *Great Britain and*

Her World, 1750–1914: Essays in Honour of W. O. Henderson (Manchester, 1975), pp.219–21; W. Schlote, *British Overseas Trade from 1700 to the 1930's* (Oxford, 1952), pp.161–2, Table 20b.

12   A. Thompson and G. Magee, 'A Soft Touch? British Industry, Empire Markets, and the Self-Governing Dominions, c.1870–1914', *Economic History Review*, 56, no. 4 (2003).

13   Of whom 19.3 per cent went to British North America, 17.10 per cent to Australasia and 7.34 per cent to South Africa. See P. J. Cain, 'Economics and Empire: The Metropolitan Context', in A. N. Porter (ed.) *Oxford History of the British Empire*: Vol 3: *The Nineteenth Century* (Oxford, 1999), p.47, Table 2.5.

14   Calculated from L. E. Davis and R. A. Huttenback, *Mammon and the Pursuit of Empire: The Political Economy of British Imperialism, 1860–1912* (Cambridge, 1987), pp.40–1, 48–9, Tables 2.1 and 2.4.

15   J. H. Rose et al., *Cambridge History of the British Empire*, 8 vols (Cambridge, 1929–1959).

16   W. K. Hancock, *Survey of British Commonwealth Affairs:* Volume Two*: Problems of Economic Policy, 1918–1939*, 2 vols (London, 1942), pp.23–7.

17   J. A. Hobson, *Imperialism: A Study* (London, 1905), pp.6–7, 116, 125–8. Marxist writers, often following Hobson, had little specific to say on the dominions. For an overview, see A. Brewer, *Marxist Theories of Imperialism: A Critical Survey* (London, 1990).

18   J. T. Lang, *Why I Fight!* (Sydney, 1934); B. Fitzpatrick, *The British Empire in Australia: An Economic History, 1834–1939* (Melbourne, 1941).

19   On Hobson, see N. Etherington, *Theories of Imperialism: War, Conquest and Capital* (London, 1984), pp.81–2.

20   J. Gallagher and R. Robinson, 'The Imperialism of Free Trade', *Economic History Review*, 6, no. 1 (1953), 5.

21   R. Robinson, 'The Non-European Foundations for European Imperialism: Sketch for a Theory of Collaboration', in R. Owen and B. Sutcliffe (eds) *Studies in the Theory of Imperialism* (London, 1972), p.124; idem, 'The Excentric Idea of Imperialism: With or Without Europe', in W. J. Mommsen and J. Osterhammel (eds) *Imperialism and After: Continuities and Discontinuities* (London, 1986), p.274.

22   Their classic analysed the Scramble for Africa. See R. Robinson, J. Gallagher, and A. Denny, *Africa and the Victorians: The Official Mind of Imperialism* (London, 1961).

23   A. G. Hopkins, 'Back to the Future: From National History to Imperial History', *Past and Present*, 164, no. 1 (1999); P. A. Buckner and R. D. Francis (eds) *Rediscovering the British World* (Calgary, 2005), pp.10–13. The main exceptions were comparative studies of economic development, in part in the context of debates about dependency thesis and 'world systems theory'. The classic is D. Denoon, *Settler Capitalism: The Dynamics of Dependent Development in the Southern Hemisphere* (Oxford, 1983). See also, B. Dyster, 'Argentine and Australian Development Compared', *Past and Present*, no. 84 (1979); D. C. M. Platt and G. Di Tella (eds) *Argentina, Australia and Canada: Studies in Comparative Development 1870–1965* (London, 1985); C. B. Schedvin, 'Staples and Regions of Pax Britannica', *Economic History Review*, 43, no. 4 (1990). For an attempts to apply dependency thesis to various dominions, see P. Cochrane, *Industrial-*

ization and Dependence: Australia's Road to Economic Development 1870–1939
(Brisbane, 1980); P. Ehrensaft and W. Armstrong, 'Dominion Capitalism:
A First Statement', *Australian And New Zealand Journal of Sociology*, 14, no. 3
(1978); H. M. Schwartz, *In the Dominions of Debt: Historical Perspectives on
Dependent Development* (Ithaca, N.Y., 1989).

24 P. A. Buckner and R. D. Francis, 'Introduction', in idem (eds) *Rediscovering
the British World* (Calgary, 2005), p.13. See also C. Bridge and K. Fedorowich
(eds) *The British World: Diaspora, Culture, and Identity* (London, 2003);
P. A. Buckner and R. D. Francis (eds) *Canada and the British World: Culture,
Migration, and Identity* (Vancouver, 2006).

25 See Buckner and Francis, 'Introduction', p.13; J. G. A. Pocock, 'British
History: A Plea for a New Subject', *Journal of Modern History*, 47, no. 4
(1975).

26 C. Bridge and K. Fedorowich, 'Mapping the British World', in idem (eds)
The British World: Diaspora, Culture, and Identity (London, 2003), p.8. Philip
Buckner places the dominions squarely at the heart of the British World.
See Buckner and Francis, 'Introduction', pp.13–16.

27 Bridge and Fedorowich, 'The British World', 7.

28 R. Bright, 'Asian Migration and the British World, 1850–1914', in K. Fedorowich and A. Thompson (eds) *Empire, Identity and Migration in the British World*
(Manchester, forthcoming). On the need to 'decentre' empire, see T. Ballantyne,
'Race and the Webs of Empire', *Journal of Colonialism and Colonial History*, 2,
no. 3 (2001).

29 Although Simon Potter's work is sensitive to business dynamics; see Potter,
News and the British World.

30 J. Belich, *Replenishing the Earth: The Settler Revolution and the Rise of
the Anglo-World, 1783–1939* (Oxford, 2009), pp.180–209. Belich's work is
discussed further in Chapter 2.

31 G. B. Magee and A. S. Thompson, *Empire and Globalisation: Networks of
People, Goods and Capital in the British World, c.1850–1914* (Cambridge,
2010).

32 Belich leaves open the possibility for such an analysis but does not attempt
it himself, see Belich, *Replenishing the Earth*, p.548.

33 Bridge and Fedorowich, 'The British World', pp.2, 7. See also P. Buckner,
'Introduction', in idem (ed.) *Canada and the British Empire* (Oxford, 2008),
p.13; P. Buckner, 'The Creation of the Dominion of Canada, 1860–1901', in
ibid., pp.68–9.

34 Magee and Thompson, *Empire and Globalisation*, p.26.

35 Bridge and Fedorowich, 'The British World', p.8.

36 Z. Laidlaw, *Colonial Connections, 1815–45: Patronage, the Information
Revolution and Colonial Government* (Manchester, 2005); A. Lester, *Imperial
Networks: Creating Identities in Nineteenth Century South Africa and Britain*
(London, 2001).

37 S. J. Potter, 'The Imperial Significance of the Canadian-American Reciprocity
Proposals of 1911', *Historical Journal*, 47, no. 1 (2004).

38 For a similar critique of network theory, see idem, 'Webs, Networks
and Systems: Globalization and the Mass Media in the Nineteenth- and
Twentieth-Century British Empire', *Journal of British Studies*, 46, no. 3
(2007).

39 P. J. Cain and A. G. Hopkins, *British Imperialism, 1688–2000* (Harlow, 2001). For an overview, see A. R. Dilley, 'The Economics of Empire', in S. E. Stockwell (ed.) *The British Empire: Themes and Perspectives* (Oxford, 2008), pp.106–8.

40 Cain and Hopkins, *British Imperialism, 1688–2000*, quotes at pp.208, 240.

41 Ibid., chs 8, 21; A. Smith, *British Businessmen and Canadian Confederation: Constitution-Making in an Era of Anglo-Globalization* (Kingston, 2008); B. Attard, 'From Free-Trade Imperialism to Structural Power: New Zealand and the Capital Market, 1856–68', *Journal of Imperial and Commonwealth History*, 35, no. 4 (2007).

42 Quote from R. V. Kubicek, 'Economic Power at the Periphery: Canada, Australia, and South Africa, 1850–1914', in R. E. Dumett (ed.) *Gentlemanly Capitalism and British Imperialism: The New Debate on Empire* (London, 1999), p.125; J. McAloon, 'Gentlemanly Capitalism and Settler Capitalists: Imperialism, Dependent Development and Colonial Wealth in the South Island of New Zealand', *Australian Economic History Review*, 42, no. 2 (2002). See also, L. E. Davis, 'The Late Nineteenth-Century British Imperialist: Specification, Quantification and Controlled Conjectures', in Dumett (ed.) *Gentlemanly Capitalism*; A. Redish, 'British Financial Imperialism after the First World War', in ibid.

43 P. J. Cain and A. G. Hopkins, 'Afterword: The Theory and Practice of British Imperialism', in ibid., p.204. See also A. G. Hopkins, 'Informal Empire in Argentina: An Alternative View', *Journal of Latin American Studies*, 26, no. 2 (1994), 476–82. For the original usage of these terms, see S. Strange, *States and Markets* (London, 1988), pp.24–41.

44 A. G. Hopkins, 'Gentlemanly Capitalism in New Zealand', *Australian Economic History Review*, 43, no. 3 (2003), 292.

45 Attard, 'Free-Trade Imperialism to Structural Power', 521.

46 A. R. Dilley, '"The Rules of the Game": London Finance, Australia and Canada, c.1900–1914', *Economic History Review*, 63 (2010).

47 Darwin, *Empire Project*, p.xii.

48 Ibid., pp.9–12, chs 13–14.

49 Ibid., p.145.

50 Ibid., p.282.

51 Ibid., pp.162–8.

52 Ward, *Australia and the British Embrace*; idem, 'Sentiment and Self-Interest: The Imperial Idea in Anglo-Australian Commercial Culture', *Australian Historical Studies*, 32 (2001). See also N. Meaney, 'Britishness and Australian Identity: The Problem of Nationalism in Australian History and Historiography', *Australian Historical Studies*, 32, no. April (2001).

53 I am grateful to John Darwin for first suggesting the phrase. I have probably invested it with more significance than he originally intended.

54 There is little reason to suppose that New Zealand or Newfoundland would radically alter the picture presented here. South Africa's history and historiography have had a very different trajectory.

55 J. Darwin, 'A Third British Empire? The Dominion Idea in Imperial Politics', in J. M. Brown and W. R. Louis (eds) *Oxford History of the British Empire: Volume Four: The Twentieth Century* (Oxford, 1999), pp.65–6.

56 See Chapter 2.

57 These points have been helpfully clarified by reading, C. Mahar, R. Harker and C. Wilkes, 'The Basic Theoretical Position', in R. Harker, C. Mahar and C. Wilkes (eds) *An Introduction to the Work of Pierre Bourdieu* (Basingstoke, 1990).

58 For further interrogation, see A. Lester, 'Imperial Circuits and Networks: Geographies of the British Empire', *History Compass*, 4, no. 1 (2006).

59 Denoon, *Settler Capitalism*, e.g. p.93. I am indebted to Bernard Attard for drawing my attention to this aspect of Denoon's work.

60 This is a more fluid conception of structure than that used by Cain and Hopkins. For discussion, and a critique of the equation of structure to a simple 'framework', see A. Giddens, *The Constitution of Society: Outlines of the Theory of Structuration* (Cambridge, 1984), esp. pp.16–25.

Chapter 1   Capital Imports and Economic Development in Two Settler Societies

1 For overviews, see Belich, *Replenishing the Earth*; Schedvin, 'Staples and Regions'; J. Foreman-Peck, *A History of the World Economy: International Economic Relations since 1850* (New York, 1995); B. R. Tomlinson, 'Economics and Empire: The Periphery and the Imperial Economy', in Porter (ed.) *Oxford History of the British Empire*: Vol. 3. For the classic study of British multilateral settlements, see S. B. Saul, *Studies in British Overseas Trade, 1870–1914* (Liverpool, 1960), pp.43–88.

2 Ehrensaft and Armstrong, 'Dominion Capitalism', 354. For a recent study of British ideas about political economy in 'young countries', see E. Rogers, 'The Impact of the New World on Economic and Social Debates in Britain, c.1860–1914' (Ph.D., University of Cambridge, 2008).

3 J. M. Keynes, *Economic Consequences of the Peace* (New York, 1920), pp.9–26, quotes at 12 and 22.

4 Denoon, *Settler Capitalism*. See also D. Denoon, 'Settler Capitalism Unsettled', *New Zealand Journal of History*, 29 (1995).

5 For Innis's own work see for example, H. A. Innis, *The Fur-Trade of Canada* (Toronto, 1927), pp.1–96. See also, C. Berger, *The Writing of Canadian History: Aspects of English-Canadian Historical Writing since 1900* (Toronto, 1976), pp.85–100. For a later economic history of Canada in the staples mould, see W. T. Easterbrook and H. G. J. Aitken, *Canadian Economic History* (Toronto, 1956). For attempts to formalise staples theory, see M. H. Watkins, 'A Staple Theory of Economic Growth', *Canadian Journal of Economics and Political Science*, xxix, no. 2 (1963), esp. 144–52; M. Altman, 'Staple Theory and Export-Led Growth: Constructing Differential Growth', *Australian Economic History Review*, 43, no. 3 (2003). For an Australian application, see J. W. McCarty, 'The Staple Approach in Australian Economic History', *Business Archives and History*, iv, no. 1 (1964); idem, 'Australia as a Region of Recent Settlement in the Nineteenth Century', *Australian Economic History Review*, 13 (1973).

6 Altman, 'Staple Theory', 237.

7 Watkins, 'Staple Theory', esp. 144–52; W. L. Marr and D. G. Paterson, *Canada: An Economic History* (Toronto, 1980).

8   McCarty, 'Australia', 152; J. Fogarty, 'The Comparative Method and Regions of Recent Settlement', *Historical Studies*, 19 (1981), 412–18.
9   K. Norrie, D. Owram and J. C. H. Emery, *A History of the Canadian Economy* (Toronto, 2002), p.xx.
10   Dyster, 'Argentine and Australian Development'; Fogarty, 'Comparative Method'; D. C. M. Platt and G. Di Tella, 'Introduction', in Platt and Tella (eds) *Argentina, Australia and Canada*, pp.16–17. See also the essays by Fogarty, Solberg, and Armstrong in ibid.
11   Belich, *Replenishing the Earth*, pp.187–96.
12   E. J. Chambers and D. F. Gordon, 'Primary Products and Economic Growth: An Empirical Measurement', *Journal of Political Economy*, 74, no. 4 (1966).
13   Norrie, Owram and Emery, *History of the Canadian Economy*, pp.xvii–xxviii.
14   D. Greasley and L. Oxley, 'Segmenting the Contours: Australian Economic Growth 1828–1913', *Australian Economic History Review*, 37, no. 1 (1997); idem, 'A Tale of Two Dominions: Comparing the Macroeconomic Records of Australia and Canada since 1870', *Economic History Review*, 51, no. 2 (1998).
15   A. Offer, *The First World War: An Agrarian Interpretation* (Oxford, 1989), p.137; Altman, 'Staple Theory'. See also Marr and Paterson, *Canada*; W. A. Sinclair, *The Process of Economic Development in Australia* (Melbourne, 1976).
16   Belich, *Replenishing the Earth*, p.196.
17   Belich defines this as population growth of 8.2 per cent per year (or 100 per cent over ten years) from a base of 20,000. See ibid., p.87.
18   Ibid., pp.187–96.
19   Ibid., esp. pp.85–8, 97–8, 183–208.
20   A. Smith, *The Wealth of Nations: Books IV–V* (London, 1999, 1st pub 1776), pp.146–7.
21   For the best overview, see L. E. Davis and R. E. Gallman, *Evolving Financial Markets and International Capital Flows: Britain, the Americas, and Australia, 1870–1914* (Cambridge, 2001). See also I. W. McLean, 'Saving in Settler Economies: Australian and North American Comparisons', *Explorations in Economic History*, 31, no. 4 (1994).
22   Denoon, *Settler Capitalism*, p.68.
23   This figure includes the US but excludes Russia, despite the dramatic settlement of Siberia in the late-nineteenth century. Calculated from W. Woodruff, *Impact of Western Man: A Study of Europe's Role in the World Economy, 1750–1960* (London, 1966), p.106. On the role of London as a conduit for continental savings, see D. C. M. Platt, *Britain's Investment Overseas on the Eve of the First World War* (Basingstoke, 1986), pp.32–4.
24   The following is based on Cain and Hopkins, *British Imperialism, 1688–2000*, pp.207–8; Belich, *Replenishing the Earth*, pp.86–9, 181–208.
25   For an early account, see D. B. Copland, 'Australian Banking and Exchange', *Economic Record*, 1, no. 1 (1925).
26   Offer, *First World War*, p.158.
27   Cain and Hopkins, *British Imperialism, 1688–2000*, pp.208–9, 240.
28   Belich, *Replenishing the Earth*, pp.87, 206–8, 364–405.
29   A. Maddison, *Monitoring the World Economy 1820–1992* (Paris, 1995), p.104.
30   Sinclair, *Process of Economic Development*, pp.9–13; B. Dyster and D. Meredith, *Australia in the International Economy* (Cambridge, 1990), pp.26–7.

31   Graph 2.1 is based on Angus Maddison's statistical compilation, but the original statistics are drawn from the work of Noel Butlin and M. Urquhart. Their calculations of Canadian and Australian national income will be used in the remainder of this chapter. Urquhart's figures have superseded earlier estimates by O. J. Firestone. Butlin's figures have recently been challenged by Bryan Haig. Use of Haig's revised figures would not seriously alter timings presented here, although they do revise down estimates of growth, especially in the 1880s. Maddison argues that Haig has not provided sufficient detail to justify preferring his figures. See A. Maddison, *The World Economy: A Millennial Perspective* (Paris, 2001), pp.72–5; M. C. Urquhart, 'New Estimates of Gross National Product, Canada, 1870–1927: Some Implications for Canadian Development', in S. L. Engerman and R. E. Gallman (eds) *Long-Term Factors in American Economic Growth* (Chicago, 1992); N. G. Butlin, *Australian Domestic Product, Investment, and Foreign Borrowing, 1861–1938/39* (Cambridge, 1962); B. Haig, 'New Estimates of Australian GDP, 1861–1948/49', *Australian Economic History Review*, 41, no. 1 (2001).

32   E. A. Boehm, *Prosperity and Depression in Australia, 1887–1897* (Oxford, 1971), pp.26–31; Sinclair, *Process of Economic Development*, pp.137–8.

33   Denoon, *Settler Capitalism*, pp.52–3; D. Meredith and B. Dyster, *Australia in the Global Economy: Continuity and Change* (Cambridge, 1999), pp.34–40. On relations between urban growth and rural production, see L. Frost, 'The Contribution of the Urban Sector to Australian Economic Development before 1914', *Australian Economic History Review*, 38, no. 1 (1998), 70.

34   G. Blainey, *The Tyranny of Distance: How Distance Shaped Australia's History* (Sydney, 2001), p.257.

35   Davis and Gallman, *Evolving Financial Markets*, pp.548–9.

36   G. Blainey, *The Rush That Never Ended: A History of Australian Mining* (Carlton, Vic., 1994), pp.97–9, 154–5.

37   Sinclair, *Process of Economic Development*, pp.128–9; Boehm, *Prosperity and Depression*, pp.63–6.

38   Dyster and Meredith, *Australia in the International Economy*, pp.28–31; M. Cannon, *The Land of Boomers* (Cambridge, 1966).

39   Belich, *Replenishing the Earth*, pp.358–63.

40   Boehm, *Prosperity and Depression*, pp.210, 220, 231, 254–69; A. Beaver and M. Beaver, 'Henry Gyles Turner', in R. T. Appleyard and C. B. Schedvin (eds) *Australian Financiers: Bibliographical Essays* (Melbourne, 1988), pp.112–13, 118–29.

41   Boehm, *Prosperity and Depression*, pp.128–33.

42   There were several exceptions, especially the Great Southern and Midland Railways in Western Australia, where private construction received various state subsidies. See Blainey, *Tyranny of Distance*, pp.261–2; S. Glynn, 'Private Enterprise and Public Policy: An Australian Land Grant Railway', *University Studies in History*, 4, no. 4 (1966).

43   Butlin, *Australian Domestic Product*, p.183.

44   N. G. Butlin, 'Colonial Socialism', in H. G. J. Aitken (ed.) *The State and Economic Growth* (New York, 1959).

45   J. Hirst, 'Empire, State, Nation', in Schreuder and Ward (eds) *Australia's Empire*, pp.145–7.

46   H. M. Boot, 'Government and the Colonial Economies', *Australian Economic History Review*, 38, no. 1 (1998); Blainey, *Tyranny of Distance*, pp.236–8.

47   Davis and Gallman, *Evolving Financial Markets*, p.483.
48   Schwartz, *In the Dominions of Debt*, p.67; P. Richardson, 'Collins House Financiers: W. L. Baillieu, Lionel Robinson, and Francis Govett', in Appleyard and Schedvin (eds) *Australian Financiers*; idem, 'The Origins and Development of the Collins House Group, 1914–1951', *Australian Economic History Review*, 27 (1987); W. D. Rubinstein, 'The Top-Wealth-Holders of New South Wales, 1817–1939', *Australian Economic History Review*, 20 (1980), 145–6.
49   Sinclair, *Process of Economic Development*, p.127.
50   Winslade has suggested that Butlin overestimated the size of capital formation in the sector. See S. Winslade, 'Wire-Fencing Investment in Eastern Australia, 1858–1914', *Australian Economic History Review*, 34, no. 1 (1994).
51   Meredith and Dyster, *Australia in the Global Economy*, pp.11–12. It was only in the 1920s that an Australian government successfully borrowed outside of London. See, T. Cochrane, *Blockade: The Queensland Loans Affair, 1920 to 1924* (St. Lucia, Qld., Australia, 1989), p.9.
52   G. L. Wood, *Borrowing and Business in Australia* (Oxford, 1930), pp.66–7.
53   Boehm, *Prosperity and Depression*, pp.75–95, 163–79; Dyster and Meredith, *Australia in the International Economy*, pp.44–8.
54   Boehm's definitive account stresses the internal weaknesses of the Australian banking system. Of the classic works of early-twentieth century Australian economic history, T. A. Coghlan also stressed internal causes, while Edward Shann and Brian Fitzpatrick emphasised external factors. See Boehm, *Prosperity and Depression*, pp.217–317; T. A. Coghlan, *Labour and Industry in Australia*, 4 vols (Melbourne, 1969, 1st pub 1918), iii.1633–1660; E. Shann, *An Economic History of Australia* (Cambridge, 1930), pp. 328–48; B. Fitzpatrick, *The British Empire in Australia*, 3rd edn (Melbourne, 1969), pp.253–8.
55   Boehm, *Prosperity and Depression*, pp.312–17.
56   Ibid., p.93; N. G. Butlin, *Investment in Australian Economic Development, 1861–1900* (Cambridge, 1964), p.62; G. Knibbs, *Official Yearbook of the Commonwealth of Australia* (Melbourne, 1909), p.356; Sinclair, *Process of Economic Development*, p.154.
57   It even disrupted the underlying (i.e. non-cyclical) trend in growth per capita. See Greasley and Oxley, 'Segmenting the Contours', 44–51; Greasley and Oxley, 'Tale of Two Dominions', 308.
58   A. R. Hall, *London Capital Market and Australia* (Canberra, 1963), p.205; Coghlan, *Labour and Industry*, iv.2013–17.
59   Blainey, *Rush That Never Ended*, pp.173–92.
60   S. Macintyre, *The Oxford History of Australia: Vol 4: 1901–1942: The Succeeding Age* (Melbourne, 1986), iv.25; Blainey, *Rush That Never Ended*, p.190; R. F. Holder, *Bank of New South Wales: A History*, 2 vols (Sydney 1970), ii.516–17; Sinclair, *Process of Economic Development*, p.153.
61   Sinclair, *Process of Economic Development*, p.168; Hall, *London Capital Market*, pp.180–1; Wood, *Borrowing and Business*, p.108.
62   Sinclair, *Process of Economic Development*, pp.66–7.
63   Macintyre, *Oxford History of Australia*, iv.30; Knibbs, *Official Yearbook, 1909*, p.356.
64   Sinclair, *Process of Economic Development*, p.167; E. Dunsdorfs, *The Australian Wheat-Growing Industry, 1788–1948* (Melbourne, 1956), pp.188–261.

65 Dyster and Meredith, *Australia in the International Economy*, p.41, fig. 43.41.
66 Sinclair, *Process of Economic Development*, p.168; Macintyre, *Oxford History of Australia*, iv.30; Dyster and Meredith, *Australia in the International Economy*, pp.64–5.
67 Sinclair, *Process of Economic* Development, pp.170–2.
68 Ibid., pp.169–71; W.A. Sinclair, 'Capital Formation', in C. Forster (ed.) *Australian Economic Development in the Twentieth Century* (London, 1970), pp.15–19; S. Glynn, 'Government Policy and Agricultural Development: Western Australia, 1900–1930', *Australian Economic History Review*, 7, no. 2 (1967), 133.
69 Schedvin, 'Staples and Regions', 534; K. Norrie and D. Owram, *A History of the Canadian Economy* (Toronto, 1996), Pt 1 and 2. The classic study is Innis, *Fur-Trade*.
70 D. G. Creighton, *The Commercial Empire of the St. Lawrence, 1760–1850* (1937).
71 Norrie and Owram, *History of the Canadian Economy*, pp.377–8; *The Centenary of the Bank of Montreal, 1817–1917* (Montreal, 1917), pp.7–12; Tulchinsky, G., 'The Montreal Business Community, 1837–1852', in D. S. Macmillan (ed.) *Canadian Business History: Selected Studies, 1497–1971* (Toronto, 1972), pp.125–43; idem. *The River Barons: Montreal Businessmen and the Growth of Industry and Transportation, 1837–53* (Toronto, 1977).
72 G. D. Taylor and P. A. Baskerville, *A Concise History of Business in Canada* (Oxford, 1994), pp.154–64; V. Ross, *A History of the Canadian Bank of Commerce*, 3 vols (Toronto, 1922), i.1–18.
73 Tulchinsky, 'Montreal Business Community', p.137.
74 J. Teichman, 'Businessmen and Politics in the Process of Economic Development: Argentina and Canada', *Canadian Journal of Political Science/ Revue canadienne de science politique*, 15, no. 1 (1982), 55; D. C. M. Platt and J. Aldeman, 'London Merchant Bankers in the First Phase of Heavy Borrowing: The Grand Trunk Railway of Canada', *Journal of Imperial and Commonwealth History*, 18 (1990); Norrie and Owram, *History of the Canadian Economy*, pp.224–32.
75 The economic effects of the treaty can be exaggerated. See D. C. Masters, *Reciprocity: 1846–1911* (Ottawa, 1961), pp.5–12; Norrie and Owram, *History of the Canadian Economy*, pp.216–22.
76 On confederation, see G. Martin, *Britain and the Origins of Canadian Confederation, 1837–67* (Basingstoke, 1995); Smith, *British Businessmen*.
77 A. A. Den Otter, *Civilizing the West: The Galts and the Development of Western Canada* (Edmonton, Alta., 1982).
78 Idem., 'Alexander Galt, the 1859 Tariff and Canadian Economic Nationalism', *Canadian Historical Review*, 58 (1982).
79 Norrie and Owram, *History of the Canadian Economy*, pp.312–13.
80 Easterbrook and Aitken, *Canadian Economic History*, p.390; Norrie and Owram, *History of the Canadian Economy*, pp.299–300, 307–9.
81 H. G. J. Aitken, 'Government and Business in Canada: An Interpretation', *Business History Review*, 38, no. 1 (1964), quote at 5.
82 Ibid., 20; Teichman, 'Businessmen and Politics', 55–7.
83 In part as a *quid pro quo*, federal and provincial governments also acted to regulate railways and urban utilities, and very occasionally the later were 'expropriated' (nationalised). See C. Armstrong and H. V. Nelles, *Monopoly's*

Moment: *The Organization and Regulation of Canadian Utilities, 1830–1930* (Philadelphia, 1986).

84 See Chapter 6.

85 For the best account of the Bank of Montreal's and Canadian Bank of Commerce's clusters of financial, industrial, and transportation connections, see C. Armstrong and H. V. Nelles, *Southern Exposure: Canadian Promoters in Latin America and the Caribbean 1896–1930* (Toronto, 1988), pp.1–14. See also, Taylor and Baskerville, *Concise History of Business*, pp.252–3.

86 This approach is exemplified in Easterbrook and Aitken, *Canadian Economic History*, esp. pp.395–405.

87 For summaries, see Urquhart, 'New Estimates', pp.22, 26; M. Altman, 'A Revision of Canadian Economic Growth: 1870–1910 (a Challenge to the Gradualist Interpretation)', *The Canadian Journal of Economics/Revue canadienne d'Economique*, 20, no. 1 (1987), 87. For the classic revisionist analysis, see Chambers and Gordon, 'Primary Products'.

88 Altman's calculations are reproduced in G.P. Marchildon, *Profits and Politics: Beaverbrook and the Gilded Age of Canadian Finance* (Toronto, 1996), p.9, table 1.2. GNP (Gross National Product) excludes the earnings of foreign capital invested in a country: it understates the acceleration in this period as a result.

89 Greasley and Oxley, 'Tale of Two Dominions', 307–8.

90 R. Bothwell, I. M. Drummond and J. English, *Canada, 1900–1945* (Toronto, 1987), pp.62–6; Urquhart, 'New Estimates', p.26, table 22.25.

91 Marr and Paterson, *Canada*, pp.6, 340, 355–63; J. Mouat, *Roaring Days: Rossland's Mines and the History of British Columbia* (Vancouver, 1995); P. Berton, *Klondike; The Last Great Gold Rush: 1896–1899* (Toronto, 1972).

92 Norrie, Owram and Emery, *History of the Canadian Economy*, p.210.

93 Taylor and Baskerville, *Concise History of Business*, pp.279–82.

94 R. C. MacIvor, *Canadian Monetary, Banking and Fiscal Development* (Toronto, 1958), p.72; Norrie, Owram and Emery, *History of the Canadian Economy*, p.244; Davis and Gallman, *Evolving Financial Markets*, p.415.

95 F. H. Leacy, *Historical Statistics of Canada* (Ottawa, 1983), series G200-202.

96 J. Viner, *Canada's Balance of International Indebtedness, 1900–1913* (Cambridge, 1924), p.134; Davis and Gallman, *Evolving Financial Markets*, pp.247–8; H. G. J. Aitken, *American Capital and Canadian Resources* (Harvard, 1961), pp.34–7.

Chapter 2 Australian and Canadian Borrowing in the Edwardian City

1 W. C. Van Antwerp, quoted in R. C. Michie, *The City of London: Continuity and Change, 1850–1990* (London, 1992), p.110.

2 There are a number of competing explanations for this striking phenomenon emphasising either the 'pull' of higher returns overseas, or the 'pushes' created by excessive saving or biases in the capital market. See P. L. Cottrell, *British Overseas Investment in the Nineteenth Century* (London, 1975), pp.47–55; M. Edelstein, *Overseas Investment in the Age of High Imperialism: The United Kingdom, 1850–1914* (London, 1982), pp.4–8; idem, 'Foreign Investment

and Accumulation 1860–1914', in R. Floud and D. N. McCloskey (eds) *The Economic History of Britain since 1700* (Cambridge, 1994), pp.173–4.

3   Davis and Huttenback, *Mammon and the Pursuit of Empire*, p.38.

4   The graph uses the 'indirect method' to estimate capital export, pioneered by C. K. Hobson, and adapted by Imlah. See C. K. Hobson, *Export of Capital* (London, 1914), pp.164–206; A. H. Imlah, *Economic Elements in the Pax Britannica: Studies in British Foreign Trade in the Nineteenth Century* (USA, 1969), pp.42–82; C. H. Feinstein, *National Income, Expenditure and Output of the United Kingdom, 1855–1965* (Cambridge, 1972), pp.110–28.

5   Edelstein, *Overseas Investment*, pp.3, 29; Edelstein, 'Foreign Investment and Accumulation 1860–1914', 176–92; Cottrell, *British Overseas Investment*, pp.11–15, 47–67; Hall, *London Capital Market*, pp.8–15.

6   These graphs are based on the direct estimates of the gross annual flow of British capital overseas compiled by Irvine Stone, based on works by Jenks and Simon. Little distinguishes this data from the estimates offered by Davis and Huttenback, and Davis and Gallman, however Stone's data are annual and disaggregated to a greater degree by industrial sector. For further discussion, see Davis and Huttenback, *Mammon and the Pursuit of Empire*, p.36; I. Stone, *The Global Export of Capital from Great Britain, 1865–1914: A Statistical Survey* (Basingstoke, 1999), p.5. Aggregated flows ought to be distinguished from investment stocks (the portfolio of securities held at any one time). Since debts may be repaid, repudiated, or repatriated, the stock at a particular juncture will tend to be less than the sum of the flows. Stocks tend to be harder to estimate as a result. See G. Paish, 'Great Britain's Capital Investments in Other Lands', *Journal of the Royal Statistical Society*, 72, no. 3 (1909); idem., 'Great Britain's Capital Investments in Individual Colonial and Foreign Countries', *Journal of the Royal Statistical Society*, 74, no. 2 (1911); idem., 'The Export of Capital and the Cost of Living', *Statist Supplement*, Feb 1914; Platt, *Britain's Investment Overseas*; C. Feinstein, 'Britain's Overseas Investments in 1913', *Economic History Review*, 43, no. 2 (1990).

7   For example, many Edwardian aristocrats purchased land in western Canada in response to Lloyd George's 1909 budget. See A. Offer, 'Empire and Social Reform: British Overseas Investment and Domestic Politics, 1908–1914', *Historical Journal*, 26, no. 1 (1983), 123–4.

8   Hall, *London Capital Market*, pp.115–19; J. D. Bailey, 'Australian Borrowing in Scotland in the Nineteenth Century', *Economic History Review*, 12, no. 2 (1959), 268.

9   R. C. Michie, *The London Stock Exchange: A History* (Oxford, 1999), pp.117–28; Platt, *Britain's Investment Overseas*, pp.32–5.

10 Michie, *City of London*, pp.34–62; D. Kynaston, *The City of London:* volume II: *Golden Years, 1890–1914*, 4 vols (London, 1994), ii.17–20.

11 Michie, *City of London*, pp.38–40.

12 S. D. Chapman, *The Rise of Merchant Banking* (London, 1984), pp.105–24.

13 Michie, *City of London*, pp.69–74; Kynaston, *City of London*, ii.8–10; W. Bagehot, *Lombard Street: A Description of the Money Market* (London, 1873), pp.8–9, 281–4.

14 Michie, *City of London*, pp.73–5.

15 Ibid., p.78; G. D. Ingall and G. Withers, *The Stock Exchange* (London, 1904), pp.78, 152; Michie, *London Stock Exchange*, p.134.

16   Y. Cassis, 'British Finance: Success and Controversy', in idem (ed.) *Finance and Financiers in European History, 1880–1960* (Cambridge, 1992), pp.1–2; G. R. Searle, *Corruption in British Politics: 1895–1930* (Oxford, 1987), p.10; H. Lowenfeld, *All About Investment* (London, 1909), pp.170–5; Ingall and Withers, *Stock Exchange*, pp.99–106; H. Withers, *International Finance* (London, 1916), pp.99–106; P. Tovey, *Prospectuses: How to Read and Understand Them* (London, 1920), pp.1–6.

17   Chapman, *Rise of Merchant Banking*, pp.82–100.

18   Y. Cassis, 'London Banks and International Finance, 1890–1914', in Y. Cassis and E. Bussière (eds) *London and Paris as International Financial Centres in the Twentieth Century* (Oxford, 2005), pp.107–10. On Cassel, see P. Thane, 'Financiers and the British State: The Case of Sir Ernest Cassel', *Business History*, 28, no. 1 (1986).

19   M. Wilkins, 'The Free-Standing Company, 1870–1914: An Important Type of British Foreign Direct Investment', *Economic History Review*, 41, no. 2 (1988), 265–9.

20   Lowenfeld, *All About Investment*, p.176.

21   Ingall and Withers, *Stock Exchange*, pp.78–84, 152.

22   Withers, *International Finance*, p.147.

23   Hall, *London Capital Market*, pp.75–83; Chapman, *Rise of Merchant Banking*, pp.88–9, 100–1; Lowenfeld, *All About Investment*, pp.176–9; R. P. T. Davenport-Hines, 'Lord Glendyne', in Appleyard and Schedvin (eds) *Australian Financiers*.

24   R. C. Michie, 'The Social Web of Investment in the Nineteenth Century', *Revue Internationale d'Histoire de la Banque*, 18 (1979).

25   Tovey, *Prospectuses*, p.1.

26   Beaverbrook Papers BBK/A/217: Benn to Aitken, 16 Mar. 1911.

27   UBA Papers U/119/42/3731/2: London Manager to General Manager, 26 May 1905.

28   Elites comprised 'financiers, military, "misc elite", and peers and gents'. See Davis and Huttenback, *Mammon and the Pursuit of Empire*, pp.195–217.

29   J. D. Bailey, 'Australian Company Borrowing, 1870–1893: A Study in British Overseas Investment' (D.Phil, University of Oxford, 1957), pp.57–68.

30   Davis and Huttenback acknowledge the latter point, suggesting that addresses in EC were particularly likely to fall into this category (40.7 per cent of their sample was held in London, all but 10 per cent in EC). See Davis and Huttenback, *Mammon and the Pursuit of Empire*, pp.197, 209. On aristocrats using their London addresses (unlikely to have been concentrated in EC), see D. Cannadine, *The Decline and Fall of the British Aristocracy* (New Haven, Conn., 1990), pp.9–10.

31   Lowenfeld, *All About Investment*, pp.29–32.

32   Financial writers such as Lowenfeld gave detailed advice on the different classes of investment most appropriate to different categories of investor. See ibid., pp.32–47. Moreover the fragmented way in which financiers tapped investors makes a 'typical' pattern of investment unlikely, a point discussed below.

33   C. A. E. Goodhart, *The Business of Banking, 1891–1914* (London, 1972), pp.129–31; R. S. Sayers, *Lloyds Bank in the History of English Banking* (Oxford, 1957), pp.188–9; Cottrell, *British Overseas Investment*, p.28.

34 S. R. O. NSW, Kingswood 19/8959/CGS-14335: Coghlan to Premier, 9 Feb.1909.
35 Vict. P. R. O., 1225/8/7R-1308: Dobson to Premier, 27 June 1903; Premier to Dobson, 3 July 1903.
36 Lowenfeld, *All About Investment*, p.9, 159; J. A. Hobson, *The Evolution of Modern Capitalism* (London, 1906), pp.241–3.
37 In 1909 it did issue short-term treasury bills in Australia. See S.L.W.A, 4309A/6: Crowley, *Sir John Forrest*, ii.747–8. Proposals to borrow in London are discussed in Chapter 7.
38 Ibid. ii.7–10.
39 B. E. Mansfield, 'O'Sullivan, Edward William (1846–1910)', *Australian Dictionary of Biography*, 11 (1988).
40 This total broke down: New South Wales, £67,361,246; Victoria, £50,071,275l; Queensland, £30,416,514; South Australia, £26,448,805; Western Australia, £12,709,430; Tasmania, £8,511,005. See Knibbs, *Official Yearbook*, 1908, p.728.
41 T. A. Coghlan, *A Statistical Account of the Seven Colonies of Australasia, 1901–2* (Sydney, 1902), p.1023.
42 Ibid., pp.1021–2. For example, pending renewals alarmed the New South Wales Government in 1904; see S. R. O. NSW, Kingswood 3/3159/CGS: 'Loans Maturing during Years 1903–1912', 23 Mar. 1904.
43 I. M. Drummond, 'Government Securities on Colonial New Issue Markets: Australia and Canada, 1895–1914', *Yale Economic Essays*, 1 (1961), esp. 142–3.
44 Hall, *London Capital Market*, p.104.
45 Coghlan, *Statistical Account*, pp.1024–5; N. Hicks, 'Coghlan, Sir Timothy Augustine (1855–1926)', *Australian Dictionary of Biography*, 8 (1981).
46 Davenport-Hines, 'Lord Glendyne', pp.41–4; R. S. Gilbert, 'London Financial Intermediaries and Australian Overseas Borrowing, 1900–29', *Australian Economic History Review*, 11 (1971).
47 Carruthers Papers, 1638/55/23/136-40: Sir Harry Rawson, 'Memorandum re NSW finances in London', Jan. 1906; Vict. P. R. O., 1225/9/10R-801 (Treasury Loan Files): Agent-General to Treasurer, 16 July 1909.
48 Vict. P. R. O., 1225/7/2R-1473: Agent-General to Peacock, 6 Dec. 1901; Coghlan Papers, MS 6335/14/213: Coghlan to Carruthers, 21 Sept. 1906.
49 Vict. P. R. O., 1225/8/7R-1308: Gillespie to Shields, 12 May 1903; Dobson to Irvine, 27 May 1903.
50 UBA Papers U/103/75/4422/6, 4425, 4435/2: General Manager to London Manager, 10, 16 Feb., 2 Mar. 1910; UBA Papers U/119/46/4297/9: London Manager to General Manager, 24 Mar. 1910.
51 UBA Papers U/119/45/4209: Coghlan to Willis, 26 Apr. 1909, Willis to Coghlan, 26 Apr. 1909; both enclosed with London Manager to General Manager, 30 Apr. 1909.
52 *The Economist*, 27 Sept. 1913, p.606; ibid., 15 Nov. 1913, p.1076.
53 Hall, *London Capital Market*, p.106; Davenport-Hines, 'Lord Glendyne', p.201. S. R. O. NSW, Kingswood 19/8959/CGS-14335: Coghlan to Premier, 11, 23 Sept., 23 Oct. 1908.
54 Sydney *Bulletin*, 6 Aug. 1908 quoted in Davenport-Hines, 'Lord Glendyne', p.201.
55 Hall, *London Capital Market*, p.94, Table 16.

56 R. T. Appleyard and M. Davies, 'Financiers of the Western Australian Goldfields', in Appleyard and Schedvin (eds) *Australian Financiers*, pp.165–73; J. W. McCarty, 'British Investment in Western Australian Gold Mining', *University Studies in History*, 4, no. 1 (1961–2), 16–21; Blainey, *Rush That Never Ended*, pp.174–201.

57 Kynaston, *City of London*, ii.185–6, 218–89; Blainey, *Rush That Never Ended*, p.201.

58 Richardson, 'Collins House Financiers', p.237.

59 Ibid., pp.229–43; Blainey, *Rush That Never Ended*, pp.255–6, 267–9.

60 See Table 2.5.

61 Hall, *London Capital Market*, pp.109–12; Boehm, *Prosperity and Depression*, pp.161–3.

62 S. P. Ville, *The Rural Entrepreneurs: A History of the Stock and Station Agent Industry in Australia and New Zealand* (Cambridge, 2000); N. G. Butlin and A. Barnard, 'Pastoral Finance and Capital Requirements, 1860–1960', in A. Barnard (ed.) *The Simple Fleece: Studies in the Australian Wool Industry* (Melbourne, 1962).

63 Schwartz, *In the Dominions of Debt*, pp.65–7.

64 Ville, *Rural Entrepreneurs*, pp.18–45; J. D. Bailey, *A Hundred Years of Pastoral Banking: A History of the Australian Mercantile Land & Finance Company, 1863–1963* (Oxford, 1966), ch. 1.

65 M. J. Daunton, 'Family and Firm in the City of London in the Nineteenth Century: The Case of F. G. Dalgety', *Historical Research*, 62 (1989).

66 A. S. J. Baster, *The Imperial Banks* (London, 1929), pp.2–4; G. Jones, *British Multinational Banking* (Oxford, 1993), ch. 2.

67 Boehm, *Prosperity and Depression*, pp.210–13, 219–31, 271–317; Hall, *London Capital Market*, pp.108, 115–16.

68 Two of its directors, W. Capel Slaughter and Andrew Williamson joined a London Chamber of Commerce delegation to protest to the Australian Prime Minister Andrew Fisher in 1911 against the 1910 federal land tax. See *CCJ*, July 1911; *Directory of Directors* (1911).

69 *SEYB* (1915).

70 Ibid., pp.30–1, 59, 91, 99, 112–13, 119, 123–5, 141, 143, 147, 163–4, 167, 174–5, 235, 287, 621–2, 885, 1291, 1373–4, 1620, 1973, 2085; J. Viner, *Canada's Balance of International Indebtedness, 1900–1913* (Cambridge, 1924), p.118.

71 *Centenary of the Bank of Montreal*, p.49; M. Denison, *Canada's First Bank: A History of the Bank of Montreal*, 2 vols. (Montreal, 1966), ii.61.

72 Davenport-Hines, 'Lord Glendyne', p.191.

73 *SEYB* (1915) pp.30–1.

74 Laurier Papers MG-26-G/c873/561/162035: Taylor to Clouston, 10 Feb. 1909 enclosed with Clouston to Laurier, 6 May 1909.

75 Ross, *History of the Canadian Bank of Commerce*, ii.61.

76 *SEYB* (1915), pp.23, 92, 141, 167, 226, 1335, 2043.

77 Walker Papers 1/A/9/49: Jones to Walker, 3 Nov. 1911.

78 Walker Papers, 1/A/7/19: Jones to Walker, 11 Oct. 1906; I.M. Drummond, 'Capital Markets in Australia and Canada, 1895–1914: A Study in Colonial Economic History' (Ph.D., Yale University, 1959), p.144; G.P. Marchildon, '"Hands across the Water": Canadian Industrial Financiers in the City of London, 1905–20', *Business History*, 34, no. 3 (1992), 71–4.

79 His annual speeches to the bank's AGM were widely published in London and he was consulted by journalists and others upon Canadian finances. See for example, Walker Papers, 1/A/7/13: Jones to Walker, 13 Feb. 1906; Ibid., 1/A/11/17: Lefroy to Walker, 9 June 1906; Ibid., 1/A/8/32: Just to Walker, 16 Feb. 1910.

80 *SEYB* (1915), pp.59–60, 157–8, 225, 228, 571, 1826, 1915, 1928–9, 2063–4, 2175.

81 Sayers, *Lloyds Bank*, pp.215–16; T. D. Regehr, *The Canadian Northern Railway: Pioneer Road of the Northern Prairies, 1895–1918* (Toronto, 1976), pp.339, 357.

82 *SEYB* (1915), pp.113, 141, 173, 237, 570, 604–5, 1154, 1303–4, 1361, 1362, 1373, 1658, 1723, 1754–5, 1775, 2099, 2125.

83 Ibid., pp.164, 906.

84 D. A. Farnie, 'Wilson, Sir Charles Rivers (1831–1916)', *Oxford Dictionary of National Biography* (Oxford, 2004).

85 *SEYB* (1915), p.287; Hays Letterbooks, MG30/a18/2, p.719: Rivers-Wilson to Hays, 16 Nov. 1904; A. W. Currie, *The Grand Trunk Railway of Canada* (Toronto, 1957), p.371.

86 *SEYB* (1915), pp.223–7; Regehr, *Canadian Northern Railway*, pp.215–16; D. B. Hanna, *Trains of Recollection* (Toronto, 1924), pp.191–203.

87 F. Williams-Taylor, 'Canadian Loans in London', *United Empire*, 3, no. 12 (1912), 987.

88 *SEYB* (1915), p.230; Taylor and Baskerville, *Concise History of Business*, pp.236, 237–47; W. K. Lamb, *History of the Canadian Pacific Railway* (New York, 1977), pp.275–7; H. A. Innis, *A History of the Canadian Pacific Railway* (Toronto, 1923) pp.270–86.

89 Innis, *Canadian Pacific Railway*, pp.283–4.

90 F. W. Field, *Capital Investments in Canada* (Montreal, 1914), p.124. See also Innis, *Canadian Pacific Railway*, p.276.

91 Field, *Capital Investments in Canada*, p.126.

92 Currie, *Grand Trunk Railway*, pp.430–1. The Association sought to safeguard the interests of English investors in North America; see *Canada*, 23 Oct. 1909; *SEYB* (1914), p.1855.

93 Maurice Wright, 'Welby, Reginald Earle, Baron Welby (1832–1915)', *Oxford Dictionary of National Biography* (Oxford, 2004).

94 Currie, *Grand Trunk Railway*, pp.394–415.

95 *SEYB* (1915), pp.286–8.

96 R. B. Fleming, *The Railway King of Canada: Sir William Mackenzie, 1849–1923* (Vancouver, 1991), pp.23–89; Armstrong and Nelles, *Southern Exposure*, ch. 2.

97 Regehr, *Canadian Northern Railway*, pp.102–4; R. T. Naylor, *The History of Canadian Business, 1867–1914*, 2 vols (Toronto, 1975), i.290; P. Roy, 'The Fine Arts of Lobbying and Persuading: The Case of the B.C. Electric Railway, 1897–1917', in Macmillan (ed.) *Canadian Business* History, p.239; idem, 'The British Columbia Electric Railway, 1897–1929: A British Company in British Columbia' (Ph.D., University of British Columbia, 1970), pp.44–85; Armstrong and Nelles, *Monopoly's Moment*, p.117.

98 *SEYB* (1915), p.695. Of the 19 companies in which the Trust held shares, Mackenzie was director of 12. See White Papers, MG 27-II-D-18/2/10(a)/ 725800: *Annual Report of British Empire Trust Co*, 30 Apr. 1913; *Directory of Directors* (1915) p.674.

99 NAC, RG 30/1437/2: Minutes of CNR Board Meeting, 5 Jan. 1907; *SEYB* (1915), p.277; White Papers, MG 27-II-D-18/2/10(b)/73000: Wood to White, 3 July 1914; *Directory of Directors* (1915), pp.525, 674

100 NAC, RG 30/1439/82: Minutes of CNR Meeting, 23 Aug. 1909.

101 Hanna, *Trains of Recollection*, p.244.

102 *SEYB* (1915), pp.226–7.

103 Mouat, *Roaring Days*, pp.52–63.

104 *SEYB* (1915), pp.2034–5; J. Mouat, *Metal Mining in Canada* (Ottawa, 2000), pp.1–3, 32–3.

105 K. Burk, 'Grenfell, A. M.', in D. J. Jeremy (ed.) *Dictionary of Business Biography: A Biographical Dictionary of Business Leaders Active in Britain in the Period 1860–1980* (London, 1984); *CAR* (1907), p.414.

106 Strathcona Papers MG 25/C/2: Grenfell to Strathcona, 2 Nov. 1906.

107 Michie, 'Social Web', 165–8. Whitney Papers, F 5/MU 3125: Lefroy to Whitney, 21 Aug. 1908. Lefroy edited *Canada*.

108 Beaverbrook Papers, BBK/A/167: Aitken to Scrigemeour, 22 Jan. 1909. See also *CAR* (1912), p.156; *The Times*, 10 Nov. 1910, p.8.

109 Strathcona Papers MG25/C.2: 'High Court of Justice, No 00218 of 1914. Matter of Companies Consolidation Act of 1908 and the Canadian Agency', p.8.

110 Burk, 'Grenfell, A. M.', p.651.

111 Ibid; Kynaston, *City of London*, ii.592. *The Economist*, 6, 27 June 1914, pp.427, 1538.

112 Marchildon, *Profits and Politics*, pp.139–40.

113 R. C. Michie, 'Dunn, Fischer and Co. in the City of London', *Business History*, 30, no. 2 (1988).

114 G. P. Marchildon, '"Hands across the Water": Canadian Industrial Financiers in the City of London, 1905–20', Ibid., 34, no. 3 (1992).

115 On 'bridgeheads', see J. Darwin, 'Imperialism and the Victorians: The Dynamics of Territorial Expansion', *English Historical Review*, 112, no. 447 (1997), 629.

Chapter 3   The Rules of the Game

1 A more concise version of this chapter can be found in, Dilley, 'Rules of the Game'.

2 Robinson, Gallagher, and Denny, *Africa and the Victorians*, ch. 1. See also, Darwin, 'Imperialism and the Victorians', 614–17.

3 Keynes had Lord Rothschild, Sir John Lubbock and Sir Samuel Montague in mind. See J. M. Keynes, *Indian Currency and Finance* (London, 1913), p.24.

4 S. G. Checkland, 'The Mind of the City, 1870–1914', *Oxford Economic Papers*, 9, no. 3 (1957), 278.

5 Tovey, *Prospectuses*, pp.2–4; Lowenfeld, *All About Investment*, pp.32–47; R. J. A. Skidelsky, *John Maynard Keynes: Vol. 1: Hope Betrayed, 1883–1920*, 3 vols (London, 1983), i.208.

6 Tovey, *Prospectuses*, p.16.

7 Ibid., pp.30–45.

8 H. Lowenfeld, *Investment an Exact Science* (London, 1909).

9 'Colonial Finance', *Financial Times*, 11 July 1910.
10 Lowenfeld, *All About Investment*, p.263. For large investors seeking high returns and accepting high risk, see R.C. Michie, 'Options, Concessions, Syndicates, and the Provision of Venture Capital, 1880–1913', *Business History*, 23, no. 2 (1981).
11 Lowenfeld, *All About Investment*, p.8.
12 *CCJ*, May 1904, p.107.
13 D. Porter, '"A Trusted Guide of the Investing Public": Harry Marks and the *Financial News*, 1884–1916', *Business History*, 28, no. 1 (1986), 1–6.
14 S. J. Potter, 'Nationalism, Imperialism, and the Press in Britain and the Dominions' (D.Phil, University of Oxford, 2000), p.41.
15 Withers, *International Finance*, p.95.
16 E. T. Powell, *The Mechanism of the City* (London, 1910), pp.78–81.
17 Offer, 'Empire and Social Reform'.
18 Potter, *News and the British World*, p.107.
19 *The Economist*, 21 Dec. 1901, p.1889.
20 Kynaston, *City of London*, ii.179.
21 Porter, 'A Trusted Guide', 6–14.
22 *The Economist*, 1 Nov. 1913, p.943.
23 James Papers, MSS 412/1/34-5: James to Daglish, 9 Dec. 1904. See also Powell, *Mechanism of the City*, p.133; Searle, *Corruption in British Politics*, p.35; Kynaston, *City of London*, ii.181; R. D. Edwards, *The Pursuit of Reason: The Economist 1843–1993* (London, 1993), pp.433–8.
24 See J. A. La Nauze, *Alfred Deakin: A Biography* (Sydney 1979), ii.348–53.
25 Deakin Papers: 1540/15/2137: Walter James, 'Memorandum for the Consideration of Agents General on the Question of Advertising the Resources and Developments of the Commonwealth', Aug. 1905.
26 Potter, *News and the British World*, pp.167–70.
27 *TSDC*, pp.13–14.
28 *The Economist*, 15 Sept. 1906, p.1539.
29 Tovey, *Prospectuses*, p.15; Lowenfeld, *All About Investment*, p.120. See also N. Angell, *The Great Illusion* (London, 1910), p.60.
30 W. R. Lawson, *Canada and the Empire* (London, 1911), pp.250–1.
31 Ibid., pp.128–40.
32 Melbourne Correspondent, *The Economist*, 3 May 1902, p.686.
33 On returns, see Tovey, *Prospectuses*, p.36; Lowenfeld, *All About Investment*, p.43. On the political exposure of railways and utilities, see Armstrong and Nelles, *Monopoly's Moment*, pp.141–2.
34 GTRC Letterbooks, RG30/10712/64: Smithers to Borden, 30 Dec. 1913.
35 *The Economist*, 19 Mar. 1904, p.492; MRC Papers 1557A/447 (London Letterbook): Barber to Brounlie, 23 Jan. 1903, 26 June 1903, 10 July 1903, 1 Sept. 1903.
36 The company reproduced these in a pamphlet distributed to shareholders and Western Australian politicians. See *C.MRC.CS.*, pp.10–50. See also MRC Papers 1557A/448: Barber to Murcott, 18 Dec. 1903; W.A.A.G. Papers, 1150/969/17 (Official Reports): *Official Report of the Agent-General* (1903), p.15.
37 *The Economist*, 27 Feb. 1904, p.351. For similar comments, see for example *Financial Times*, 10, 11, 12, 21, 29 Dec. 1903; *Financial News*, 10, 14, 19, 29

Dec. 1903; *Statist*, 19 Dec. 1903; *Investor's Review*, 2 Jan. 1904, all quoted in *C.MRC.CS.*, pp.10–30.

38 'Midland Railway Company and Western Australia', *Investor's Review*, 12 Dec. 1903.

39 'Midland Railway of Australia', *Stock Exchange Gazette*, 1 Jan. 1904; 'Midland Railway Co of Western Australia', *Statist*, 2 Jan. 1904; 'Western Australia', *Tattler*, 1 Jan. 1904; MRC Papers 1557A/449: Barber to Murcott, 8 Jan. 1904.

40 For the background, see H. V. Nelles, *The Politics of Development: Forests, Mines, and Hydro-Electric Power in Ontario, 1849–1941* (Toronto, 1974), pp.215–305.

41 Fielding Papers MG2/514/48/2805: W. R. Lawson, *Financial Times* (no date on cutting).

42 *Financier*, 7 May 1909, quoted in A. V. Dicey, *The Credit of Canada: How It Is Affected by the Ontario Power Legislation* (Toronto, 1909), p.13.

43 *Standard*, 7 May 1909; *Statist*, 10 July 1909; *Investor's Review*, 11 Sept. 1909; *Outlook*, 13 Mar. 1909, quoted in Dicey, *Credit of Canada*, pp.9–10, 19–20, 35–6.

44 *The Economist*, 28 Aug. 1909, pp.381, 425. See also ibid. 9 Oct. 1909, pp.692–3.

45 Lawson, *Canada and the Empire*, pp.77–87.

46 Angell, *Great Illusion*. For the minority who supported Angell, see Offer, 'Empire and Social Reform', 128.

47 Tovey, *Prospectuses*, p.15.

48 D. Mackenzie, 'Canada, the North Atlantic Triangle and the Empire', in Brown and W. R. Louis (eds) *Oxford History of the British Empire*, iv.576–7.

49 J. Darwin, *After Tamerlane: The Global History of Empire since 1405* (London, 2007), pp.349–59.

50 For an overview, see D. Day, 'The White Australia Policy', in B. Attard and C. Bridge (eds) *Between Empire and Nation: Australia's External Relations from Federation to the Second World War* (Melbourne, 2000).

51 Melbourne Correspondent, *The Economist*, 8 June 1907, p.979.

52 *The Times*, 24 Oct. 1905, p.9.

53 *CAR* (1908), pp.604–5.

54 *The Times*, 10 July 1900, p.9.

55 Davis and Huttenback, *Mammon and the Pursuit of Empire*, pp.147–57, 161. However, see A. Offer, 'The British Empire, 1870–1914: A Waste of Money?' *Economic History Review*, 46, no. 2 (1993), 222–8.

56 *The Economist*, 13 Apr. 1907, p.626. See also Lawson, *Canada and the Empire*, p.89.

57 O.R.CCCE, 1900, p.8.

58 *The Economist*, 5 May 1900, p.623; 'British North America Co.', ibid., 3 Mar. 1900, p.315; 'London Bank of Australia AGM', ibid., 26 May 1900, pp.747–8; 'EASB AGM', ibid. 10 Nov. 1900, p.1583; B. Wilson, *The Life of Lord Strathcona and Mount Royal* (London, 1914), p.518.

59 Cain and Hopkins, *British Imperialism, 1688–2000*, pp.383–6, 389–96.

60 H. G. Turner, *The First Decade of the Australian Commonwealth* (Melbourne, 1911), pp.246–7, 275–5, 295.

61 *The Times*, 24 Aug. 1909, p.7; ibid., 29 May 1913, p.9.

62 O. D. Skelton, *Life and Letters of Sir Wilfrid Laurier* (London, 1922), pp.288–98; N.W. Rowell, 'Canada and the Empire', in J. Holland-Rose (ed.) *Cambridge History of the British Empire*, 9 vols (Cambridge, 1929–1963), iii.717–18.

63 Skelton, *Life and Letters*, pp.327–8.

64 R. C. Brown, *Robert Laird Borden: A Biography*, 2 vols (Toronto, 1975), i.156–62, 235–45.

65 'English Association of American Bondholders AGM', *The Economist*, 20 Feb. 1913, p.482.

66 Ibid., 4 Apr., pp.812–13; ibid., 7 June 1913, p.1391.

67 *CCJ*, Jan. 1913, p.33.

68 *The Globe*, 20 Oct. 1913 quoted in *CAR* (1913), p.26.

69 Michie, *City of London*, pp.69–70; Y. Cassis, *City Bankers, 1890–1914* (Cambridge, 1994), pp.8, 299–301; Kynaston, *City of London*, ii.143–4; M. D. Bordo and H. Rockoff, 'The Gold Standard as a "Good Housekeeping Seal of Approval"', *Journal of Economic History*, 56, no. 2 (1996).

70 N. Ferguson, *The Cash Nexus: Money and Power in the Modern World, 1700–2000* (London, 2001), p.284.

71 Keynes, *Indian Currency and Finance*, pp.22–5, quote at 25.

72 S. B. R. Smith, 'British Nationalism, Imperialism, and the City of London' (Ph.D., University of London, 1985), pp.71–5; Cassis, *City Bankers*, pp.299–301. See also Bordo and Rockoff, 'Gold Standard'.

73 Sydney Correspondent, *Economist*, 6 Dec. 1902, p.1887; Melbourne Correspondent, ibid., 22 Jan. 1904, p.9.

74 Idem, ibid., 20 Sept. 1902, p.1455.

75 Idem, ibid., 27 Aug. 1910, p.434; S. J. Butlin, 'British Banking in Australia', *Journal of the Royal Australian Historical Society*, 49 (1963), 99.

76 *The Times*, 27 Nov. 1907; Fielding Papers, MG2/517/50/2956: *The World*, probably 1910, p.155.

77 *The Economist*, 11 Jan. 1908, p.62.

78 *CCJ*, July 1905, p.152.

79 J. F. Gilpin, 'The Poor Relation Has Come into Her Fortune: The British Investment Boom in Canada, 1905–1915', *Canada House Lecture Series*, 55 (1992).

80 *The Economist*, 25 Jan. 1913, p.159.

81 He spoke at British Empire Trust Co. AGM, 18 June 1913. For this, and the mayor of Winnipeg's indignant reaction, see *CAR* (1913), pp.34–5.

82 *The Economist*, 25 Jan. 1913, p.159; ibid., 27 Sept. 1913, p.558.

83 Cain and Hopkins, *British Imperialism, 1688–2000*, pp.135–6, 216, 224; Cain and Hopkins, 'Theory and Practice', p.204.

84 Many of Wilson's writings on Australia were reprinted in 1909. See A. J. Wilson, *An Empire in Pawn* (London, 1909), pp.103–33. *The Economist* thought Wilson excessively pessimistic. See *The Economist*, 31 June 1909, p.241.

85 Withers, *International Finance*, p.43. Australia's defenders argued that British capital had largely been devoted to the construction of railways, the reproductive work par excellence, a point dismissed by Wilson. See Wilson, *An Empire in Pawn*, pp.104–5.

86 'Australian loans imminent', *Daily Mail*, 30 June 1903.

87 Wood, *Borrowing and Business*, pp.107–8. See also 'Bondholder' to Editor, *Morning Post*, 27 July 1903.
88 *The Economist*, 26 May 1906, p.879.
89 *The Economist*, 17 May 1913, p.1142.
90 'ESAB AGM', *The Economist*, 31 Oct. 1903, p.1857; Wilson, *An Empire in Pawn*, pp.98–9.
91 Melbourne Correspondent, *The Economist*, 3 May 1902, p.689; ibid., 28 Mar. 1903, p.554; *The Times*, 23 Feb. 1910, p.11.
92 'Perth Electric Tramways, AGM', *The Economist*, 4 May 1904, p.660; ibid., 13 April 1907, p.652.
93 *The Times*, 17 Apr. 1900, p.7. See also *The Economist*, 14 Oct. 1905, p.1626; ibid., 26 May 1906, p.877.
94 Ottawa Correspondent, ibid., 27 June 1908, p.1354. See also, ibid., 3 July 1909, p.12.
95 Anon to Editor, ibid., 13 Nov. 1909, p.981.
96 Cassis, *City Bankers*, pp.302–10; A. Howe, *Free Trade and Liberal England, 1846–1946* (Oxford, 1997), pp.233–5; Cain and Hopkins, 'Theory and Practice', pp.201–2; P. J. Cain and A. G. Hopkins, 'The Peculiarities of British Capitalism: Imperialism and World Development', in S. Akita (ed.) *Gentlemanly Capitalism, Imperialism and Global History* (Basingstoke, 2002), pp.196–9.
97 Cain and Hopkins, *British Imperialism, 1688–2000*, pp.241–2, 259–60.
98 O.R.CCCE, 1903, p.131. See also, *The Economist*, 16 Aug. 1902, p.1285; Lawson, *Canada and the Empire*, p.322.
99 *Investor's Review*, 19 July 1902, in Wilson, *An Empire in Pawn*, p.145.
100 *The Economist*, 9 Nov. 1901, p.1167.
101 *CCJ*, Mar. 1902, p.56.
102 'Associate Goldmines of Western Australia AGM', *The Economist*, 26 July 1902, p.1179.
103 Editorial, *Financial News*, 5 Feb. 1911.
104 'The Canadian parliament on Annexation', *Statist*, 25 Feb. 1911.
105 For a selection of such views, see *CAR* (1911), pp.130–8.
106 BCER Papers, 40, File 'Horne Payne Correspondence to 1917': Horne-Payne to Kidd, 1 Apr. 1911.
107 *CCJ*, Dec. 1911, p.368.
108 GTRC Letterbooks RG30/1712/132: Smithers to Hays, 3 Feb. 1911.
109 'English Association of American Bond and Shareholders AGM', *The Economist*, 25 Feb. 1911, p.394; *The Times*, 25 Feb. 1911, p.9; *CAR* 1911, pp.126; *CCJ*, Dec. 1911, p.369.
110 A. S. Thompson, 'Tariff Reform: An Imperial Strategy, 1903–1913', *Historical Journal*, 40, no. 4 (1997).
111 Howe, *Free Trade and Liberal England*, pp.239–43.
112 On the measure, see E. Sullivan, 'Revealing a Preference: Imperial Preference and the Australian Tariff, 1901–1914', *Journal of Imperial and Commonwealth History*, 29, no. 1 (2001), 42–8.
113 Howe, *Free Trade and Liberal England*, pp.241–3.
114 *The Times* quoted in *CCJ*, Oct. 1907, p.266. See also Melbourne Correspondent, *The Economist*, 10 Aug. 1907, p.1354.
115 'ESAB AGM', *The Economist*, 2 Nov. 1907, p.1876.

116 For the resultant transatlantic politicking, see Potter, 'Imperial Significance'.
117 Ottawa Cor., *The Economist*, 4 Mar. 1911, pp.428–9.
118 See for example, Montreal *Star*, 27 Feb. 1911, quoted in *CAR* (1911), p.139.
119 For further analysis, see Rogers, 'Impact of the New World'.
120 D. Rock, *Argentina, 1516–1982* (London, 1986), p.xxi.
121 Bodleian Library, MSS Brand 26/2AP/1912-15: Brand to Steel Maitland, 10 Feb. 1913.
122 *The Times*, 10 Oct. 1901, p.7.
123 Ingall and Withers, *Stock Exchange*, p.124.
124 *The Economist*, 9 June 1906, p.959.
125 W. A. Carrothers, *Emigration from the British Isles* (London, 1965), pp.305–6.
126 *The Times*, 25 Oct. 1905, p.9.
127 Melbourne Correspondent, *The Economist*, 30 Apr. 1904, p.740.
128 A. P Stoneham at 'Perth Electric Tramways AGM', *The Economist*, 23 May 1908, p.1108.
129 *The Times*, 24 Oct. 1905, p.9. I am grateful to Dr Rachel Bright for reminding me of this case.
130 Barton to Editor, *The Economist*, 18 July 1903, 1259.
131 'ESAB AGM', ibid., 4 Nov. 1905, p.1765.
132 'The Scandal of New South Wales', *Daily Mail*, 15 Dec. 1905.
133 'UBA AGM', *The Economist*, 30 July 1910, p.236.
134 'Dalgety AGM', ibid., 4 Nov. 1905, p.1809. See also C. J. Hegan's comments, 'ESAB AGM', ibid., 3 Nov. 1906, p.1796.
135 'New South Wales and the Investor', *Daily Mail*, 16 Jan 1907.
136 At the ACCUK, Sept. 1900, see *CCJ (Supplement)*, Oct. 1900, p.4.
137 G. R. Searle, *A New England? Peace and War, 1886–1918* (Oxford, 2004), pp.93–4, 352–9, 452–3.
138 GTRC Letterbooks RG30/1712/287: Smithers to Hays, 6 Feb. 1912.
139 Lawson, *Canada and the Empire*, p.143.
140 *CCJ*, Dec. 1911, p.369.
141 'Grand Trunk Railway HYGM', *The Economist*, 10 Oct. 1908, p.682; GTRC Letterbooks RG30/1712/287: Smithers to Hays, 6 Feb. 1912.
142 GTRC Letterbooks RG30/1712/287: Smithers to Hays, 6 Feb. 1912.
143 Canadian businessmen were less optimistic. See M. Bliss, '"Dyspepsia of the Mind": The Canadian Businessman and His Enemies, 1880–1914', in Macmillan (ed.) *Canadian Business History*, pp.180–2.
144 *CCJ*, Jan. 1910, p.6.
145 'Zinc Corp AGM', *The Economist*, 14 May 1910, p.1092.
146 Editorial, *Australasian World*, 13 May 1909.
147 See Samuel Bagster Boulton's comments in O.R.CCE, 1903, p.131.
148 G. Patmore, *Australian Labour History* (Melbourne, 1991), pp.101–21.
149 'Zinc Corp AGM', *The Economist*, 14 May 1910, p.1092.
150 Whitney Papers, F5/MU3122: Extract from Grenfell to Grey, 29 Mar. 1907, enclosed with Mortimer-Clarke to Whitney, 2 Apr. 1907.
151 *The Times*, 10 Oct. 1901, p.7.
152 *The Economist*, 6 Dec. 1902, p.1887.
153 Melbourne Correspondent, *The Economist*, 3 May 1902, p.686. See also his comments in ibid., 30 Jan. 1904, p.172; ibid., 11 June 1904, pp.985–6. The London editorial writers agreed; see ibid., 26 July 1902, p.1166.

154 'English View of the Federal Government', Melbourne *Age*, 1 June 1904.
155 Carruthers Papers, MSS 1683/55/23: Sir H. Rawson, 'Memorandum re NSW finances in London' (Jan. 1906), p.143.
156 'Australian Estates Co. AGM', *The Economist*, 17 June 1911, 1314. See also C. J. Hegan's comments, 'ESAB AGM', ibid., 29 Oct. 1910, p.877.
157 Withers, *International Finance*, p.77.
158 *CCJ Supplement*, Feb. 1911, p.2.

Chapter 4 Risk, Empire, and Britishness

1 'Merchants' Trust AGM', *The Economist*, 10 Mar. 1906, p.412.
2 *CAR* (1914), p.28; R. A. Lehfeldt, 'The Rate of Interest on British and Foreign Investments', *Journal of the Royal Statistical Society*, 76, no. 2 (1913); Paish, 'Great Britain's Capital Investments', 475.
3 L. E. Davis and R. A. Huttenback, *Mammon and the Pursuit of Empire: The Economics of British Imperialism* (Cambridge, 1988), p.149; N. Ferguson and M. Schularick, 'The Empire Effect: The Determinants of Country Risk in the First Age of Globalization, 1880–1913', *Journal of Economic History*, 66, no. 2 (2006); A. Offer, 'Costs and Benefits, Prosperity and Security, 1870–1914', in Porter (ed.) *Oxford History of the British Empire*, iii.700–1.
4 Ferguson and Schularick, 'Empire Effect', 286–7, 307–88.
5 Magee and Thompson, *Empire and Globalisation*, p.184.
6 Ferguson and Schularick, 'Empire Effect', 299, table 293.
7 Startt, *Journalists for Empire*.
8 N. Ferguson, 'The City of London and British Imperialism: New Light on an Old Question', in Cassis and Bussièr (eds) *London and Paris*, p.61.
9 A. F. Madden and J. Darwin (eds) *Select Documents on the Constitutional History of the British Empire and Commonwealth: The Dominions and India since 1900*, 7 vols (London, 1993), vi.6.
10 *The Economist*, 6 July 1901, p.1007.
11 'Investor' to Editor, ibid., 10 Mar. 1906, p.959.
12 Young to Lyettelton, 19 Nov. 1903, Bertram Cox to MRC, 4 Dec. 1903, Young to Lyttleton, 8 Dec. 1903, Cox to MRC, 22 Dec. 1903 quoted in *C.MRC.CS*, pp.2–4, 7, 10.
13 A. Lyttleton, 'The Empire', in W. J. S. Ashley (ed.) *British Dominions: Their Present Commercial and Industrial Condition* (London, 1911), p.13.
14 P. Girard, 'British Justice, English Law, and Canadian Legal Culture', in Buckner (ed.) *Canada and the British Empire*, pp.269–71.
15 *AIBR*, 19 April 1900, p.252.
16 A. Page, 'The Legal Problems of the Empire', in A. J. H. Herbertson and O. J. R. Howarth (eds) *The Oxford Survey of the British Empire* (Oxford, 1914), p.99.
17 Laurier Papers, MG 26-G/c797/226/63537-9: Clouston to Laurier, 10 Mar. 1902.
18 Quoted in Fleming, *Railway King*, p.153.
19 For one Australian radical's views, see F. Bongiorno, 'From Republican to Anti-Billite: Bernard O'Dowd and Federation', *The New Federalist*, 4 (1999).

20   C. M. H. Clark, *A Short History of Australia* (New York, 1987), pp.181–8;
     L. Trainor, *British Imperialism and Australian Nationalism: Manipulation,
     Conflict, and Compromise in the Late Nineteenth Century* (Cambridge, 1994),
     p.157.
21   La Nauze, *Alfred Deakin*, i.190; P. T. Marsh, *Joseph Chamberlain: Entre-
     preneur in Politics* (London, 1994), p.491.
22   *The Times*, 28 Apr. 1900, 11.
23   UBA Papers U/103/58 /2531/5: General Manager to London Manager,
     23 Mar. 1900.
24   *The Economist*, 19 May 1900, p.699.
25   *CCJ*, May 1900, p.80.
26   A. Deakin, *The Federal Story: The Inner Story of the Federal Cause* (Melbourne,
     1944), pp.141–9.
27   Marsh, *Joseph Chamberlain*, p.492.
28   *The Times*, 18 Dec. 1913, p.9.
29   *CCJ*, June 1907, p.155.
30   Davis and Huttenback, *Mammon and the Pursuit of Empire*, p.169.
31   D. Jessop, 'The Colonial Stock Act of 1900: A Symptom of New Imperialism?'
     Journal of Imperial and Commonwealth History, 4 (1975), 154–9.
32   Quoted in A. S. J. Baster, 'A Note on the Colonial Stock Acts and
     Dominion Borrowing', *Economic History*, 8 (1933), 603.
33   'More Colonial Trustee Investments', *Westminster Gazette*, 14 Mar.
     1901.
34   Quoted in *The Economist*, 26 May 1900, p.738.
35   Ibid. p.738; *AIBR.*, 19 Aug. 1900, p.596.
36   Baster, 'Colonial Stock Acts', 605–6.
37   S. R. O. NSW, Kingswood 19/8959/CGS-14335 (Treasury Files): Coghlan to
     Premier, 9 Feb. 1909.
38   Vict. P. R. O., 1225/8/7R-2071 (Treasury Loan Files): Agent-General to
     Treasurer, 8 Mar. 1901; S. R. O. NSW, Kingswood 3/3158/CGS-14335:
     Agent-General to Treasurer, 17 May 1901.
39   Whitney Papers, F5/MU3122: Whitney to Laurier, 26 Feb. 1907; Fielding
     Papers, MG2/511/40/2173: Linkater and Co. to Lyttleton, 'Memorandum
     on Behalf of the Canadian Northern Railway Company', Dec. 1905; Field,
     Capital Investments in Canada, p.178; Offer, 'Empire and Social Reform',
     136.
40   Correspondent to Editor, 'Answers to Questions', *Investor's Review*, 31 Jan.
     1914.
41   Coghlan, *Statistical Account*, p.1032.
42   'Answers to Questions', *Investor's Review*, 31 Jan. 1914.
43   Potter, *News and the British World*.
44   The *Canadian Annual Review* often listed parties of visiting London jour-
     nalists. See, *CAR* (1905), p.499; ibid. (1907), pp.361–3; ibid. (1908),
     pp.608–11.
45   Walker Papers 1/20/60: Walker to Grey, 3 Sept. 1908.
46   Ibid., Walker to Jones, 11 Nov. 1908.
47   *The Economist*, 17 Nov. 1900, p.1612.
48   S. R. O. NSW, Kingswood 3/3158/CGS-14335 (Treasury Files): Jersey to
     Premier, 11, 22 Nov., 8, 16, 23 Dec. 1904; Coghlan Papers, MS6335/6/1:

NSW Cabinet Minute, 'Re-organisation of the Agent-General's Department', 31 Jan. 1905.

49   R. P. T. Davenport-Hines, 'Blackwood, Frederick Temple Hamilton-Temple, First Marquess of Dufferin and Ava', *Oxford Dictionary of National Biography*.

50   Kynaston, *City of London*, ii.140.; 'British America Corp. AGM', *The Economist*, 3 Mar. 1900, p.315; ibid., 5 Jan. 1901, pp.4–5.

51   Ibid., 12 Jan. 1901, p.43.

52   'London and Globe Finance Corp. AGM', ibid., 12 Jan. 1901, pp.52–4.

53   Miss Mack quoted in M. Shanahan, 'Tracing the Crimson Thread: United Kingdom Residents Holding Probated South Australian Assets, 1905–1915', *Australian Economic History Review*, 43, no. 3 (2003), 223.

54   Fleming, *Railway King*, p.164.

55   J. E. Kendle, *The Colonial and Imperial Conferences. 1887–1911: A Study in Imperial Organization* (London, 1967).

56   Fielding Papers, MG2/505/11a/798A: Fielding to Davies, 1 Nov. 1897.

57   W. J. S. Ashley, 'Introduction', in Ashley (ed.) *British Dominions*, pp.xiv–xv; Smith, 'British Nationalism', p.19.

58   O. R. CCCE, 1900, 1903, 1906, 1909, 1912.

59   *CCJ*, July 1906, p.174.

60   James Papers, MSS 412/5/315: James to Waxman, 3 Aug. 1906.

61   Laurier Papers MG 26-G/c792/226/63545: Fielding to Laurier, 10 Mar. 1902.

62   *CCJ*, Jan. 1903.

63   Deakin Papers, MS1540/1/1501: James to Deakin, 17 Aug. 1906.

64   W. A. A. G. Papers, 1150/298/18: R. C. Hare, *Official Report of the Agent General*, Feb. 1909, p.34.

65   O. R. CCCE, 1909, p.1; *CCJ*, Jan. 1910, pp.4–9. See also A. Spicer, 'Australia', in Ashley (ed.) *British Dominions*.

66   Hobson, *Export of Capital*, p.26.

67   O. R. CCCE, 1903, pp.137–41.

68   *CCJ*, Sept. 1903, p.209.

69   Turner, *First Decade*, p.142.

70   Deakin Papers, MS1540/15/42/1/1446: Gwynne to Deakin, 20 Apr. 1907. See also ibid., 1540/43/29/1547: Rason to Deakin, 20 May 1907.

71   'Australian Credit Enhanced in Great Britain', *SMH*, 2 July 1907.

72   R. G. Moyles and D. Owram, *Imperial Dreams and Colonial Realities: British Views of Canada 1880–1914* (Toronto, 1988), p.142.

73   'White Pass and Yukon Railway AGM', *The Economist*, 31 July 1909, p.931.

74   *CCJ*, Dec. 1911, p.368.

75   'British Empire Trust Co. AGM', *The Economist*, 16 July 1910, p.128.

76   Anonymous to Editor, ibid., 10 Dec. 1910, p.1173.

77   Ottawa Correspondent, ibid., 7 July 1906, p.1126.

78   *CCJ*, Aug. 1906, p.187; *The Times*, 10 Apr. 1914, p.7.

79   Wilson, *An Empire in Pawn*, p.173.

80   P. J. Cain, 'Character and Imperialism: The British Financial Administration of Egypt, 1878–1914', *Journal of Imperial and Commonwealth History*, 34, no. 2 (2006).

81   H. O. O'Hagan, *Leaves from My Life* (London, 1929), ii.148.

82   'Merchants' Trust AGM', *The Economist*, 10 Mar. 1906, p.412.

83 'What Every Financier Ought to Know!', *Australasian World*, 11 Mar. 1909.

84 'Midland Railway Company of Australia and the State', *Financial World*, 17 Jan. 1914.

85 A. Offer, 'Pacific Rim Societies: Asian Labour and White Nationalism', in Eddy and Schreuder (eds) *The Rise of Colonial Nationalism*; Bright, 'Asian Migration and the British World, 1850–1914'.

86 NAC, MG 30/A93 (Sir Alfred W. Smithers Papers): C. Rivers Wilson, 'Memo: Visit to Canada, 22nd July to 27th Sept, 15,000 miles', pp.3–4.

87 C. J. Hegan at 'ESAB AGM', *The Economist*, 4 Nov. 1905, p.1765. See also G. F. Malcomson at 'Australian Estates Company AGM', ibid., 9 June 1906, p.972.

88 Ibid. 8 July 1911, p.61.

89 *The Times*, 24 Oct. 1905, p.9.

90 *CCJ*, Oct. 1910, p.7.

91 B. Attard, 'The Australian High Commissioner's Office: Politics and Anglo-Australian Relations, 1901–1939' (D.Phil, University of Oxford, 1991), pp.13–29.

92 James Papers 412/1/15: James to Rason, 2 Dec. 1904.

93 A. Reford, 'Smith, Donald Alexander, 1st Baron Strathcona and Mount Royal', *Canadian Dictionary of National Biography* (Ottawa, 2005); available from http://www.biographi.ca/009004-119.01-e.php?&id_nbr=7710&&PHP-SESSID=49viocasr16adm1c2pkph5kdi1.

94 Quoted in Wilson, *Lord Strathcona*, p.463.

95 He spoke at least five times to the London Chamber of Commerce, including at the dinner held for the Australian federal delegates in April 1900. See *CCJ* May 1900, May 1904, May 1907, Feb. 1911, Aug. 1912.

96 Wilson, *Lord Strathcona*, p.464.

97 Ibid., pp.466–555.

98 *CAR*, 1906, p.622.

99 Williams-Taylor, 'Canadian Loans', 986.

100 Wilson, *Lord Strathcona*, p.476.

101 Walker Papers, 1/B/19/52: Walker to Jones, 5 Jan. 1903.

102 White Papers MG 27-I-D-18/2/9a/1140: Wood to White, 18 Nov. 1912.

103 Williams-Taylor, 'Canadian Loans'.

104 Ibid., 992–3.

105 Ibid., 993.

106 Ibid., 995–6.

107 White Papers, MG 27-II-D-18/2/9a/1159: Foster to Borden, 10 Dec. 1912.

108 See for example, Anon to Editor, *The Economist*, 4 Jan. 1913, p.26.

109 Borden Papers MG 26-H-1a/c4202/10/70287: Strathcona to Borden, 21 Feb. 1913. See also Wilson, *Lord Strathcona*, p.572.

110 Quoted in *The Times*, 31 Jan. 1906, p.7.

111 Vict. P. R. O., 1225/8/7R-1308 (Treasury Loan Files): Dobson to Premier, 11 Sept. 1903.

112 Carruthers Papers, MSS 1683/6/140: Jersey to Carruthers, 23 Feb. 1905.

113 Deakin Papers, MS 1540/1/1893: Coghlan to Deakin, 27 Apr. 1906.

114 'The Scandal of New South Wales', *Daily Mail*, 15 Dec. 1905.

115 Coghlan to Editor, 'New South Wales Scandal', *Daily Mail*, 18 Dec. 1905.

116 Deakin Papers, MS 1540/15/1/484: Wise to Deakin, 27 Dec. 1905.

117 James Papers, MSS412/6, pp.209–15: Coghlan to Belliers (London Standard), 24 May 1905; Belliers to Coghlan, 25 May 1905; Coghlan to Gwynne, 26 May 1905; Gwynne to Coghlan, 26 May 1905.
118 Ibid., MS 1540/1/1911: Coghlan to Deakin, 5 Mar. 1908.
119 Deakin Papers, MS 1540/1/2137: W. James, 'Memorandum of for the Consideration of Agents General on the Question of Advertising the Resources and Developments of the Commonwealth', Aug. 1905.
120 Ibid. MS 1540/1/2138.
121 James Papers, MSS 412/1, pp.24–5: James to Rason, 26 May 1905.
122 W.A.A.G. Papers 1150/298/18 (Agent-Generals' Reports): Sir Newton Moore, *Annual Report: 1911–1912*, 1 Sept. 1912. Joseph Carruthers made similar recommendations to the New South Wales Government in 1908, see Carruthers Papers 1638/12/293-295: Carruthers to Wade, 9 July 1908.
123 Ibid.
124 Carruthers Papers, MSS 1638/12/323: Caruthers to Wade, 31 July 1908.
125 Deakin Papers MS 1540/1/2139: James, 'Memorandum'.
126 'Australia in London', *SMH*, 15 Jan. 1910.
127 Turner, *First Decade*, p.10.
128 Attard, 'Australian High Commissioner's Office', pp.19–23, 54–69.
129 G. Reid, *My Reminiscences* (1917), p.271.
130 'Enter Sir George', *Pall Mall Gazette*, 1 Mar. 1910.
131 'An Australian Loan', *Daily News*, 2 Mar. 1910.
132 Attard, 'Australian High Commissioner's Office', p.82.
133 Reid, *My Reminiscences*, p.277.
134 *CCJ Supplement*, Feb. 1911, p.3.
135 The term used dismissively by D. C. M. Platt; see D. C. M. Platt, 'Canada and Argentina: The First Preference of the British Investor, 1904–1914', *Journal of Imperial and Commonwealth History*, 8 (1985), 85.
136 'Merchants' Trust AGM', *The Economist*, 10 Mar. 1906, p.412.

Chapter 5   Canadian Politics and London Finance, 1896–1914

1 See R. C. Brown and R. Cook, *Canada, 1896–1921: A Nation Transformed* (Toronto, 1974).
2 Taylor and Baskerville, *Concise History of Business*, p.254; Armstrong and Nelles, *Southern Exposure*, p.6.
3 *CAR* (1913), p.58.
4 Ibid., pp.57–8.
5 Taylor and Baskerville, *Concise History of Business*, pp.252, 258–61; Armstrong and Nelles, *Southern Exposure*, pp.6–9. *CAR* (1913), p.58.
6 Although the *CAR* studiously reproduced other points of views, its asides, structure, and commentary reflected this role. Six of its 14 founders appear in a list of leading Canadian directors produced by the Manitoba *Grain Grower's Guide* in 1913, while another, A. E. Ames might plausibly be added. See *CAR* (1913), pp.1, 57–8.
7 A. A. Den Otter, *The Philosophy of Railways: The Transcontinental Railway Idea in British North America* (Toronto, 1997).

8   O. D. Skelton, 'General Economic History, 1867–1912', in A. Shortt and A. G. Doughty (eds) *Canada and Its Provinces*, 23 vols (Toronto, 1913), ix.274.

9   Ibid., ix.269.

10   *CAR* (1909), p.165.

11   White Papers M2/27/II/D/18/10/43/7300: Wood to White, 3 July 1914.

12   K. Levitt, *Silent Surrender: The Multinational Corporation in Canada* (Toronto, 1970), pp.51–2.

13   CMA Papers, MG28-I-230/3/26: Minutes, 15 May 1902.

14   Viner, *Canada's Balance*, pp.113–15, 126.

15   Calculated from Field, *Capital Investments in Canada*, p.9.

16   E. R. Wood, *Review of the Bond Market in Canada for 1911* (Toronto, 1911), p.22.

17   *CAR* (1907), p.600.

18   'Canadian Bank of Commerce AGM', *The Economist*, 26 Jan. 1907, p.153.

19   'Canadian Bank of Commerce AGM', ibid., 13 Feb. 1904, p.273.

20   Quoted in *CAR* (1908), p.604.

21   *Toronto Globe*, 25 Apr. 1910 quoted in *CAR* (1910), p.81. Similar comments from *The Halifax Chronicle*, *Toronto News*, *Toronto Star*, *Medicine Hat News*, *Nelson News*, *Montreal Witness*, *Montreal Gazette*, the *Manitoba Free Press*, the *Vancouver Advertizer*, and the *Toronto Telegraph* were reproduced in Field's 1914 edition, see Field, *Capital Investments in Canada*, pp.223–9, 260.

22   Naylor, *History of Canadian Business*, i.85.

23   Ross, *History of the Canadian Bank of Commerce*, ii.237–9; A. B. Jamieson, *Chartered Banking in Canada* (Toronto, 1957), pp.37–8.

24   Walker Papers, MS 1/B/20/38: Walker to Megan, 26 Mar. 1908.

25   Ibid., 1/20/69: Walker to Allen, 29 Dec. 1908.

26   'Canadian Bank of Commerce AGM', *The Economist*, 1 Feb. 1908, 234.

27   Denison, *Canada's First Bank*, ii.295; Field, *Capital Investments in Canada*, p.13; Moyles and Owram, *Imperial Dreams and Colonial Realities: British Views of Canada 1880–1914*, pp.147–8.

28   E. R. Wood, *Review of the Bond Market in Canada for 1908* (Toronto, 1908), p.7.

29   Field, *Capital Investments in Canada*, p.170.

30   'Bank of Montreal AGM', *The Economist*, 1 Jan. 1910, p.30.

31   A phrase used by Williams-Taylor, see Field, *Capital Investments in Canada*, pp.170–1. See also W. Miller's comments at 'Bank of Montreal AGM', *The Economist*, 21 Dec. 1912, p.1288.

32   *CAR* (1913), pp.17–18; Jamieson, *Chartered Banking*, p.40.

33   George Drummond at 'Bank of Montreal AGM', *The Economist*, 1 Jan. 1910, p.30.

34   Naylor, *History of Canadian Business*, ii.89–91; Anon, *The Story of Mond Nickel* (N.P., 1951), pp.16–18.

35   Laurier Papers, MG 26-G/c785/196/55947: Clouston to Laurier, 6 May 1901. Walker concurred; see Naylor, *History of Canadian Business*, ii.91.

36   Laurier Papers, MG 26-G/c785/196/55951: Laurier to Clouston, 7 May 1901.

37   Naylor, *History of Canadian Business*, ii.91.

38   For the best account, see Nelles, *Politics of Development*, pp.215–305.

39 B. E. Walker, *Canadian Credit and Enterprise* (Toronto, 1908), p.7.
40 Ibid., p.3.
41 Ibid., pp.7–8.
42 Whitney Papers MU3127: Williams-Taylor to Whitney, 12 May 1909.
43 Laurier Papers, MG 26G/c.877/575/156477-8: Walker to Laurier, 5 June 1909.
44 Ibid., MG 26G/c.877/575/157057-59: Wood to Laurier, 17 June 1909.
45 Dicey, *The Credit of Canada*, pp.67–73.
46 Whitney Office Records: RG3/2: Aylesworth to Governor-General in Council, 29 March 1910.
47 Laurier Papers, MG 26G/c877/575/156482: Laurier to Walker, 11 June 1909; Ibid. MG 26G/c881/593/160980: Lyon to Laurier, 16 Oct. 1909; Whitney Papers, MU2138: Brodser to Whitney, 24 Dec. 1909.
48 The politics of finance in the Canadian provinces would be worth further exploration.
49 DDEAP RG 25/B/1a/83: Courtney to High Commissioner, 26 Mar.1900.
50 Ibid., RG25/B/1a/83: Courtney to High Commission, High Commission to Courtney, 19, 20 Apr. 1900.
51 Ibid., RG25/B/1a/885: Fielding to High Commission, 20 Oct. 1902.
52 Borden Papers, MG 26-H-1a/c4353/132/70235: Unattributed to Griffith, 24 Sept. 1912; White Papers, MG 27-II-D-18/1/1/33: Williams-Taylor to White, 1 May 1913.
53 D. O. Carrigan, *Canadian Party Platforms, 1867–1968* (Urbana, 1968), pp.34–5, 37.
54 Contemporaries distinguished between capital and current expenditure hence the deficit appearing in the table would have seemed smaller by contemporary reckoning than on the basis of these later statistics. On the distinction, see Fielding's comments in the Canadian parliament, *CAR* (1905), p.403.
55 J. Lewis, 'The British Preference', *Annals of the American Academy of Political and Social Science*, 107 (1923), 200.
56 E. McInnis and M. Horn, *Canada: A Political & Social History* (Toronto, 1982), p.460; Skelton, 'General Economic History, 1867–1912', pp.206–10.
57 *The Times*, 26 Apr., 4, 28 May 1897.
58 Moyles and Owram, *Imperial Dreams and Colonial Realities*, p.17.
59 Marsh, *Joseph Chamberlain*, pp.423–6.
60 Skelton, *Life and Letters*, p.73.
61 'The Canadian Prefence', *Daily News*, 3 May 1897.
62 London Correspondent, *Toronto Globe*, 28 Apr. 1897. The London correspondent of the *New York Times* concurred; see Skelton, *Life and Letters*, pp.57–8.
63 Quoted in ibid., p.71.
64 Fielding Papers MG 2/505/11/765: Davies to Fielding, 20 July 1897.
65 Ibid., MG 2/11a/798A: Fielding to Davies, 1 Nov. 1897.
66 Laurier Papers MG 26-G/c751/54/17376: Fielding to Laurier, 3 Nov. 1897.
67 *DHC* (1902), i.1291, 1294.
68 Laurier Papers MG 26-G/c771/136/40484: Fielding, 'Confidential Departmental Circular', 1900.

69 Ibid., MG 26-G/c786/198/56559A: Fielding, 'Confidential Departmental Circular', May 1901. See also DDEAP, RG 25-B/1a/92278: Fielding to 'Colleagues', 16 Nov. 1904.
70 Laurier Papers, MG 26-G/c825/375/99996-8: Fielding to Laurier, 25 July 1905; Fielding to 'Colleagues', 25 July 1905.
71 Ibid., MG 26-G/c927/386/102573-4: Fielding to 'Colleagues', 31 Oct. 1905.
72 Fielding Papers, MG 2/517/50/2954/8-9: 'Memorandum of the Finances of Canada', undated, probably 1908.
73 *SEYB* (1915), p.30.
74 Laurier Papers, MG 26-G/c870/550/149010-1: Clouston to Laurier, 17 Dec. 1908.
75 Ibid. MG 26-G/c870/550/149013: Laurier to Clouston, 21 Dec. 1908.
76 Ibid., MG 26-G/c873/561/152036: Williams-Taylor to Clouston, 10 Feb. 1909; Fielding Papers MG2/517/50/2912, 2930-1: Fielding to Williams-Taylor, 22 Dec. 1908, Williams-Taylor to Hirst, 20, 23 Jan. 1909.
77 Laurier Papers, MG 26-G/c872/558/151316: Clouston to Laurier, 2 Feb. 1909.
78 Ibid. MG 26G/c872/558/151317: Laurier to Clouston, 4 Dec. 1909.
79 Borden Papers, MG 26/H/1(a)/8/856: W. T. White, *Budget Speech: 12 May 1913* (Ottawa, 1913), pp.9–10.
80 Ibid., p.20.
81 Innis, *Canadian Pacific Railway*, pp.173, 182, 292.
82 J. H. Gray, *R. B. Bennett: The Calgary Years* (Toronto, 1991), pp.37–8.
83 McInnis and Horn, *Canada*, pp.442–5; Offer, *First World War*, pp.159–62.
84 Easterbrook and Aitken, *Canadian Economic History*, p.495.
85 C. F. Wilson, *A Century of Canadian Grain: Government Policy to 1951* (Saskatoon, 1978), p.5.
86 *DHC* (1902), i.1294, 1391.
87 G. R. Stevens, *Canadian National Railways* (Toronto, 1962), pp.24–39.
88 Laurier Papers, MG 26-G/c796/243/67896: Cox et al. to Laurier, 3 Nov. 1902. The American railway magnate (and another former member of the CPR syndicate), J. J. Hill's Great Northern Railway had been probing north from Minnesota since the early 1890s.
89 Ibid.
90 For Laurier's attitude, see Stevens, *Canadian National Railways*, pp.275–6.
91 Hays Letterbooks, MG30/a18/1/18: Hays to Rivers Wilson, 22 Sept. 1902. See also, Currie, *Grand Trunk Railway*, pp.394–8.
92 Fleming, *Railway King*, p.98; Regehr, *Canadian Northern Railway*, pp.108–12; Stevens, *Canadian National Railways*, pp.129–43; Taylor and Baskerville, *Concise History of Business*, p.283.
93 See for example, Hays Letterbooks MG 30/a18/1, pp.27–8: Rivers Wilson to Hays, 7 Oct. 1902.
94 Stevens, *Canadian National Railways*, pp.455–524.
95 Regehr, *Canadian Northern Railway*, p.102. See also Hays Letterbooks MG 30/a18/1/229: Rivers Wilson to Hays, 20 July 1903.
96 Regehr, *Canadian Northern Railway*, pp.210–11.
97 As Laurier described it; see *DHC* (1903), v.7678.
98 Hays Letterbooks MG 30/a18/1/179-80: Hays to Rivers Wilson, 29 June 1903.

99   Ibid. MG 30/a18/2./797: Rivers-Wilson to Hays, 22 Jan. 1905.
100 Currie, *Grand Trunk Railway*, pp.389–90; Stevens, *Canadian National Railways*, pp.136–44.
101 *DHC* (1903), v.7660.
102 Ibid., v.7660.
103 Ibid., v.7675–86.
104 Ibid., v.7695.
105 Brown, *Robert Laird Borden*, pp.69–70.
106 *DHC* (1903), v.8462–3.
107 Skelton, *Life and Letters*, p.193.
108 *CAR* (1904), p.195.
109 Ibid., p.196.
110 Anon, *Grand Trunk Pacific: A History of a Project* (n.d.), pp.46–7.
111 Laurier Papers MG 26-G/c817/344/92105-7: Rivers Wilson to Laurier, 11 Nov. 1904; Laurier to Rivers Wilson, 22 Nov. 1904.
112 Quoted in *CAR* (1907), p.542.
113 *CAR* (1908), p.219
114 *Toronto Star*, 11 July 1910.
115 Fielding Papers MG 2/514/45/2247-8: Fielding, 'To the Electoral District of Shelburne and Queens', 9 Sept. 1908.
116 Hays Letterbooks, MG 30/a18/3/986, 1011, 1017–18: Fielding to Hays, 3 Nov. 1905, Hays to Rivers-Wilson, 6 Dec. 1905, 13 Dec. 1905; Laurier Papers, MG 26-G/c828/367/103054-9: Rivers-Wilson to Laurier, 10 Nov. 1905; Ibid., MG 26/c820/391/103910: Fielding to Laurier, 2 Dec. 1905.
117 Ibid., MG 26-G/c828/367/1113: Rivers-Wilson Hays, 30 Nov. 1906; *CAR* (1906), p.582.
118 Stevens, *Canadian National Railways*, pp.210–15.
119 Currie, *Grand Trunk Railway*, p.410.
120 *CAR* (1911), p.644.
121 GTRC Letterbooks RG30/1712/108: Smithers to Laurier, 9 Dec. 1910.
122 Quoted in Brown, *Robert Laird Borden*, i.23.
123 Williams-Taylor, 'Canadian Loans', 990.
124 GTRC Letterbooks RG30/1712/251: Smithers to Hays, 13 Dec. 1911.
125 Ibid. RG30/1712/318: Smithers to Chamberlain, 28 June 1912.
126 Brown, *Robert Laird Borden*, i.223–6; H. Borden (ed.) *Robert Laird Borden: His Memoirs* (Toronto, 1938), pp.324–5.
127 White Papers, MG 27-II-D-18/1/1/33: Williams-Taylor to White, 1 May 1913. See also ibid., MG 27-II-D-18/10/40/62410: Williams-Taylor to White, 8 Apr. 1913.
128 Borden (ed.) *Robert Laird Borden*, i.226.
129 Stevens, *Canadian National Railways*, pp.462–523.
130 Offer, *First World War*, pp.81–6.
131 *CAR* (1905), pp.390–4.
132 B. Fergusson, *Rt Hon W. S. Fielding*, 2 vols (Windsor, N. S., 1971), ii.58.
133 Marr and Paterson, *Canada*, p.7; Norrie and Owram, *History of the Canadian Economy*, pp.218–19.
134 Quoted in Masters, *Reciprocity*, p.16. See also McInnis and Horn, *Canada*, pp.381–7, 422–6; Fergusson, *Rt Hon W. S. Fielding*, ii.101; L. E. Ellis,

Reciprocity, 1911: A Study in Canadian-American Relations (New Haven, 1939), p.4.

135 McInnis and Horn, *Canada*, p.470; Ellis, *Reciprocity, 1911*, pp.2–10, 25–35.
136 Offer, *First World War*, pp.161–2.
137 *CAR* (1911), pp.28–30.
138 Quoted in Fergusson, *Rt Hon W. S. Fielding*, ii.101–2.
139 Fielding Papers MG 2/521/72/4908: Griffith to Fielding, 8 Feb 1911.
140 Fergusson, *Rt Hon W. S. Fielding*, ii.108.
141 Potter, 'Imperial Significance'.
142 Masters, *Reciprocity*, p.18.
143 Fielding Papers MG 2/511/40/2225/5-6: Grey to Fielding, 10 Mar. 1911.
144 Ibid. MG 2/511/40/2225/5-6: Grey to Fielding, 10 Mar. 1911.
145 Ibid. MG 2/521/72/4867, 4898, 4908: Griffith to Fielding, 8, 11 Feb. 1911.
146 Ibid. MG 2/522a/B35: Fielding to Strathcona, n.d. Feb. 1911. For example, responses in *The Times*, the *Manchester Guardian*, *The Standard*, *Daily News*, and *Daily Chronicle*, were cabled to Fielding. See ibid. MG 2/522a/B36: High Commission to Fielding, n.d. Feb. 1911.
147 *CAR* (1911), p.79.
148 Ibid., p.84.
149 Ibid., p.104.
150 Walker Papers 1/B/21/43: Walker to Hemming, 30 Jan. 1911; *CAR* (1911), p.39.
151 Ibid., p.49.
152 R. Cuff, 'The Toronto Eighteen and the Election of 1911', *Ontario History*, 57 (1965), 177–8.
153 Walker Papers 1/C/32/1: Z. A. Lash, *Reciprocity with the United States: Canadian Nationality, the British Connection and Fiscal Independence* (Toronto, 1911), 11–13.
154 Potter, 'Nationalism, Imperialism, and the Press', p.277.
155 Fielding Papers MG 2/521/72/4883-4: Griffith to Fielding, 30 Mar. 1911.
156 McCurdy and Co. to Editor, *Halifax Chronicle*, 25 Feb. 1911.
157 'An "Infant Industry" and Reciprocity', *Halifax Chronicle*, 6 July 1911.
158 Offer, *First World War*, p.162.

Chapter 6   The Politics of Finance in Three Australian States: Victoria, New South Wales, and Western Australia, 1901–1914

1 Trainor, *British Imperialism*, pp.9–12.
2 Ibid., pp.155–6.
3 Clark, *A Short History of Australia*, pp.184–91.
4 R. Norris, *The Emergent Commonwealth: Australian Federation, Expectations and Fulfilment, 1889–1910* (Melbourne, 1975), pp.14–15.
5 W. G. Spence, *Australia's Awakening* (Sydney, 1909), pp.221–9; D. Murphy (ed.) *Labor in Politics* (St Lucia, Queensland: 1975), pp.3–4.
6 P. Love, *Labour and the Money Power: Australian Labour Populism 1890–1950* (Carlton, Victoria, 1984), pp.7, 29–31; R. Markey, *The Making of the Labor Party in New South Wales, 1880–1900* (Sydney, 1988), pp.14–15.

7 P. Loveday, A. W. Martin and R. S. Parker (eds) *The Emergence of the Australian Party System* (Sydney, 1977).

8 On business lobbying more generally, see J. Rickard, *Class and Politics: New South Wales, Victoria and the Early Commonwealth* (Canberra, 1976); T. V. Matthews, 'Trends in Public, Private Relations, 1901–75', in B. Head (ed.) *State and Economy in Australia* (Melbourne, 1983).

9 *AIBR*, 20 Sept. 1901, 711–19; Fitzpatrick, *The British Empire in Australia*, p.300.; CD 7171, 'Dominions Royal Commission: Minutes of Evidence Taken in Australia', in *Reports Commissioners*, xvii (1914), pp.292–5.

10 Hicks, 'Coghlan', 2.

11 P. D. Groenewegen and B. McFarlane, *A History of Australian Economic Thought* (London, 1990), p.105.

12 Coghlan, *Statistical Account* quotes at pp.753–4, 761, 1043.

13 Ibid.; T. A. Coghlan, *The Wealth and Progress of New South Wales 1898–9* (Sydney, 1900). A view implicitly confirmed in his 1918 classic, which had little to say on the role of British capital in facilitating development. See Coghlan, *Labour and Industry*. On Coghlan's elliptical methods of argument, see S. S. Holton, 'T. A. Coghlan's *Labour and Industry in Australia*: An Enigma in Australian Historiography', *Historical Studies*, 22, no. 88 (1987).

14 Butlin, 'Colonial Socialism'.

15 J. Rydon and R. N. Spann, *New South Wales Politics, 1901–1910* (Melbourne, 1962), pp.1–2, 21; J. Hagan and K. Turner, *A History of the Labor Party in New South Wales 1891–1991* (Melbourne, 1991), pp.95–7.

16 Love, *Labour and the Money Power*.

17 The evolving thought of Frank Anstey, a 'monetary radical' reflected this. See P. Love, 'Frank Anstey and the Monetary Radicals', in Appleyard and Schedvin (eds) *Australian Financiers*, pp.258–9.

18 L. F. Crisp, *The Australian Federal Labour Party, 1901–1951* (London, 1954), p.263.

19 Quoted in de Norbury Rogers, *Australian Case against John Bull & Co.*, p.24. See also, *SMH*, 22 July 1904, p.5.

20 Love, *Labour and the Money Power*, pp.37–47.

21 B. R. Wise, *The Commonwealth of Australia* (London, 1909), p.20.

22 Quoted in Melbourne *Argus*, 9 Oct. 1903, p.4. For uses of 'Bull Cohen', see *Brisbane Courier*, 31 Dec. 1910, p.5; Perth *Sunday Times*, 23 May 1909, p.1.

23 Melbourne *Argus*, 9 Oct. 1903, p.4.

24 Mitchell Library, MSS 5706/6/11: Minutes of the Tenth Annual Meeting of the Associated Chambers of Commerce of the Commonwealth of Australia, 17–20 June 1913, pp.126–7.

25 *AIBR*, 19 Nov. 1900, p.845.

26 'Reform Loan Policy', *SMH*, 9 July 1906.

27 *AIBR*, Sept. 1901, p.719.

28 'Borrowing Locally or Abroad', *SMH*, 20 Mar. 1905.

29 AMLF Papers, Dep. 162/3121/850/466-7: General Manager to London Office, 25 Feb. 1901.

30 *AIBR*, 20 June 1901, p.430. See also 'Loans and Loan Policy', *SMH*, 12 Feb. 1906.

31 Public Library of Victoria, MS 10917/1(Melbourne Chamber of Commerce Papers): Minutes, 19 May 1903, 113.

32   'The State Loan', Melbourne *Argus*, 10 Feb. 1906.
33   'The Mining Outlook', *Coolgardie Miner*, 17 May 1905.
34   'The State Loan', Melbourne *Argus*, 5 Feb. 1906.
35   Vict. P. R. O., 1225/9/8R-22510 (Treasury Loan Files): Agent-General
     to Premier, 21 Sept. 1904. See also, 'Australian Credit', *Financial Times*,
     11 Sept. 1902; 'Victorian Loans', *The Capitalist*, 6 Oct. 1906.
36   'The Money Lender', *SMH*, 14 Jan. 1907.
37   CD 7171, 'Dominions Royal Commission: Minutes of Evidence Taken in
     Australia', 295.
38   *Morning Post*, 12 Feb. 1901, quoted in J. A. La Nauze (ed.) *Federated
     Australia: Selections from Letters to the 'Morning Post' 1900–1910, by Alfred
     Deakin* (London, 1968), p.22.
39   See Chapter 5.
40   Macintyre, *Oxford History of Australia*, iv.77.
41   Since the statistics used combine loan and ordinary expenditure, the size
     of the deficits is greater than by contemporary reckoning.
42   Norris, *Emergent Commonwealth*, p.184.
43   P. Loveday, R. S. Parker, and P. Weller, 'New South Wales', in Loveday,
     Martin and Weller (eds) *Emergence of the Australian Party System*, pp.221–2.
44   *AIBR*, 20 Aug. 1902.
45   F. Bongiorno, *The People's Party: Victorian Labor and the Radical Tradition,
     1875–1914* (Carlton, Vic., 1996), p.52.
46   *AIBR*, 20 Aug. 1902, p.93.
47   *AIBR*, 19 July 1902, p.541.
48   Rickard, *Class and Politics*, pp.177–9; Bongiorno, *People's Party*, pp.55–6,
     81.
49   Bongiorno, *People's Party*, p.58.
50   *AIBR*, 20 Sept. 1902, p.733.
51   C. A. Hughes, Graham, and B. D. Graham, *A Handbook of Australian
     Government and Politics, 1890–1964* (Canberra, 1968), p.473.
52   D. W. Rawson, 'Victoria', in Loveday, Martin and Parker (eds) *Emergence of
     the Australian Party System*, p.93.
53   Vict. P. R. O., 1225/8/7R-1308 (Treasury Loan Files): Agent-General to
     Irvine, 12 Oct. 1903.
54   Bongiorno, *People's Party*, p.71; Rickard, *Class and Politics*, pp.192–3;
     Rawson, 'Victoria', p.93.
55   Vict. P. R. O., 1225/8/7R-1308 (Treasury Loan Files): Agent-General to
     Irvine, 3 July 1903. For typical praise for a 'premier with backbone', see
     MRC Papers 1557A/447 (London Letterbook): Barber to Brounlie, 5 June
     1903. See also UBA Papers U/119/40/3319/4: London Manager to General
     Manager, 13 May 1903.
56   Vict. P. R. O., 1225/8/7R-1308 (Treasury Loan Files): Agent-General to
     Premier, 11 Jan. 1907.
57   Bongiorno, *People's Party*, pp.73–91. A minority Labor government held
     power briefly in December 1913 due to divisions in the Liberal party.
58   Rydon and Spann, *New South Wales Politics*, pp.30–1; Mansfield, 'O'Sullivan',
     p.104.
59   Markey, *Making of the Labor Party*, pp.6, 57–66; Hagan and Turner, *History
     of the Labor Party*, pp.33–58.

60 *AIBR*, Jan. 1902, p.8.
61 *AIBR*, 20 Mar. 1902, p.182. See also ibid., 20 Feb. 1902, p.93
62 See for example: 'The Public Finances', *SMH*, 29 Mar. 1902; 'How the Track was Missed', 3 Apr. 1902; 'Groping our way out', ibid., 9 Apr. 1902; 'The Public Finances', ibid., 16 Apr. 1902; 'The Only Way Out', ibid., 26 Apr. 1902; 'Crying Need for Retrenchment', *SDT*, 25 Mar. 1902; 'Crying Need for Retrenchment II', ibid. 26 Mar. 1902; 'Expenditure and Extravagance', ibid., 1 Apr. 1902; 'When Parliament Meets'.
63 Ibid., 3 Apr. 1902; 'The Government Boom', ibid., 7 Apr. 1902. *SDT*, 3 and 7 Apr. 1902.
64 AMLF Papers, Dep. 162/3122/926/320: Sydney Manager to London Office, 9 Mar. 1902.
65 Rickard, *Class and Politics*, pp.121–3.
66 Carruthers Papers MSS1638/135/39: 'State Politics: Manifesto of the Liberal and Reform Party', undated, unattributed cutting.
67 'State Politics', *SMH*, 17 Mar. 1903.
68 Carruthers Papers MSS1638/135/7: 'Remarks by Mr Carruthers: The value of the Arbitration Bill', undated, unattributed cutting.
69 AMLF Papers, Dep. 162/3122/970/458: Sydney Manager to London Office, 27 Oct. 1902.
70 See Chapter 3.
71 Sydney Correspondent, 'The New South Wales Ministry', *The Times*, 28 June 1904. See also 'N. S. W. Finances', *The Financier*, 4 Mar. 1904; Rydon and Spann, *New South Wales Politics*, pp.40–7.
72 Frustrated ambition and differences on local government also played a role. See Deakin Papers, MS1540/1/1004: Wise to Waddell enclosed with Wise to Deakin, 14 June 1904; J.A. Ryan, 'Wise, Bernhard Ringrose (1858–1916)', *Australian Dictionary of Biography*, 12 (1990).
73 'Proposed Fighting Platform', *SMH*, 20, 27 Jan. 1904, Rydon and Spann, *New South Wales Politics*, p.2.
74 'The Inadequate Budget', *SMH*, 10 Oct. 1904.
75 'The Budget', ibid., 17 Oct. 1904.
76 'State Finances', ibid., 4 Jan. 1905.
77 'Assure Our Creditors', ibid., 9 Jan. 1905.
78 'Our Improving Credit', ibid., 17 July 1905.
79 'Revenue and Reform', ibid., 3 Apr. 1906.
80 Carruthers Papers MSS.1638/55/11-2: 'Notes for Premier's Speech at Arncliffe', 18 June 1906.
81 Rydon and Spann, *New South Wales Politics*, p.74.
82 Macintyre, *Oxford History of Australia*, iv.80.
83 Loveday, Parker and Weller, 'New South Wales', p.234.
84 'The Financial Statement', *SMH*, 31 Oct. 1907.
85 Waddell Papers MSS.3134 (Correspondence): Jersey to Waddell, 11 Dec. 1908.
86 Rickard, *Class and Politics*, p.195.
87 Macintyre, *Oxford History of Australia*, iv.114–16.
88 Hagan and Turner, *History of the Labor Party*, p.40.
89 Ibid., pp.94–6. See also AMLF Papers, Dep. 162/3129/1522/107-8, 1543/226-7: General Manager to London Office, 13 Dec. 1910, 24 Apr. 1911.

90 T. Waddell, 'Finance: A Critical Position', *SDT*, 24 Dec. 1913.
91 Ibid.
92 'State Finances', ibid., 27 Oct. 1913.
93 N. G. Butlin, 'Trends in Public, Private Relations, 1901–75', in Head (ed.) *State and Economy*, pp.82–6.
94 Glynn, 'Government Policy', 119. S. L. W. A, 4309A/6: Crowley, *Forrest the Politician, 1891–1918*, ii.7–10.
95 B. De Garis, 'Western Australia', in Loveday, Martin and Parker (eds) *Emergence of the Australian Party System*, pp.299, 329–30.
96 D. I. Wright, 'The Politics of Federal Finance: The First Decade', *Historical Studies*, 8 (1969), 461–3.
97 De Garis, 'Western Australia', p.342; B. Attard, 'New Estimates of Australian Public Borrowing and Capital Raised in London, 1849–1914', *Australian Economic History Review*, 47, no. 2 (2007), 176, Appendix 2.
98 'The State's Finances', *West Australian*, 1 Nov. 1904.
99 'The Daglish Ministry', *Coolgardie Miner*, 1 Nov. 1904.
100 'New Railways Schemes', *West Australian*, 16 May 1905.
101 De Garis, 'Western Australia', pp.342–3; Glynn, 'Government Policy', 129–33; J. R. Robertson, 'Scaddan, John (1876–1934)', *Australian Dictionary of Biography*, 11 (1988).
102 G. Blainey, 'Herbert Hoover's Forgotten Years', *Business Archives and History*, 3, no. 1 (1963), 62.
103 James Papers MSS 412/6/321: *Agent-General's Annual Report* (2 June 1905).
104 Ibid., 351.
105 Ibid., MSS 412/6/179: W. James 'Circular to Mine owners', 26 Apr. 1905.
106 Ibid., MSS 412/1/330: James to Rason, 27 Oct. 1905.
107 Ibid., MSS 412/1/145: James to Daglish, 14 Apr. 1905.
108 Ibid., MSS 412/6/184-6: Govett to W. James, 28, 29 Apr. 1905.
109 Quoted in ibid. MSS.412/6/346: *Agent-General's Annual Report*, 2 June 1905.
110 Ibid., MSS 412/1/271: James to Rason, 15 Sept. 1905.
111 Ibid., MSS 412/1/147: James to Daglish, 14 Apr. 1905.
112 Ibid., MSS 412/1/213-4: James to Daglish, 6–7 July 1905.
113 Daglish Papers MN 553/2397A/19: Daglish to James, 3 June 1905.
114 Richardson, 'Collins House Financiers', pp. 239–40; *The Economist*, 17 Dec. 1910, 1243.
115 Glynn, 'Government Policy', pp.115, 119–20, 131–3; De Garis, 'Western Australia', p.344.
116 Glynn, 'Private Enterprise', pp.42–3.
117 Ibid., pp.48–50; Spence, *Australia's Awakening*, p.360; MRC Papers 1557A/1055 (Company Histories): M. Lukeus, *History of the Midland Railway Company in Western Australia* (no place, no date), pp.2–5.
118 Glynn, 'Private Enterprise', pp.53–4.
119 Lukeus, *History of the Midland Railway Company*, pp.4–5.
120 See for example, 'The Midland Railway', Perth *Morning Herald*, 7 June 1905.
121 Lukeus, *History of the Midland* Railway, pp.4–5; Glynn, 'Private Enterprise', p.54.

122 *The Economist*, 19 Mar. 1904, p.492; MRC Papers 1557A/447: Barber to de Bels Brounlie, 23 Jan., 26 June, 10 July 1903.
123 Ibid., 1557A/449: Barber to Murcott, 8 Jan. 1904.
124 Ibid., 1557A/450: Barber to Murcott, 14 Oct. 1904.
125 *SMH*, 10 Aug. 1905; James Papers MSS 412/1/39, 69–7: James to Daglish, 16 Dec. 1904, 20 Jan. 1905.
126 See his comments in, 'Western Australian Politics', Adelaide *Advertizer*, 22 June 1905.
127 'The Midland Railway Question', Perth *Morning Herald*, 22 July 1905.
128 'The State Finances', ibid., 2 Mar. 1905.
129 Daglish Papers, MN 553/2397A/19: Daglish to James, 29 May, 3 June 1905. See also 'The Western Australian Loan', *West Australian*, 7 June 1905; 'Recent Loan Floatation', Perth *Morning Herald*, 8 June 1905.
130 'The Financial Crisis', Perth *Sunday Times*, 11 June 1905.
131 'The Political Outlook', *West Australian*, 19 Aug. 1905.
132 Spence, *Australia's Awakening*, pp.357–61, quote at p.361.
133 MRC Papers, 1557A/450 (London Letterbook): Barber to Murcott, 14 Oct. 1904; ibid. 1557A/452: Rason to Barber, 9 Nov. 1905; Smith to Barber, 11 Nov. 1905; Barber to Murcott, 17 Nov. and 1 Dec. 1905; James Papers, MSS 412/1/254: James to Daglish, 25 Aug. 1905.
134 Quoted in Glynn, 'Private Enterprise', p.56. For one promotional leaflet, see Midland Railway Company of Western Australia, *Unlocking the Land* (Perth, 1909).
135 Glynn, 'Private Enterprise', pp.56–7.

Chapter 7   Influence Stumped? The Commonwealth and the City, 1901–1913

1 'Australia's Finances', *The Financier*, 23 June 1908.
2 Deakin Papers, 1540/1/2182: Coghlan to Deakin, 3 Nov. 1908.
3 Hughes and Graham, *A Handbook of Australian Government and Politics*, p.280.
4 Wise, *Commonwealth of Australia*, pp.202–3.
5 P. Loveday, 'The Federal Parties', in Loveday, Martin and Weller (eds) *Emergence of the Australian Party System*, p.385.
6 Sullivan, 'Revealing a Prefence'.
7 P. Loveday, 'Support in Return for Concessions', *Australian Historical Studies*, 55, no. 376–405 (1970).
8 Macintyre, *Oxford History of Australia*, iv.87–8; Patmore, *Australian Labour History*, pp.120–1.
9 Crisp, *Australian Federal Labour Party*, pp.4–6.
10 For the views of one Deakinite, see Wise, *Commonwealth of Australia*, p.67.
11 Loveday, 'Support in Return for Concessions', 393.
12 Ibid., pp.175–7.
13 Macintyre, *Oxford History of Australia*, p.101.
14 Wright, 'Politics of Federal Finance', 463–4.
15 Norris, *Emergent Commonwealth*, p.15.

16 Calculated from W. Vamplew (ed.) *Australians: Historical Statistics* (Broadway, N.S.W, 1987), Series A104-107, G108-114.
17 'The Federal Budget', *SMH*, 19 Oct. 1904.
18 Spence, *Australia's Awakening*, p.483.
19 La Nauze, *Alfred Deakin*, ii.252–4.
20 G. Serle, 'Turner, Sir George', *Australian Dictionary of Biography*, 12 (1990).
21 S. L. W. A., MN 34/766A/3/5/324 (John Forrest Papers): Lord Knutsford to Forrest, 3 Oct. 1905.
22 Ibid., MN 34/766A/3/6/358, 361: R (illegible, of Carlton House Terrace, London) to Forrest, 13 Sept. 1906; see also Jersey to Forrest, 17 Oct. 1906.
23 'S. L. W. A., 4309A/6: Crowley, *Forrest the Politician*, iii.675; S. L. W. A., MN 34/768A (John Forrest Papers): Middleton Campbell to Forrest, 16 May 1907; enclosed memoranda by A. C. Cole, May 1907; ibid. MN 34/766A/4/6/385: Revelstoke to Forrest, 21 Mar. 1907.
24 *Morning Post*, 23 Oct. 1904 in La Nauze (ed.) *Federated Australia*, p.155.
25 S. L. W. A. 530A (John Forrest Papers): W. Lyne, 'Memorandum on the Subject of the Transfer of State Debts to the Commonwealth', 5 May 1908, 2; *Morning Post*, 12 May 1902 in La Nauze (ed.) *Federated Australia*, p.97.
26 D. Elder, 'Transfer of State Debts', Melbourne *Age*, 30 July 1905; Knibbs, *Official Yearbook* (1908), p.695, table 5.
27 He contacted the agents-general of Victoria, New South Wales, and South Australia; the Bank of England and its broker; the London and Westminster Bank; Robert Nivison; Lord Revelstoke; Lord Goschen (who converted consuls to a lower rate of interest in 1888); W. Hamilton (Goschen's assistant); and the ubiquitous earl of Jersey. Deakin Papers MS 1540/15/460, 480501, 509: Forrest to Deakin, 25 Oct., 5 Dec. 1905, 2, 23 March 1906.
28 *TSDC*, quotes at pp.11, 12, 16.
29 Coghlan Papers MS.6335/6: Tavener to Coghlan, 6 March 1906.
30 Deakin Papers MS.1540/1/1365: Coghlan to Deakin, 20 March 1906; Coghlan Papers MS.6335/13/172: Coghlan to Deakin, 27 July 1906.
31 S. L. W. A., MN.34/768A (John Forrest Papers): Forrest to Deakin, 5 March 1907.
32 Lyne, 'Memorandum on the Subject of the Transfer', 5 May 1908, pp.2–4.
33 Turner, *First Decade*, p.247.
34 Deakin Papers MS 1540/15/46/59/2994: Collins to Deakin, 23 July 1909; Ibid. 1540/15/46/60/3022-4: Collins to Deakin, 19 Nov. 1909; Bank of England Archive, AC30/325: *Proposed Issue of Loans for the Commonwealth of Australia*.
35 'Arrival of Sir George Reid', *Financial News*, 1 Mar. 1910.
36 Turner, *First Decade*, p.247.
37 Wright, 'Politics of Federal Finance', 71–3.
38 Deakin Papers, 1540/15/1789: *Speech by the Hon Alfred Deakin on the Constitution Alteration Finance Bill*, 8 Sept. 1909, p.21.
39 Wright, 'Politics of Federal Finance', 473–5; Fitzpatrick, *The British Empire in Australia*, pp.303–4.
40 'English View of the Federal Government', Melbourne *Age*, 1 June 1904.
41 S. L. W. A., MN 34/766A/3/3/277 (John Forrest Papers): Clarke to Forrest, 17 Feb. 1904.
42 'Mr Reid in Sydney', *SMH*, 6 Mar. 1905.

43 *Morning Post*, 19 Feb. 1905, in La Nauze (ed.) *Federated Australia*, p.175.
44 Reid Papers, MS 7842/2: Reid to Governor-General, 3 July 1905.
45 Deakin Papers MS 1540/1/1170: 'Against Socialism. Fighting Organisations formed. All electorates invaded tomorrow', undated, unattributed clipping.
46 Ibid.
47 'Politics and the London Market', *SMH*, 18 June 1906.
48 B. R. Wise, *The Commonwealth of Australia*, 2nd edn (London, 1913), p.235, note 231.
49 Spence, *Australia's Awakening*, p.431.
50 S. L. W. A., MN 34/766A/3/3/285 (John Forrest Papers): Forrest to Deakin, 24 Apr. 1904; Ibid. MN 34/766A/4/2/401: Forrest to Deakin, 27 July 1907; Loveday, 'The Federal Parties', 383.
51 PLV, MS 10917/I/367 (Melbourne Chamber of Commerce Papers): AGM Minutes, 23 May 1907.
52 'The Fall in Consuls', *SMH*, 13 Aug. 1907.
53 Deakin Papers MS 1540/1/416: Carruthers to Deakin, 18 July 1905.
54 *Morning Post*, 19 April 1905, in La Nauze (ed.) *Federated Australia*, 175–6. For a similar defence, see Wise, *Commonwealth of Australia*, pp.53–74.
55 Deakin Papers MS 1540/15/42/24/1566-7: Telegraphed extract from the *Adelaide Register*, 21 May 1907.
56 Macintyre, *Oxford History of Australia*, iv.92.
57 C. Lloyd, 'Andrew Fisher', in M. Grattan (ed.) *Australian Prime Ministers* (Sydney, 2000), pp.79–80.
58 Turner, *First Decade*, p.248.
59 Rickard, *Class and Politics*, pp.249–51.
60 Quoted in Crisp, *Australian Federal Labour Party*, p.275.
61 Patmore, *Australian Labour History*, p.92.
62 Love, *Labour and the Money Power*, pp.44–5.
63 Quoted in ibid., p.51.
64 *Sydney Worker*, 7 Sept. 1911, quoted in ibid., p.52.
65 Ibid., p.53; Turner, *First Decade*, pp.277–81.
66 Butlin, 'British Banking in Australia', 99.
67 Coghlan Papers 6335/15: Coghlan to Fisher, 28 Oct. 1911; *Sunday Times*, 17 Dec. 1911, 24 Dec. 1911.
68 Love, *Labour and the Money Power*, p.54.
69 Love, 'Frank Anstey', p.262.
70 ESAB Papers E/143/16/827: General Manager to London Manager, 22 May 1912. See also ibid., pp.206–12.
71 I. R. Harper and C. B. Schedvin, 'Sir Denison Millar', in Appleyard and Schedvin (eds) *Australian Financiers*, pp.213–16.
72 For discussion see Cochrane, *Blockade*; B. Schedvin, 'E. G. Theodore and the London Pastoral Lobby', *Politics*, vi (1971).
73 K. Buckley and T. Wheelwright, *No Paradise for Workers: Capitalism and the Common People in Australia 1788–1914* (Melbourne, 1988), pp.204–7; Love, *Labour and the Money Power*, p.29; Markey, *Making of the Labor Party*, pp.297–303.
74 F. Anstey, *Monopoly and Democracy* (Melbourne, 1906), p.39.
75 Idem, 'The Means of Exchange', *Labor Call*, 6 Feb. 1908.
76 Wise, *Commonwealth of Australia*, p.127.

77 J. Forrest, 'Australia of to-Day', *Empire Review*, 11 (1906), 339, 349.
78 Wise, *Commonwealth of Australia*, pp.129, 140.
79 Spence, *Australia's Awakening*, pp.597–624.
80 Crisp, *Australian Federal Labour Party*, pp.263–4.
81 S. L. W. A. MN 1379/4309A/5 (Frank Crowley Papers): Federal Labour Party W. A. Division, 'Labour Manifesto' (Melbourne, 4 Oct. 1906).
82 ANA A2863/1 (Prime Minister's Office Papers): Extracts from A. Fisher's Speech at Gympie', 30 Mar. 1909.
83 Turner, *First Decade*, p.211.
84 Spence, *Australia's Awakening*, p.410.
85 Melbourne *Argus*, 1 Apr. 1909; *SMH*, 6 May 1909; *Morning Post*, 22 Apr. 1909 in La Nauze (ed.) *Federated Australia*, p.283.
86 Turner, *First Decade*, p.287.
87 'The Labour Manifesto', Hobart *Mercury*, 7 Mar. 1910.
88 H. Heaton, 'The Taxation of Unimproved Value of Land in Australia', *Quarterly Journal of Economics*, 39, no. 3 (1925), 422.
89 Turner, *First Decade*, pp.287–9.
90 Heaton, 'Taxation of Unimproved Value', 423.
91 Ibid., 424.
92 Turner, *First Decade*, pp.217–19.
93 ANA, A2863/1/2907 (Prime Minister's Office): Forrest to Fisher, 1 Oct. 1910.
94 'Effect on Credit', Melbourne *Argus*, 2 Sept. 1910.
95 Turner, *First Decade*, p.287.
96 'Federal Land Tax', Hobart *Mercury*, 19 Aug. 1910; 'Federal Land Tax', Melbourne *Argus* 19 Aug 1910; 'Federal Land Tax', *SMH*, 19 Aug. 1910.
97 Turner, *First Decade*, pp.287–9; Heaton, 'Taxation of Unimproved Value', 423.
98 AMLF Papers Dep. 162/3129/1511/68A: Kidd to London Office, Sept. 1910; Doxat Letterbook N8/30 pp.535–6: Doxat to Fairbairn, 15 Sept. 1910.
99 ANA A2863/1/2774 (Prime Minister's Office Papers): British Australasian Society Cable to Fisher, 29 Sept. 1910. See also ibid., Doxat to Fisher, 7 Oct. 1910.
100 See for example, ESAB AGM, *The Economist*, 29 Oct. 1910, p.877.
101 UBA Papers U/103/4521/2: General Manager to London Manager, 17 Aug. 1910.
102 In particular, individual shareholders (not firms) would be taxed as absentees and the treatment of mortgages was altered. See, ESAB Papers E/143/16/378: General Manager to London Office, 24 Sept. 1910.
103 AMLF Papers Dep. 162/3129/1514/76-77: Kidd to London Office, 16 Oct. 1910; UBA Papers U/119/42/4349: London Manager to General Manager, 28 Oct. 1910.
104 'Federal Land Tax', *SMH*, 28 Nov. 1910.
105 Turner, *First Decade*, p.290.
106 GL MS 16511/1/157 (LCC Australasian Trade Section Minute Books): Minutes, Feb. 1911.
107 Ibid.; GL MS16459/4/2, 423 (LCC Council Minute Books): 'Report inserted in minutes for consideration by the Council as a matter of urgency under Bye Law II: Australian Federal Land Tax', 11 May 1911.

108   The following two paragraphs are based on the report in *CCJ*, July 1911, pp.205–7.
109   'Federal Land Tax', *SMH*, 15 June 1911.
110   Ibid.
111   Heaton, 'Taxation of Unimproved Value', 424–8.
112   On the deadlock, see Lloyd, 'Andrew Fisher', p.82.
113   Doxat Letterbooks N8/30, pp.572–3: Doxat to Fairbairn, 2 December 1910. On private investment see Andrew Williamson's comments at, 'Australian Estates Company AGM', *The Economist*, 17 June 1911, pp.1312–14.

Conclusion

1   Belich, *Replenishing the Earth*, pp.206–8.
2   For a similar critique of new British history, which shares similar intellectual roots to the British World, see R. Bourke, 'Pocock and the Presuppositions of the New British History', *Historical Journal*, 53, no. 3 (2010).
3   This is not to support their central claims about 'gentlemanly capitalism'. Despite their interaction with the ideas and institutions of empire, there is little evidence that the City's conceptions of its interests – the evolving 'rules' – were affected by the policy priorities of the British state. This was indeed a 'commercial republic' as Darwin has suggested, and as far as it was populated by gentlemanly capitalists, they were supremely uninfluenced by their counterparts in Whitehall.
4   Strange, *States and Markets*, p.25.

Select Bibliography

Manuscript and Archival Sources

Australia

Canberra

National Archives of Australia
Prime Minister's Department
A2863/1: Papers Relating to the Land Tax

National Library of Australia
Alfred Deakin Papers (MS 1540)
Timothy Coghlan Papers (MS 6335)
George Reid Papers (MS 7842)

Noel Butlin Archives Centre, Australian National University
Australian Mercantile, Land and Finance Co. Papers. Dep. 97
Dalgety and Co. Papers. Dep. N8/28-31

Melbourne

ANZ Group Archive
English Scottish and Australian Bank Ltd Papers (E)
Union Bank of Australia Ltd Papers (U)

Public Library of Victoria
Melbourne Chamber of Commerce Papers (MS 10917)

Public Record Office of Victoria
Treasury of Victoria Papers. VPRO 1225/7-11

Perth

State Library of Western Australia
Frank Crowley Papers (MN 1379/4309A)
Henry Daglish Papers (MN 553-2397A)
John Forrest Papers (MN 34, Acc. 532A, Acc. 766A/3-4, Acc. 768A, Acc. 530A)
Midland Railway Co. of Western Australia Papers (1557A)

State Record Office of Western Australia
Agent-General's Papers (1150)

Sydney

Mitchell Library
Walter James Papers (MSS 412)
Joseph Carruthers Papers (MSS 1638)
Sydney Chamber of Commerce Papers (MSS 5706)

State Record Office of New South Wales, Kingswood
Treasury Papers CGS-1433

Canada

Halifax

Public Archives of Nova Scotia
W. S. Fielding Papers (MG 2)

Ottawa

National Archives of Canada
W. T. White Papers (MG 27-II-D-18)
Strathcona Papers (MG 25)
Wilfred Laurier Papers (MG 26-G)
Robert Laird Borden Papers (MG 26-H-1-A)
Canadian Manufacturers Association Papers (MG 28-I-230)
C. M. Hays Letterbooks (MG 30-a18)
A. W. Smithers Papers (MG 30-A-93)
Department of Finance Papers (RG 19)
Department of External Affairs Papers (RG 25)
Canadian National Railways Papers (RG 30)

Toronto

Public Archives of Ontario
J. P. Whitney Papers (F5)
Premier James Whitney Office Records (RG 3-2)

Thomas Fisher Rare Books Library, University of Toronto
B E Walker Papers (MS Col 1)

Vancouver

University of British Columbia Library
British Columbia Electric Railway Papers (MSS Col Rare Books and Special
   Collections)

United Kingdom
London

Bank of England Archive
Bank of England Papers (AC30/189/H20, AC30/325/S9)

Guildhall Library
London Chamber of Commerce Papers. (MS 16459, MS 16511)
Federation of Commonwealth Chambers of Commerce Papers (MS 18287)

House of Lords Record Office
Beaverbrook Papers (BBK)

Oxford

Bodleian Library, Collection of Western Manuscripts
R. Brand Papers (MSS Brand)

Printed Primary Sources

Official Publications
Colonial Office List
Commonwealth of Australia Parliamentary Debates
Debates of the Commons of the Dominion of Canada
CD 7171, 'Dominions Royal Commission: Minutes of Evidence Taken in Australia',
  in *Reports Commissions and c*, xvii (1914)

Newspapers and Journals
Australian

Adelaide *Advertiser*
Australasian Insurance and Banking Record (Melbourne)
Brisbane Courier
Brisbane *Worker*
Coolgardie Miner
Hobart *Mercury*
Labor Call (Melbourne)
Melbourne *Age*
Melbourne *Argus*
Perth *Morning Herald*
Perth *Sunday Times*
Perth *West Australian*
Sydney *Bulletin*
Sydney *Daily Telegraph*
Sydney Morning Herald
Sydney *Worker*

Canadian

Canadian Annual Review of Public Affairs (Toronto)
Halifax Morning Chronicle
Manitoba Free Press
Manitoba *Grain Growers Guide*
Montreal Daily Witness
Montreal Gazette
Montreal Star
Nelson News
Toronto Globe
Toronto News
Toronto Saturday Night
Toronto Star
Toronto Telegraph
Vancouver Advertiser

United Kingdom

Australasian World
Capitalist
Chamber of Commerce Journal
Daily Mail
Daily News
Economist
Financial News
Financial Times
Financial World
Financier
Globe
Investor's Review
Morning Post
Pall Mall Gazette
Standard
Statist
Stock Exchange Gazette
Stock Exchange Official Intelligence
Stock Exchange Yearbook
Tatler
Times
Westminster Gazette

Pre-1918 Publications

Angell, N., *The Great Illusion* (London, 1910).
Anon, *Grand Trunk Pacific: A History of a Project* (n.d., probably 1904).
Anon, *The Centenary of the Bank of Montreal, 1817–1917* (Montreal, 1917).
Ashley, W. J. S. 'Introduction', in Ashley, W. J. S. (ed.) *British Dominions: Their Present Commercial and Industrial Condition* (London, 1911).
Ashley, W. J. S. (ed.) *British Dominions: Their Present Commercial and Industrial Condition* (London, 1911).
Bagehot, W., *Lombard Street: A Description of the Money Market* (London, 1873).

Coghlan, T. A., *The Wealth and Progress of New South Wales 1898–9* (Sydney, 1900).
——, *A Statistical Account of the Seven Colonies of Australasia, 1901–2* (Sydney, 1902).
——, *Labour and Industry in Australia* (Melbourne, 1969, 1st pub. 1918).
Curzon, G. N., *Speeches on India, Delivered by Lord Curzon ... While in England in July–August, 1904* (London, 1904).
Dicey, A. V., *The Credit of Canada: How It is Affected by the Ontario Power Legislation* (Toronto, 1909).
Dilke, C. W., *Greater Britain: A Record of Travel in English-Speaking Countries During 1866 and 1867* (London, 1868).
——, *Problems of Greater Britain* (London, 1890).
Field, F. W., *Capital Investments in Canada*, 3rd edn (Montreal, 1914).
Forrest, J., 'Australia of To-Day', *Empire Review*, 11 (1906), 339–50.
Hobson, C. K., *Export of Capital* (London, 1914).
Hobson, J. A., *Imperialism: A Study* (London, 1905).
——, *The Evolution of Modern Capitalism* (New Edn, London, 1906).
Ingall, G. D. and G. Withers, *The Stock Exchange* (London, 1904).
Keynes, J. M., *Indian Currency and Finance* (London, 1913).
Knibbs, G., *Official Yearbook of the Commonwealth of Australia* (Melbourne, 1908).
——, *Official Yearbook of the Commonwealth of Australia* (Melbourne, 1909).
Lawson, W. R., *Canada and the Empire* (London, 1911).
Lehfeldt, R. A., 'The Rate of Interest on British and Foreign Investments', *Journal of the Royal Statistical Society*, 76 (1913), 196–207.
Lowenfeld, H., *All About Investment* (London, 1909).
——, *Investment an Exact Science* (London, 1909).
Lyttleton, A., 'The Empire', in Ashley, W. J. S. (ed.) *British Dominions: Their Present Commercial and Industrial Condition* (London, 1911), 2–23.
Midland Railway Company of Western Australia, *Unlocking the Land* (Perth, 1909).
Page, A., 'The Legal Problems of the Empire', in Herbertson, A. J. H. and O. J. R. Howarth (eds) *The Oxford Survey of the British Empire* (Oxford, 1914), pp.87–112.
Paish, G., 'Great Britain's Capital Investments in Other Lands', *Journal of the Royal Statistical Society*, 72 (1909), 465–95.
——, 'Great Britain's Capital Investments in Individual Colonial and Foreign Countries', *Journal of the Royal Statistical Society*, 74 (1911), 167–200.
——, 'The Export of Capital and the Cost of Living', in *Statist Supplement*, (London, 1914), 167–200.
Powell, E. T., *The Mechanism of the City* (London, 1910).
de Norbury Rogers, E., *The Australian Case against John Bull & Co* (Sydney, 1905).
Seeley, J. R., *The Expansion of England* (London, 1883).
Smith, A., *The Wealth of Nations: Books IV–V* (London, 1999, 1st pub. 1776).
Spence, W. G., *Australia's Awakening* (Sydney, 1909).
Spicer, A., 'Australia', in Ashley, W. J. S. (ed.) *British Dominions: Their Present Commercial and Industrial Condition* (London, 1911), pp.36–67.
Tovey, P., *Prospectuses: How to Read and Understand Them* (London, 1920, 1st pub. 1912).
Turner, H. G., *The First Decade of the Australian Commonwealth* (Melbourne, 1911).
Walker, B. E., *Canadian Credit and Enterprise* (Toronto, 1908).
Williams-Taylor, F., 'Canadian Loans in London', *United Empire*, 3 (1912), 985–97.

Wilson, A. J., *An Empire in Pawn* (London, 1909).
Wilson, B., *The Life of Lord Strathcona and Mount Royal* (London, 1914).
Wise, B. R., *The Commonwealth of Australia* (London, 1909).
——, *The Commonwealth of Australia* (2nd edn, London, 1913).
Withers, H., *International Finance* (London, 1916).
Wood, E. R., *Review of the Bond Market in Canada for 1908* (Toronto, 1908).
——, *Review of the Bond Market in Canada for 1911* (Toronto, 1911).

Post-1918 Publications

Anon, *The Story of Mond Nickel* (N. P., 1951).
Aitken, H. G. J., 'Government and Business in Canada: An Interpretation', *Business History Review*, 38 (1964), 4–21.
Altman, M., 'A Revision of Canadian Economic Growth: 1870–1910 (A Challenge to the Gradualist Interpretation)', *The Canadian Journal of Economics/Revue canadienne d'Economique*, 20 (1987), 86–113.
——, 'Staple Theory and Export-Led Growth: Constructing Differential Growth', *Australian Economic History Review*, 43 (2003), 230–255.
Anstey, F., *Monopoly and Democracy* (Melbourne, 1906).
Appleyard, R. T. and M. Davies, 'Financiers of the Western Australian Goldfields', in Appleyard, R. T. and C. B. Schedvin (eds) *Australian Financiers: Bibliographical Essays* (Melbourne, 1988), pp.160–86.
Armstrong, C. and H. V. Nelles, *Monopoly's Moment: The Organization and Regulation of Canadian Utilities, 1830–1930* (Philadelphia, 1986).
——, *Southern Exposure: Canadian Promoters in Latin America and the Caribbean 1896–1930* (Toronto, 1988).
Attard, B., 'From Free-Trade Imperialism to Structural Power: New Zealand and the Capital Market, 1856–68', *Journal of Imperial and Commonwealth History*, 35 (2007), 505–27.
——, 'New Estimates of Australian Public Borrowing and Capital Raised in London, 1849–1914', *Australian Economic History Review*, 47 (2007), 155–77.
Bailey, J. D., 'Australian Borrowing in Scotland in the Nineteenth Century', *Economic History Review*, 12 (1959), 268–79.
——, *A Hundred Years of Pastoral Banking: A History of the Australian Mercantile Land & Finance Company, 1863–1963* (Oxford, 1966).
Ballantyne, T., 'Race and the Webs of Empire', *Journal of Colonialism and Colonial History*, 2 (2001).
Baster, A. S. J., *The Imperial Banks* (London, 1929).
——, 'A Note on the Colonial Stock Acts and Dominion Borrowing', *Economic History*, 8 (1933), 602–8.
Beaver, A. and M. Beaver, 'Henry Gyles Turner', in Appleyard, R. T. and C. B. Schedvin (eds) *Australian Financiers: Bibliographical Essays* (Melbourne, 1988).
Belich, J., *Replenishing the Earth: The Settler Revolution and the Rise of the Anglo-World, 1783–1939* (Oxford, 2009).
Bell, D., *The Idea of Greater Britain: Empire and the Future of World Order, 1860–1900* (Princeton, N.J., 2007).
Berger, C., *The Writing of Canadian History: Aspects of English-Canadian Historical Writing since 1900* (Toronto, 1976).
Berton, P., *Klondike; The Last Great Gold Rush: 1896–1899* (Toronto, 1972).
Blainey, G., 'Herbert Hoover's Forgotten Years', *Business Archives and History*, 3 (1963), 53–70.

——, *The Rush That Never Ended: A History of Australian Mining* (Carlton, Vic., 1994).

——, *The Tyranny of Distance: How Distance Shaped Australia's History* (Sydney, 2001).

Bliss, M. '"Dyspepsia of the Mind": The Canadian Businessman and His Enemies, 1880–1914', in Macmillan, D. S. (ed.) *Canadian Business History: Selected Studies, 1497–1971* (Toronto, 1972), pp.144–91.

Boehm, E. A., *Prosperity and Depression in Australia, 1887–1897* (Oxford, 1971).

Bongiorno, F., *The People's Party: Victorian Labor and the Radical Tradition, 1875–1914* (Carlton, Vic., 1996).

——, 'From Republican to Anti-Billite: Bernard O'dowd and Federation', *The New Federalist*, 4 (1999), 49–57.

Boot, H. M., 'Government and the Colonial Economies', *Australian Economic History Review*, 38 (1998), 74–101.

Borden, H. (ed.), *Robert Laird Borden: His Memoirs* (Toronto, 1938).

Bordo, M. D. and H. Rockoff, 'The Gold Standard as a "Good Housekeeping Seal of Approval"', *Journal of Economic History*, 56 (1996), 389–428.

Bothwell, R., M. Drummond and J. English, *Canada, 1900–1945* (Toronto, 1987).

Bourke, R., 'Pocock and the Presuppositions of the New British History', *Historical Journal*, 53 (2010), 747–70.

Brewer, A., *Marxist Theories of Imperialism: A Critical Survey* (London, 1990).

Bridge, C. and K. Fedorowich (eds) *The British World: Diaspora, Culture, and Identity* (London, 2003).

Bridge, C. and K. Fedorowich, 'Mapping the British World', in Bridge, C. and K. Fedorowich (eds) *The British World: Diaspora, Culture, and Identity* (London, 2003), pp.1–15.

Bright, R., 'Asian Migration and the British World, 1850–1914', in Fedorowich, K. and A. Thompson (eds) *Empire, Identity and Migration in the British World* (Manchester, forthcoming).

Brown, R. C., *Robert Laird Borden: A Biography* (Toronto, 1975).

Brown, R. C. and R. Cook, *Canada, 1896–1921: A Nation Transformed* (Toronto, 1974).

Buckley, K. and T. Wheelwright, *No Paradise for Workers: Capitalism and the Common People in Australia 1788–1914* (Melbourne, 1988).

Buckner, P., 'The Creation of the Dominion of Canada, 1860–1901', in Buckner, P. (ed.) *Canada and the British Empire* (Oxford, 2008), pp.66–87.

——, 'Introduction', in Buckner, P. (ed.) *Canada and the British Empire* (Oxford, 2008), pp.1–22.

Buckner, P. A. and R. D. Francis, 'Introduction', in Buckner, P. A. and R. D. Francis (eds) *Rediscovering the British World* (Calgary, 2005), pp.10–17.

—— (eds), *Rediscovering the British World* (Calgary, 2005).

—— (eds), *Canada and the British World: Culture, Migration, and Identity* (Vancouver, 2006).

Burk, K., 'Grenfell, A. M.', in Jeremy, D. J. (ed.) *Dictionary of Business Biography: A Biographical Dictionary of Business Leaders Active in Britain in the Period 1860–1980* (London, 1984), pp.648–52.

Burroughs, P. P., 'Colonial Self-Government', in Eldridge, C. C. (ed.) *British Imperialism in the Nineteenth Century* (London, 1984), pp.39–63.

Butlin, N. G. 'Colonial Socialism', in Aitken, H. G. J. (ed.) *The State and Economic Growth*. (New York, 1959), pp.22–78.

——, *Australian Domestic Product, Investment, and Foreign Borrowing, 1861–1938/39* (Cambridge, 1962).

——, *Investment in Australian Economic Development, 1861–1900* (Cambridge, 1964).

——, 'Trends in Public, Private Relations, 1901–75', in Head, B. (ed.) *State and Economy in Australia* (Melbourne, 1983), pp.75–115.

Butlin, N. G. and A. Barnard, 'Pastoral Finance and Capital Requirements, 1860–1960', in Barnard, A. (ed.) *The Simple Fleece: Studies in the Australian Wool Industry* (Melbourne, 1962), pp.383–401.

Butlin, S. J., 'British Banking in Australia', *Journal of the Royal Australian Historical Society*, 49 (1963), 81–100.

Cain, P. J., 'Economics and Empire: The Metropolitan Context', in Porter, A. N. (ed.) *Oxford History of the British Empire: Vol. 3: The Nineteenth Century* (Oxford, 1999), pp.31–52.

——, 'Character and Imperialism: The British Financial Administration of Egypt, 1878–1914', *Journal of Imperial and Commonwealth History*, 34 (2006), 177–200.

Cain, P. J. and A. G. Hopkins, 'Afterword: The Theory and Practice of British Imperialism', in Dumett, R. E. (ed.) *Gentlemanly Capitalism and British Imperialism: The New Debate on Empire* (London, 1999), pp.196–220.

——, *British Imperialism, 1688–2000* (Harlow, 2001).

——, 'The Peculiarities of British Capitalism: Imperialism and World Development', in Akita, S. (ed.) *Gentlemanly Capitalism, Imperialism and Global History* (Basingstoke, 2002), pp.207–64.

Cannadine, D., *The Decline and Fall of the British Aristocracy* (New Haven, Conn., 1990).

Cannon, M., *The Land Boomers* (Cambridge, 1966).

Carrigan, D. O., *Canadian Party Platforms, 1867–1968* (Urbana, 1968).

Carrothers, W. A., *Emigration from the British Isles* (London, 1965).

Cassis, Y., 'British Finance: Success and Controversy', in Cassis, Y. (ed.) *Finance and Financiers in European History, 1880–1960* (Cambridge, 1992), pp.1–22.

——, *City Bankers, 1890–1914* (Cambridge, 1994).

——, 'London Banks and International Finance, 1890–1914', in Cassis, Y. and E. Bussière (eds) *London and Paris as International Financial Centres in the Twentieth Century* (Oxford, 2005), pp.75–110.

Chambers, E. J. and D. F. Gordon, 'Primary Products and Economic Growth: An Empirical Measurement', *Journal of Political Economy*, 74 (1966), 315–32.

Chapman, S. D., *The Rise of Merchant Banking* (London, 1984).

Checkland, S. G., 'The Mind of the City, 1870–1914', *Oxford Economic Papers*, 9 (1957), 261–78.

Clark, C. M. H., *A Short History of Australia* (New York, 1987).

Cochrane, P., *Industrialization and Dependence: Australia's Road to Economic Development 1870–1939* (Brisbane, 1980).

Cochrane, T., *Blockade: The Queensland Loans Affair, 1920 to 1924* (St. Lucia, Queensland, 1989).

Copland, D. B., 'Australian Banking and Exchange', *Economic Record*, 1 (1925), 18–28.

Cottrell, P. L., *British Overseas Investment in the Nineteenth Century* (London, 1975).

Creighton, D. G., *The Commercial Empire of the St. Lawrence, 1760–1850* (Toronto, 1937).

Crisp, L. F., *The Australian Federal Labour Party, 1901–1951* (London, 1954).

Crouzet, F., 'Trade and Empire: The British Experience from the Establishment of Free Trade until the First World War', in Ratcliffe, B. M. (ed.) *Great Britain and Her World, 1750–1914: Essays in Honour of W. O. Henderson* (Manchester, 1975), pp.209–27.

Cuff, R., 'The Toronto Eighteen and the Election of 1911', *Ontario History*, 57 (1965), 169–80.

Currie, A. W., *The Grand Trunk Railway of Canada* (Toronto, 1957).

Darwin, J., 'Imperialism and the Victorians: The Dynamics of Territorial Expansion', *English Historical Review*, 112 (1997), 614–42.

——, 'A Third British Empire? The Dominion Idea in Impersial Politics', in Brown, J. M. and W. R. Louis (eds) *Oxford History of the British Empire: Vol. 4: The Twentieth Century* (Oxford, 1999), pp.64–87.

——, *After Tamerlane: The Global History of Empire since 1405* (London, 2007).

——, *The Empire Project: The Rise and Fall of the British World-System, 1830–1970* (Cambridge, 2009).

Daunton, M. J., 'Family and Firm in the City of London in the Nineteenth Century: The Case of F. G. Dalgety', *Historical Research*, 62 (1989), 152–78.

Davenport-Hines, R. P. T. 'Lord Glendyne', in Appleyard, R. T. and C. B. Schedvin (eds) *Australian Financiers: Bibliographical Essays* (Melbourne, 1988), pp.191–203.

——, 'Blackwood, Frederick Temple Hamilton-Temple, First Marquess of Dufferin and Ava', *Oxford Dictionary of National Biography* (2004).

Davis, L. E., 'The Late Nineteenth-Century British Imperialist: Specification, Quantification and Controlled Conjectures', in Dumett, R. E. (ed.) *Gentlemanly Capitalism and British Imperialism: The New Debate on Empire* (London, 1999), pp.82–112.

Davis, L. E. and R. A. Huttenback, *Mammon and the Pursuit of Empire: The Political Economy of British Imperialism, 1860–1912* (Cambridge, 1987).

——, *Mammon and the Pursuit of Empire: The Economics of British Imperialism* (Cambridge, 1988).

Davis, L. E. and R. E. Gallman, *Evolving Financial Markets and International Capital Flows: Britain, the Americas, and Australia, 1870–1914* (Cambridge, 2001).

Day, D., 'The White Australia Policy', in Attard, B. and C. Bridge (eds) *Between Empire and Nation: Australia's External Relations from Federation to the Second World War* (Melbourne, 2000), 35–54.

De Garis, B., 'Western Australia', in Loveday, P., A. W. Martin and R. S. Parker (eds) *The Emergence of the Australian Party System* (Sydney, 1977), pp.298–354.

Deakin, A., *The Federal Story: The Inner Story of the Federal Cause* (Melbourne, 1944).

Den Otter, A. A., 'Alexander Galt, the 1859 Tariff and Canadian Economic Nationalism', *Canadian Historical Review*, 58 (1982), 151–78.

——, *Civilizing the West: The Galts and the Development of Western Canada* (Edmonton, Alta., 1982).

——, *The Philosophy of Railways: The Transcontinental Railway Idea in British North America* (Toronto, 1997).

Denison, M., *Canada's First Bank: A History of the Bank of Montreal* (Montreal, 1966).

Denoon, D., *Settler Capitalism: The Dynamics of Dependent Development in the Southern Hemisphere* (Oxford, 1983).

——, 'Settler Capitalism Unsettled', *New Zealand Journal of History*, 29 (1995), 131–7.

Dilley, A. R., 'The Economics of Empire', in Stockwell, S. E. (ed.) *The British Empire: Themes and Perspectives* (Oxford, 2008), pp.101–30.

——, '"The Rules of the Game": London Finance, Australia and Canada, c.1900–1914', *Economic History Review*, 63 (2010), 1003–31.

Drummond, I. M., 'Government Securities on Colonial New Issue Markets: Australia and Canada, 1895–1914', *Yale Economic Essays*, 1 (1961), 137–75.

Dunsdorfs, E., *The Australian Wheat-Growing Industry, 1788–1948* (Melbourne, 1956).

Dyster, B., 'Argentine and Australian Development Compared', *Past and Present*, 84 (1979), 91–110.

Dyster, B. and D. Meredith, *Australia in the International Economy* (Cambridge, 1990).

Easterbrook, W. T. and H. G. J. Aitken, *Canadian Economic History* (Toronto, 1956).

Eddy, J. and D. Schreuder, 'The Context: The Edwardian Empire in Transformation and Decline, 1902–1914', in Eddy, J. and D. Schreuder (eds) *The Rise of Colonial Nationalism: Australia, New Zealand, Canada and South Africa First Assert Their Nationalities, 1880–1914* (Sydney, 1988), pp.19–62.

Edelstein, M., *Overseas Investment in the Age of High Imperialism: The United Kingdom, 1850–1914* (London, 1982).

——, 'Foreign Investment and Accumulation 1860–1914', in Floud, R. and D. N. McCloskey (eds) *The Economic History of Britain since 1700* (Cambridge, 1994), pp.173–96.

Edwards, R. D., *The Pursuit of Reason: The Economist 1843–1993* (London, 1993).

Ehrensaft, P. and W. Armstrong, 'Dominion Capitalism: A First Statement', *Australian and New Zealand Journal of Sociology*, 14 (1978), 352–63.

Ellis, L. E., *Reciprocity, 1911: A Study in Canadian-American Relations* (New Haven, 1939).

Etherington, N., *Theories of Imperialism: War, Conquest and Capital* (London, 1984).

Feinstein, C. H., *National Income, Expenditure and Output of the United Kingdom, 1855–1965* (Cambridge, 1972).

——, 'Britain's Overseas Investments in 1913', *Economic History Review*, 43 (1990), 288–95.

Ferguson, N., *The Cash Nexus: Money and Power in the Modern World, 1700–2000* (London, 2001).

——, 'The City of London and British Imperialism: New Light on an Old Question', in Cassis, Y. and É. Bussièr (eds) *London and Paris as International Financial Centres in the Twentieth Century* (Oxford, 2005), pp.57–78.

Ferguson, N. and M. Schularick, 'The Empire Effect: The Determinants of Country Risk in the First Age of Globalization, 1880–1913', *Journal of Economic History*, 66 (2006), 283–312.

Fergusson, B., *Rt Hon W. S. Fielding* (Windsor, N. S., 1971).

Fitzpatrick, B., *The British Empire in Australia: An Economic History, 1834–1939* (Melbourne, 1941).

——, *The British Empire in Australia*, 3ʳᵈ edn (Melbourne, 1969).

Fleming, R. B., *The Railway King of Canada: Sir William Mackenzie, 1849–1923* (Vancouver, 1991).

Fogarty, J., 'The Comparative Method and Regions of Recent Settlement', *Historical Studies*, 19 (1981), 412–30.

Foreman-Peck, J., *A History of the World Economy: International Economic Relations since 1850* (New York, 1995).

Frost, L., 'The Contribution of the Urban Sector to Australian Economic Development before 1914', *Australian Economic History Review*, 38 (1998), 42–71.

Gallagher, J. and R. Robinson, 'The Imperialism of Free Trade', *Economic History Review*, 6 (1953), 1–15.

Giddens, A., *The Constitution of Society: Outlines of the Theory of Structuration* (Cambridge, 1984).

Gilbert, R. S., 'London Financial Intermediaries and Australian Overseas Borrowing, 1900–29', *Australian Economic History Review*, 11 (1971), 39–47.

Gilpin, J. F., 'The Poor Relation Has Come into Her Fortune: The British Investment Boom in Canada, 1905–1915', *Canada House Lecture Series*, 55 (1992), 3–20.

Girard, P. 'British Justice, English Law, and Canadian Legal Culture', in Buckner, P. (ed.) *Canada and the British Empire* (Oxford, 2008), pp.259–79.

Glynn, S., 'Private Enterprise and Public Policy: An Australian Land Grant Railway', *University Studies in History*, 4 (1966), 41–61.

——, 'Government Policy and Agricultural Development: Western Australia, 1900–1930', *Australian Economic History Review*, 7 (1967), 115–35.

Goodhart, C. A. E., *The Business of Banking, 1891–1914* (London, 1972).

Gray, J. H., *R. B. Bennett: The Calgary Years* (Toronto, 1991).

Greasley, D. and L. Oxley, 'Segmenting the Contours: Australian Economic Growth 1828–1913', *Australian Economic History Review*, 37 (1997), 39–53.

——, 'A Tale of Two Dominions: Comparing the Macroeconomic Records of Australia and Canada since 1870', *Economic History Review*, 51 (1998), 294–318.

Groenewegen, P. D. and B. McFarlane, *A History of Australian Economic Thought* (London, 1990).

Hagan, J. and K. Turner, *A History of the Labor Party in New South Wales 1891–1991* (Melbourne, 1991).

Haig, B., 'New Estimates of Australian GDP, 1861–1948/49', *Australian Economic History Review*, 41 (2001), 1–34.

Hall, A. R., *London Capital Market and Australia* (Canberra, 1963).

Hancock, W. K., *Survey of British Commonwealth Affairs: Vol. 2: Problems of Economic Policy, 1918–1939*, 2 vols (London, 1942).

Hanna, D. B., *Trains of Recollection* (Toronto, 1924).

Harper, I. R. and C. B. Schedvin, 'Sir Denison Millar', in Appleyard, R. T. and C. B. Schedvin (eds) *Australian Financiers: Bibliographical Essays* (Melbourne, 1988), pp.206–25.

Heaton, H., 'The Taxation of Unimproved Value of Land in Australia', *The Quarterly Journal of Economics*, 39 (1925), 410–49.

Hicks, N., 'Coghlan, Sir Timothy Augustine (1855–1926)', *Australian Dictionary of Biography*, 8 (1981), 48–51.

Hirst, J., 'Empire, State, Nation', in Schreuder, D. and S. Ward (eds) *Australia's Empire* (Oxford, 2008), pp.141–63.

Holder, R. F., *Bank of New South Wales: A History* (Sydney, 1970).

Holton, S. S., 'T.A. Coghlan's Labour and Industry in Australia: An Enigma in Australian Historiography', *Historical Studies*, 22 (1987), 336–51.

Hopkins, A. G., 'Informal Empire in Argentina: An Alternative View', *Journal of Latin American Studies*, 26 (1994), 469–84.

——, 'Back to the Future: From National History to Imperial History', *Past and Present*, 164 (1999), 198–243.

——, 'Gentlemanly Capitalism in New Zealand', *Australian Economic History Review*, 43 (2003), 287–97.

Howe, A., *Free Trade and Liberal England, 1846–1946* (Oxford, 1997).

Hughes, C. A., Graham and B. D. Graham, *A Handbook of Australian Government and Politics, 1890–1964* (Canberra, 1968).

Imlah, A. H., *Economic Elements in the Pax Britannica: Studies in British Foreign Trade in the Nineteenth Century* (USA, 1969).

Innis, H. A., *A History of the Canadian Pacific Railway* (Toronto, 1923).

——, *The Fur-Trade of Canada* (Toronto, 1927).

Jamieson, A. B., *Chartered Banking in Canada* (Toronto, 1957).

Jessop, D., 'The Colonial Stock Act of 1900: A Symptom of New Imperialism?' *Journal of Imperial and Commonwealth History*, 4 (1975), 166–3.

Jones, G., *British Multinational Banking* (Oxford, 1993).

Kendle, J. E., *The Colonial and Imperial Conferences, 1887–1911: A Study in Imperial Organization* (London, 1967).

Keynes, J. M., *Economic Consequences of the Peace* (New York, 1920).

Kubicek, R. V., 'Economic Power at the Periphery: Canada, Australia, and South Africa, 1850–1914', in Dumett, R. E. (ed.) *Gentlemanly Capitalism and British Imperialism: The New Debate on Empire* (London, 1999), pp.113–27.

Kynaston, D., *The City of London*, Vol. II, *Golden Years, 1890–1914*, 4 vols (London, 1994).

La Nauze, J. A., *Alfred Deakin: A Biography*, 2 vols (Sydney, 1979).

—— (ed.), *Federated Australia: Selections from Letters to the 'Morning Post' 1900–1910, by Alfred Deakin* (London, 1968).

Laidlaw, Z., *Colonial Connections, 1815–45: Patronage, the Information Revolution and Colonial Government* (Manchester, 2005).

Lamb, W. K., *History of the Canadian Pacific Railway* (New York, 1977).

Lang, J. T., *Why I Fight!* (Sydney, 1934).

Leacy, F. H., *Historical Statistics of Canada* (Ottawa, 1983).

Lester, A., *Imperial Networks: Creating Identities in Nineteenth Century South Africa and Britain* (London, 2001).

——, 'Imperial Circuits and Networks: Geographies of the British Empire', *History Compass*, 4 (2006), 124–41.

Levitt, K., *Silent Surrender: The Multinational Corporation in Canada* (Toronto, 1970).

Lewis, J., 'The British Preference', *Annals of the American Academy of Political and Social Science*, 107 (1923), 198–203.

Lloyd, C. 'Andrew Fisher', in Grattan, M. (ed.) *Australian Prime Ministers* (Sydney, 2000), pp.74–94.

Love, P., *Labour and the Money Power: Australian Labour Populism 1890–1950* (Carlton, Victoria, 1984).

——, 'Frank Anstey and the Monetary Radicals', in Appleyard, R. T. and C. B. Schedvin (eds) *Australian Financiers: Bibliographical Essays* (Melbourne, 1988), pp.254–73.

Loveday, P., 'Support in Return for Concessions', *Australian Historical Studies*, 55 (1970), 376–405.

——, 'The Federal Parties', in Loveday, P., A. W. Martin and P. Weller (eds) *Emergence of the Australian Party System* (Sydney, 1977), pp.383–451.

Loveday, P., A. W. Martin and R. S. Parker (eds), *The Emergence of the Australian Party System* (Sydney, 1977).

Loveday, P., R. S. Parker and P. Weller, 'New South Wales', in Loveday, P., A. W. Martin and P. Weller (eds) *Emergence of the Australian Party System* (Sydney, 1977), pp.172–248.

Macintyre, S., *The Oxford History of Australia*: Vol. 4: *1901–1942: The Succeeding Age* (Melbourne, 1986).

MacIvor, R. C., *Canadian Monetary, Banking and Fiscal Development* (Toronto, 1958).

Mackenzie, D., 'Canada, the North Atlantic Triangle and the Empire', in Brown, J. M. and W. R. Louis (eds) *Oxford History of the British Empire*: Vol. 4: *The Twentieth Century* (Oxford, 1999), 574–95.

Madden, A. F., 'Changing Attitudes, Widening Responsibilities, 1895–1914', in Benians, E. A., J. Butler and C. E. Carrington (eds) *Cambridge History of the British Empire*, 9 vols (Cambridge, 1959), iii.399–405.

Madden, A. F. and J. Darwin (eds), *Select Documents on the Constitutional History of the British Empire and Commonwealth: The Dominions and India since 1900* (London, 1993).

Maddison, A., *Monitoring the World Economy 1820–1992* (Paris, 1995).

——, *The World Economy: A Millennial Perspective* (Paris, 2001).

Magee, G. B. and A. S. Thompson, *Empire and Globalisation: Networks of People, Goods and Capital in the British World, c.1850–1914* (Cambridge, 2010).

Mahar, C., R. Harker and C. Wilkes, 'The Basic Theoretical Position', in Harker, R., C. Mahar and C. Wilkes (eds) *An Introduction to the Work of Pierre Bourdieu* (Basingstoke, 1990), pp.1–26.

Mansfield, B. E., 'O'Sullivan, Edward William (1846–1910)', *Australian Dictionary of Biography*, 11 (1988), 106–8.

Marchildon, G. P., '"Hands across the Water": Canadian Industrial Financiers in the City of London, 1905–20', *Business History*, 34 (1992), 69–95.

——, *Profits and Politics: Beaverbrook and the Gilded Age of Canadian Finance* (Toronto, 1996).

Markey, R., *The Making of the Labor Party in New South Wales, 1880–1900* (Sydney, 1988).

Marr, W. L. and D. G. Paterson, *Canada: An Economic History* (Toronto, 1980).

Marsh, P. T., *Joseph Chamberlain: Entrepreneur in Politics* (London, 1994).

Martin, G., *Britain and the Origins of Canadian Confederation, 1837–67* (Basingstoke, 1995).

Masters, D. C., *Reciprocity: 1846–1911* (Ottawa, 1961).

Matthews, T. V., 'Trends in Public, Private Relations, 1901–75', in Head, B. (ed.) *State and Economy in Australia* (Melbourne, 1983), pp.116–40.

McAloon, J., 'Gentlemanly Capitalism and Settler Capitalists: Imperialism, Dependent Development and Colonial Wealth in the South Island of New Zealand', *Australian Economic History Review*, 42 (2002), 204–24.

McCarty, J. W., 'British Investment in Western Australian Gold Mining', *University Studies in History*, 4 (1961–2), 7–22.

——, 'The Staple Approach in Australian Economic History', *Business Archives and History*, iv (1964), 1–22.

——, 'Australia as a Region of Recent Settlement in the Nineteenth Century', *Australian Economic History Review*, 13 (1973), 148–67.

McInnis, E. and M. Horn, *Canada: A Political & Social History* (Toronto, 1982).

McLean, I. W., 'Saving in Settler Economies: Australian and North American Comparisons', *Explorations in Economic History*, 31 (1994), 432–52.

Meaney, N., 'Britishness and Australian Identity: The Problem of Nationalism in Australian History and Historiography', *Australian Historical Studies*, 32 (2001), 76–96.

Meredith, D. and B. Dyster, *Australia in the Global Economy: Continuity and Change* (Cambridge, 1999).

Michie, R. C., 'The Social Web of Investment in the Nineteenth Century', *Revue Internationale d'Histoire de la Banque*, 18 (1979), 158–75.

——, 'Options, Concessions, Syndicates, and the Provision of Venture Capital, 1880–1913', *Business History*, 23 (1981), 147–64.

——, 'Dunn, Fischer and Co. in the City of London', *Business History*, 30 (1988), 194–214.

——, *The City of London: Continuity and Change, 1850–1990* (London, 1992).

——, *The London Stock Exchange: A History* (Oxford, 1999).

Mouat, J., *Roaring Days: Rossland's Mines and the History of British Columbia* (Vancouver, 1995).

——, *Metal Mining in Canada* (Ottawa, 2000).

Moyles, R. G. and D. Owram, *Imperial Dreams and Colonial Realities: British Views of Canada 1880–1914* (Toronto, London, 1988).

Murphy, D. (ed.), *Labor in Politics* (St Lucia, Queensland, 1975).

Naylor, R. T., *The History of Canadian Business, 1867–1914*, 2 vols (Toronto, 1975).

Nelles, H. V., *The Politics of Development: Forests, Mines, and Hydro-Electric Power in Ontario, 1849–1941* (Toronto, 1974).

Norrie, K. and D. Owram, *A History of the Canadian Economy* (Toronto, 1996).

Norrie, K., D. Owram and J. C. H. Emery, *A History of the Canadian Economy* (Toronto, 2002).

Norris, R., *The Emergent Commonwealth: Australian Federation, Expectations and Fulfilment, 1889–1910* (Melbourne, 1975).

O'Hagan, H. O., *Leaves from My Life*, 2 vols (London, 1929).

Offer, A., 'Empire and Social Reform: British Overseas Investment and Domestic Politics, 1908–1914', *Historical Journal*, 26 (1983), 119–38.

——, 'Pacific Rim Societies: Asian Labour and White Nationalism', in Eddy, J. and D. Schreuder (eds) *The Rise of Colonial Nationalism: Australia, New Zealand, Canada and South Africa First Assert Their Nationalities, 1880–1914* (Sydney, 1988).

——, *The First World War: An Agrarian Interpretation* (Oxford, 1989).

——, 'The British Empire, 1870–1914: A Waste of Money?', *Economic History Review*, 46 (1993), 215–38.

——, 'Costs and Benefits, Prosperity and Security, 1870–1914', in Porter, A. N. (ed.) *Oxford History of the British Empire*: Vol. 3: *The Nineteenth Century* (Oxford, 1999), pp.546–73.

Patmore, G., *Australian Labour History* (Melbourne, 1991).

Platt, D. C. M., 'Canada and Argentina: The First Preference of the British Investor, 1904–1914', *Journal of Imperial and Commonwealth History*, 8 (1985), 77–88.

——, *Britain's Investment Overseas on the Eve of the First World War* (Basingstoke, 1986).

Platt, D. C. M. and J. Aldeman, 'London Merchant Bankers in the First Phase of Heavy Borrowing: The Grand Trunk Railway of Canada', *Journal of Imperial and Commonwealth History*, 18 (1990), 208–27.

Platt, D. C. M. and G. Di Tella (eds), *Argentina, Australia and Canada: Studies in Comparative Development 1870–1965* (London, 1985).

Platt, D. C. M. and G. Di Tella, 'Introduction', in Platt, D. C. M. and G. Di Tella (eds) *Argentina, Australia and Canada: Studies in Comparative Development 1870–1965* (London, 1985), pp.1–40.

Pocock, J. G. A., 'British History: A Plea for a New Subject', *Journal of Modern History*, 47 (1975), 601–21.

Porter, D., '"A Trusted Guide of the Investing Public": Harry Marks and the *Financial News*, 1884–1916', *Business History*, 28 (1986), 1–17.

Potter, S. J., *News and the British World: The Emergence of an Imperial Press System, 1876–1922* (Oxford, 2003).

——, 'The Imperial Significance of the Canadian-American Reciprocity Proposals of 1911', *Historical Journal*, 47 (2004), 81–100.

——, 'Empire, Cultures and Identities in Nineteenth- and Twentieth-Century Britain', *History Compass*, 5 (2007), 51–71.

——, 'Richard Jebb, John S. Ewart and the Round Table, 1898–1926', *English Historical Review*, CXXII (2007), 105–32.

——, 'Webs, Networks and Systems: Globalization and the Mass Media in the Nineteenth- and Twentieth-Century British Empire', *Journal of British Studies*, 46 (2007), 621–46.

Rawson, D. W., 'Victoria', in Loveday, P., A. W. Martin and R. S. Parker (eds) *The Emergence of the Australian Party System* (Sydney, 1977), pp.45–115.

Redish, A., 'British Financial Imperialism after the First World War', in Dumett, R. E. (ed.) *Gentlemanly Capitalism and British Imperialism: The New Debate on Empire* (London, 1999), pp.113–27.

Reford, A., 'Smith, Donald Alexander, 1st Baron Strathcona and Mount Royal', in *Dictionary of Canadian Biography On-line* (Ottawa, 2005).

Regehr, T. D., *The Canadian Northern Railway: Pioneer Road of the Northern Prairies, 1895–1918* (Toronto, 1976).

Richardson, P., 'The Origins and Development of the Collins House Group, 1914–1951', *Australian Economic History Review*, 27 (1987), 77–92.

——, 'Collins House Financiers: W. L. Baillieu, Lionel Robinson, and Francis Govett', in Appleyard, R. T. and C. B. Schedvin (eds) *Australian Financiers: Bibliographical Essays* (Melbourne, 1988), pp.226–49.

Rickard, J., *Class and Politics: New South Wales, Victoria and the Early Commonwealth* (Canberra, 1976).

Robertson, J. R., 'Scaddan, John (1876–1934)', *Australian Dictionary of Biography*, 11 (1988), 526–9.

Robinson, R. 'The Non-European Foundations for European Imperialism: Sketch for a Theory of Collaboration', in Owen, R. and B. Sutcliffe (eds) *Studies in the Theory of Imperialism* (London, 1972), pp.117–39.

——, 'The Excentric Idea of Imperialism: With or Without Europe', in Mommsen, W. J. and J. Osterhammel (eds) *Imperialism and After: Continuities and Discontinuities* (London, 1986), pp.267–90.

Robinson, R., J. Gallagher and A. Denny, *Africa and the Victorians: The Official Mind of Imperialism* (London, 1961).

Rock, D., *Argentina, 1516–1982* (London, 1986).

Rose, J. H. et al. (eds), *Cambridge History of the British Empire*, 8 vols (Cambridge, 1929–1959).

Ross, V., *A History of the Canadian Bank of Commerce* (Toronto, 1922).

Rowell, N. W. 'Canada and the Empire', in Holland-Rose, J. et al. (eds) *Cambridge History of the British Empire* (Cambridge, 1929–1963).

Roy, P. 'The Fine Arts of Lobbying and Persuading: The Case of the B. C. Electric Railway, 1897–1917', in Macmillan, D. S. (ed.) *Canadian Business History: Selected Studies, 1497–1971* (Toronto, 1972), pp.239–54.

Rubinstein, W. D., 'The Top-Wealth-Holders of New South Wales, 1817–1939', *Australian Economic History Review*, 20 (1980), 138–51.

Ryan, J. A., 'Wise, Bernhard Ringrose (1858–1916)', *Australian Dictionary of Biography*, 12 (1990), 546–9.

Rydon, J. and R. N. Spann, *New South Wales Politics, 1901–1910* (Melbourne, 1962).

Saul, S. B., *Studies in British Overseas Trade, 1870–1914* (Liverpool, 1960).

Sayers, R. S., *Lloyds Bank in the History of English Banking* (Oxford, 1957).

Schedvin, B., 'E. G. Theodore and the London Pastoral Lobby', *Politics*, vi (1971), 26–41.

Schedvin, C. B., 'Staples and Regions of Pax Britannica', *Economic History Review*, 43 (1990), 533–59.

Schlote, W., *British Overseas Trade from 1700 to the 1930's* (Oxford, 1952).

Schwartz, H. M., *In the Dominions of Debt: Historical Perspectives on Dependent Development* (Ithaca, N.Y., 1989).

Searle, G. R., *Corruption in British Politics: 1895–1930* (Oxford, 1987).

——, 'Turner, Sir George', *Australian Dictionary of Biography*, 12 (1990), 293–6.

——, *A New England? Peace and War, 1886–1918* (Oxford, 2004).

Shanahan, M., 'Tracing the Crimson Thread: United Kingdom Residents Holding Probated South Australian Assets, 1905–1915', *Australian Economic History Review*, 43 (2003), 215–29.

Shann, E., *An Economic History of Australia* (Cambridge, 1930).

Sinclair, W. A. 'Capital Formation', in Forster, C. (ed.) *Australian Economic Development in the Twentieth Century* (London, 1970), pp.13–36.

——, *The Process of Economic Development in Australia* (Melbourne, 1976).

Skelton, O. D., 'General Economic History, 1867–1912', in Shortt, A. and A. G. Doughty (eds) *Canada and Its Provinces*, 23 vols (Toronto, 1913), p.ix.

——, *Life and Letters of Sir Wilfrid Laurier* (London, 1922).

Skidelsky, R. J. A., *John Maynard Keynes: Vol. 1: Hope Betrayed, 1883–1920*, 3 vols (London, 1983).

Smith, A., *British Businessmen and Canadian Confederation: Constitution-Making in an Era of Anglo-Globalization* (Kingston, 2008).

Startt, J. D., *Journalists for Empire: The Imperial Debate in the Edwardian Stately Press, 1903–1913* (New York, 1991).

Stevens, G. R., *Canadian National Railways* (Toronto, 1962).

Stone, I., *The Global Export of Capital from Great Britain, 1865–1914: A Statistical Survey* (Basingstoke, 1999).

Strange, S., *States and Markets* (London, 1988).

Sullivan, E., 'Revealing a Preference: Imperial Preference and the Australian Tariff, 1901–1914', *Journal of Imperial and Commonwealth History*, 29 (2001), 35–62.

Taylor, G. D. and P. A. Baskerville, *A Concise History of Business in Canada* (Oxford, 1994).

Teichman, J., 'Businessmen and Politics in the Process of Economic Development: Argentina and Canada', *Canadian Journal of Political Science/Revue canadienne de science politique*, 15 (1982), 47–66.

Thane, P., 'Financiers and the British State: The Case of Sir Ernest Cassel', *Business History*, 28 (1986), 80–99.

Thompson, A. and G. Magee, 'A Soft Touch? British Industry, Empire Markets, and the Self-Governing Dominions, C.1870–1914', *Economic History Review*, 56 (2003), 689–717.

Thompson, A. S., 'The Language of Imperialism and the Meanings of Empire: Imperial Discourse in British Politics, 1895–1914', *The Journal of British Studies*, 36 (1997), 147–77.

——, 'Tariff Reform: An Imperial Strategy, 1903–1913', *Historical Journal*, 40 (1997), 1033–54.

——, *Imperial Britain: The Empire in British Politics, c.1880–1932* (London, 2000).

Tomlinson, B. R. 'Economics and Empire: The Periphery and the Imperial Economy', in Porter, A. N. (ed.) *Oxford History of the British Empire*: Vol. 3: *The Nineteenth Century* (Oxford, 1999), pp.3–74.

Trainor, L., *British Imperialism and Australian Nationalism: Manipulation, Conflict, and Compromise in the Late Nineteenth Century* (Cambridge, 1994).

Tulchinsky, G. J. J., 'The Montreal Business Community, 1837–1852', in Macmillan, D. S. (ed.) *Canadian Business History: Selected Studies, 1497–1971* (Toronto, 1972), pp.125–43.

Tulchinsky, G. J. J., *The River Barons: Montreal Businessmen and the Growth of Industry and Transportation, 1837–53* (Toronto, 1977).

Urquhart, M. C. 'New Estimates of Gross National Product, Canada, 1870–1927: Some Implications for Canadian Development', in Engerman, S. L. and R. E. Gallman (eds) *Long-Term Factors in American Economic Growth* (Chicago, 1992), pp.9–95.

Vamplew, W. (ed.), *Australians: Historical Statistics* (Broadway, N.S.W., 1987).

Ville, S. P., *The Rural Entrepreneurs: A History of the Stock and Station Agent Industry in Australia and New Zealand* (Cambridge, 2000).

Viner, J., *Canada's Balance of International Indebtedness, 1900–1913* (Cambridge, 1924).

Ward, S., *Australia and the British Embrace: The Demise of the Imperial Ideal* (Carlton South, Vic., 2001).

——, 'Sentiment and Self-Interest: The Imperial Idea in Anglo-Australian Commercial Culture', *Australian Historical Studies*, 32 (2001), 92–107.

Watkins, M. H., 'A Staple Theory of Economic Growth', *Canadian Journal of Economics and Political Science*, xxix (1963), 141–58.

Wilkins, M., 'The Free-Standing Company, 1870–1914: An Important Type of British Foreign Direct Investment', *Economic History Review*, 41 (1988), 259–82.

Wilson, C. F., *A Century of Canadian Grain: Government Policy to 1951* (Saskatoon, 1978).

Winslade, S., 'Wire-Fencing Investment in Eastern Australia, 1858–1914', *Australian Economic History Review*, 34 (1994), 22–5.

Wood, G. L., *Borrowing and Business in Australia* (Oxford, 1930).

Woodruff, W., *Impact of Western Man: A Study of Europe's Role in the World Economy, 1750–1960* (London, 1966).

Wright, D. I., 'The Politics of Federal Finance: The First Decade', *Historical Studies*, 8 (1969), 460–71.

Unpublished Theses

Attard, B., 'The Australian High Commissioner's Office: Politics and Anglo-Australian Relations, 1901–1939' (D.Phil. Thesis, University of Oxford, 1991).

Bailey, J. D. ,'Australian Company Borrowing, 1870–1893: A Study in British Overseas Investment' (D.Phil. Thesis, University of Oxford, 1957).

Drummond, I. M., 'Capital Markets in Australia and Canada, 1895–1914: A Study in Colonial Economic History' (Ph.D. Thesis, Yale, 1959).

Potter, S. J., 'Nationalism, Imperialism, and the Press in Britain and the Dominions' (D.Phil. Thesis, University of Oxford, 2000).

Rogers, E., 'The Impact of the New World on Economic and Social Debates in Britain, c.1860–1914' (Ph.D. Thesis, University of Cambridge, 2008).

Roy, P., 'The British Columbia Electric Railway, 1897–1929: A British Company in British Columbia' (Ph.D. Thesis, University of Vancouver, 1970).

Smith, S. B. R., 'British Nationalism, Imperialism, and the City of London' (Ph.D. Thesis, University of London, 1985).

Index